# MACHOS,
# MARICONES,
# AND GAYS

# IAN LUMSDEN

 Temple University Press   *Philadelphia*

# MACHOS, MARICONES, AND GAYS

## CUBA AND HOMOSEXUALITY

LATIN AMERICA BUREAU
London

Temple University Press, Philadelphia 19122
Copyright © 1996 by Temple University. All rights reserved
Published 1996
Printed in the United States of America


⊗ The paper used in this book meets the requirements of the
American National Standard for Information Sciences—Permanence
of Paper for Printed Library Materials, ANSI Z29.48-1984

Text design by Chiquita Babb


Library of Congress Cataloging-in-Publication Data
Lumsden, Ian.
    Machos, maricones, and gays : Cuba and homosexuality / Ian
Lumsden.
        p.      cm.
    Includes bibliographical references and index.
      ISBN 1-56639-370-1 (cloth). — ISBN 1-56639-371-X (paper)
        1. Homosexuality—Cuba.   2. Homosexuality—Cuba—
History—20th century.   3. Gays—Cuba.   I. Title
    HQ75.6.C9L85   1996
306.76'6'097291—dc20                        95-44233

TO

TOMASITO LA GOYESCA

AND TO

AMAURYS

# CONTENTS

Acknowledgments
*ix*

Introduction
*xi*

*ONE*
An Introduction to Contemporary Cuba
*1*

*TWO*
Machismo and Homosexuality before the Revolution
*28*

*THREE*
Institutionalized Homophobia
*55*

*FOUR*
Homosexuality and the Law
*81*

*FIVE*
Homosexuality and Sexual Education in the 1980s
*96*

*SIX*
The Erosion of Traditional Machismo
*115*

*SEVEN*
Gay Life in Havana Today
*130*


*EIGHT*
The Impact of AIDS
*160*


*NINE*
An Imperfect Revolution in an Imperfect World
*178*


*APPENDIX A*
Cuban Sexual Values and African Religious Beliefs,
by Tomás Fernández Robaina
*205*


*APPENDIX B*
El Pecado Original, by Pablo Milanés
*209*


*APPENDIX C*
Manifesto of the Gay and Lesbian Association of Cuba
*211*


Notes
*215*


Select Bibliography
*247*


Index
*255*

# ACKNOWLEDGMENTS

*PERHAPS IT* would be best to start by thanking all the unnamed gay Cubans, living in Cuba or in exile, who have helped me in countless ways. This book could not have been written without their help. I have decided not to acknowledge by name those gays who live in Cuba to save them any possible embarrassment. I would also like to thank the staff at the José Martí National Library, the National Center for Sexual Education, and the National Center for Health Education in Havana.

Many friends have supported this project throughout the years. They must be as relieved as I am that it is over. A special thanks, in no particular order, to Hugh English, Leonel Pedroso, Bob Davis, Luis Zapata, Max Mejía, David Thorstad, Ken Moffatt, Linda Briskin, and Louise Jacobs. I am very grateful to Virginia Smith, who made the final manuscript more readable, and to Karen Wald, who despite our considerable ideological differences devoted much time to drawing my attention to problematic contentions and factual errors.

Atkinson College and York University have helped me in various ways, mostly by facilitating my visits to Cuba, for which I am obliged. Last, but not least, I would like to thank the editorial staff of Temple University Press, and Elizabeth Johns, for their constructive and supportive editing of this manuscript. I am very pleased that they have chosen to publish my book since I have great respect for their work and publishing philosophy.

# INTRODUCTION

*THIS BOOK* is a gay Canadian's attempt to come to terms with the Cuban revolutionary process and the place of homosexuals within it. To understand the pages that follow the reader needs to know my own viewpoint and preconceptions. Therefore this introduction serves to introduce the author as well as the subject.

Postrevolutionary Cuba has at various times filled me with hope and admiration, exasperation and frustration, anger and despair. I have admired the social changes that have benefited countless Cubans, and I have been outraged by the Castro regime's authoritarian treatment of some of its citizens, including friends of mine, who have been jailed, forced into exile, or cowed in their daily lives. I have marveled at the formulation and implementation of programs that the rest of Latin America cries out for. Yet I have also been exasperated by the regime's bureaucratic nature and disgusted by its dogmatic imposition of policies that were foredoomed to failure and that inevitably brought hardships to ordinary Cubans. Along with many Cubans I have loved and hated Fidel Castro, a "bad daddy" if ever there was one. I have always empathized with the Cuban people—surely among the warmest and most generous people in the world—who do not deserve the hardships that have been imposed upon them, particularly by the U.S. economic blockade.

My first visit to Cuba was in 1965, when I spent six months there doing research for my Ph.D. thesis. It was an intellectually and politically stimulating time, one that was full of optimism about the future of Cuba. I stayed in a run-down hotel in Old Havana, eating my meals with fellow students in the university canteen—chiefly rice and beans. Although I enjoyed a few privileges, mostly derived from a press card that I had engineered before leaving Canada, I lived much more simply than the majority of foreign residents in Cuba, almost all of whom were working on contracts that afforded them far better lifestyles than most Cubans enjoyed. I believe that I had more exposure to the day-to-day life of ordinary Cubans than most other foreigners at the time. Since I tried to be open-minded, not restricting my contacts with any Cubans because of political preconceptions, I had friends and acquaintances who ranged from *sarampionados* (so revolutionary that they appeared to have come out in red spots as if they had measles) to *gusanos* who could hardly wait to "worm" their way off the island. I never tried to disguise my friendships and kept a copious diary of my daily experiences and feelings. The government must have been aware of me, because at the time there were very few foreigners living independently in Havana, but my freedom to do as I wished, provided that I respected Cuban laws, was never questioned (nor in subsequent visits). I wandered freely around Havana, spent much time in private homes, and traveled from Pinar del Río in the west to Santiago in the east. At times, I was only a stone's throw from Fidel Castro, which was not all that unusual in those times given that he would crop up at the most unexpected times and places. I also had the privilege of hearing him deliver his eloquent and rational speeches—primers on the problems facing Cuba and underdeveloped countries in general. Nobody who accuses him of being a ranting, demagogical maniac can possibly have heard him speak to and interact with the Cuban people.

At the time I was sexually repressed and had not yet come out. This no doubt was the primary explanation for my unawareness of the travails that had intensified for Cuban homosexuals since the 1959 revolution. The leftist political and intellectual circles in which I moved before going to Cuba were oblivious to sexual politics and to the significance of homosexual oppression. Queers, ladies, and Negroes were still in their place. The black liberation movement had only just begun, and it would be several years before it would be joined by that of women and gays.

Over the years, I returned frequently to Cuba to keep abreast of the revolution. I also traveled extensively in Latin America, drawn there by my political and academic interest in its society and politics, as well as by a personal attraction that stemmed from having been raised in Argentina. After coming out, I also became more interested, academically and personally, in gay politics. My participation in the gay liberation struggles in Toronto, which intensified in the late 1970s and early 1980s, affected my worldview and political priorities. I was angered by my growing awareness of what oppression had done to me personally and of how the Left, with which I had generally identified, had ignored the issues of gay oppression and of homophobia. I restructured my personal life around my gay identity and the gay community but did not abandon my political and social concerns, particularly regarding the fate of Cuba and the rest of Latin America.

Matters came to a head when *Improper Conduct* was shown at the 1984 Toronto Film Festival. Directed by exiled Cubans Néstor Almendros and Orlando Jiménez-Leal, the French documentary portrayed homosexual oppression in revolutionary Cuba. The film had an enormous impact upon gay people everywhere. Many of its scenes deeply disturbed me and challenged my support for the revolution. Still, I was outraged by the film's equation of overall oppression in Cuba with the oppression of Cuban gays, a view that seemed exaggerated and oversimplified. In response, I resolved to return to Cuba to study the situation of homosexuals in particular, which I felt should be given some form of comparative and historical perspective.

In 1991, thanks to sabbaticals and other extended time abroad, I published *Homosexuality, Society and the State in Mexico,*[1] the first of what was intended to be a three-part comparative study of Mexico, Costa Rica, and Cuba. I chose the first two countries for comparative purposes because they have the most visible homosexual communities (at least in their capital cities) and the most active gay liberation movements in Central America and the Caribbean. While they share a Spanish and Catholic cultural heritage with Cuba, they are also representative of the diverse socioeconomic and political conditions in Latin America.

Although it certainly contains more poverty and inequality than its image abroad suggests, Costa Rica perhaps comes closest to being a welfare state in Latin America. It has a liberal democratic political system with a tradition of democratic elections. Conversely, Mexico may not have the most repressive government in Latin America, but it is certainly authoritarian and abuses human rights with impunity. Its society and economy, notorious for their inequality, are also increasingly characterized by market-driven forces. Given that struggles for gay liberation have typically taken place in capitalist societies, one may assume that the advances made by homosexuals in those two countries indicate what rights homosexuals in other Latin American capitalist countries can realistically hope to attain.

The simultaneous study of homosexuality in these three countries underlined the fact that gays, like most people, have multifaceted identities and problems. Sometimes having sex and being in love is their most compelling activity. At other times, they are more immediately preoccupied with the economic and social problems afflicting the underdeveloped countries, with their work if they have it, or with economic survival and staying alive and healthy if they are not fortunate enough to have a decent job. Since they are social beings, day-to-day relations with their families, barrios, and society as a whole are inescapable, however marginalized gays may sometimes be or feel on account of their sexuality. Still, sex and love of other men remain central preoccupations only because we gays have been historically denied the opportunity freely to fulfill our needs for sexual and emotional intimacy, whether we live in North America or South America.

Still, gay liberation defined narrowly as sexual liberation does not sufficiently take into account all the other factors that impinge upon our capacity to express our sexuality. Freedom and liberation are not merely about the absence of constraint but also about what we need to enjoy our sexuality and, equally important, to develop our potential to be fully human in every respect. The Cuban revolution raises these issues in all their complexity.

The revolution took place in a country where homosexuals were historically oppressed in a manner similar to that elsewhere in Latin America. Their oppression was primarily social rather than politically institutionalized. Although sex with other men was relatively accessible if kept private, fuller relations with other men were rare because of the lack of material means, such as private housing and economic independence, to develop them as well as the homophobic prejudices against them.

It is not by accident that the struggle for gay liberation as we understand it has invariably been initiated first in the more developed countries whose inhabitants enjoy economic, social, and cultural opportunities that are beyond the reach of the vast majority of those who live in Latin America and the rest of the Third World. Furthermore, it has usually been more visible in the most urbanized and industrialized regions of those countries. It is more evident in New York, California, and southern Ontario, as opposed to the deep south in the United States or the Maritime provinces in Canada. Where gays have become more visible in more traditional rural or less developed regions, whether in terms of social spaces or gay organizations, they have predominantly come from the more educated and economically secure sectors of society.

If the Cuban revolution had not occurred it is possible that a minority of middle-class homosexuals in Havana might have sought to reproduce the gay liberation movement that came to the fore in North America after the 1969 Stonewall rebellion in New York, in much the same way as this emulation has occurred in Mexico City and San José. On the other hand it is probable that not much would have changed in the lives of the vast majority of those who enjoy sex with other men because the way they experienced their sexuality would continue to be determined by all the socioeconomic and political limitations that constrain the lives of the majority of the population everywhere in Latin America. These constraints include lack of economic independence and impoverishment in housing, health care, education, and culture. These factors necessarily make homosexuals more dependent on relations with their family for survival and less likely to challenge traditional customs in their communities.

The Cuban revolution could have happened without immediately affecting the lives of homosexuals. In principle it could have taken place without detriment to the private, personal dimension of gay people's lives. Pierre Trudeau said, when he partially decriminalized homosexuality in Canada, that the state has no business in people's bedrooms or in any personal behavior that does not harm others. Theoretically, Castro could have taken a similar line, but it seems inevitable that the revolutionary government should have sought to regulate gender and sexuality directly in a new way, given that almost every other aspect of Cuban society was being affected by the revolution. Ideally, a sexual policy should have emerged that befitted the humanistic, emancipatory aspirations of the revolution as a whole.

From the perspective of homosexuals who shared the oppression of the majority of citizens in prerevolutionary Cuba, the revolution had the potential of improving their lives and therefore expanding their choices. Economic, social, and cultural development ideally frees individuals and societies from traditional restraints and provides the means to fulfill an increasingly diverse human potentiality. What was previously only open to a minority, and at that in a very stunted way, might now increasingly be enjoyed more completely by everyone. For various reasons, however, the revolution has had a much more complex and less positive impact on gay Cubans than its other social achievements might suggest. This failure to deliver on its potential has tempered the support that might otherwise have been given to it.

The Cuban revolution is the most significant event in the Western hemisphere since the U.S. war of independence in the 1770s. The Cuban revolution has directly challenged the political hegemony of the United States in this hemisphere, not to mention its long-standing ambition, dating back to Jefferson, to control Cuba on behalf of its own national interest. At the same time it has contradicted many of the dominant liberal assumptions about the best way to advance people's economic, social, and cultural welfare, particularly in the Third World.

For progressive gay people the revolution also poses the challenge of reconciling its denial of individual civil rights (particularly in its treatment of gays) with its extension of human rights defined in social and material terms—for example , the provision of health care and education—to most people living in Cuba. For this reason I, myself, feel ambivalent about lending my support to the revolution.

My compromises and qualifications may also seem characteristically Canadian. There is a grain of truth to the stereotype that Canadians are generally more cautious and moderate in their political affiliations than Americans. We do not adopt and discard political causes with the passion that is more typical of American politics. We do not tend to make political heroes or demons out of politicians at home or abroad.

The U.S. government and many of its people believe that the United States is a pluralistic society in which individual rights, particularly the right to private property, should be paramount within a liberal democratic electoral system. Above and beyond these individual rights they have increasingly argued in favor of a limited role for the state and a virtually unlimited role for the market—that is, capitalist free enterprise—in the allocation of resources and provision of services such as health, education, employment, food, and shelter for the people of the United States. The majority of Americans tend to view such assumptions as natural and inherent to the human condition.

The Cuban government and many of its people have a more collectivist view of politics. Having been a colonial and neocolonial people for over four hundred and fifty years, Cubans place national sovereignty and collective self-determination at the top of their political agenda. Cuba's leaders believe that politics should primarily serve these goals because their historical experience has led them to believe that without national independence they are powerless to advance the well-being of the majority of people. Cuba's leadership defines the preservation of national unity and the integrity of the revolutionary process as basic to the country's sovereignty. Other issues such as electoral politics remain secondary. In relation to the present study, these secondary issues include individual and minority rights. This philosophy is diametrically opposite to the dominant one in the United States. Cuba's unwillingness to prioritize the individual and collective rights of Afro-Cubans, women, and gays is also problematic for North American minorities who have recently succeeded in gaining some recognition, if not always redress, of their historical oppression.

The Canadian political tradition is somewhat different from that of the United States insofar as "responsible government" is understood to include not only the executive's accountability to the legislature and to the electorate but also increasingly the expectation that the diversity of the population—regional, social, ethnic, and sexual—should be recognized and the welfare of the whole people supported. Regional equalization projects and public enterprise have historically been seen as central to Canada's survival. In short there is a social democratic component to Canadian politics that is absent in the United States. Indeed at various times there have been social democratic governments in power in almost half our provinces, containing a majority of the population.

This fact partly explains why Canada has never reacted to the Cuban revolution with the emotional intensity that the United States has. Moreover, Canada, too, has often felt bullied by the giant to its south. Cuba's right to struggle for its national independence and collective self-determination has been viewed as a legitimate option by most Canadians. Cuba's struggles have been viewed as equally legitimate to those of the African majority in South Africa. Canada did not break diplomatic relations with Cuba, and it has always been opposed to any form of economic embargo. Canada has extended aid and credit to Cuba. Many corporations have significant investments in Cuba, which is also the preferred Caribbean tourist destination of tens of thousands of Canadians who visit the island each year. Despite reservations about Cuba's relationship to the former Soviet Union and its lack of democratic institutions as understood by ordinary Canadians, neither the revolutionary regime nor its leader, Fidel Castro, have been demonized in Canada to the extent they have been in the United States. On the contrary, many Canadians have sympathized with Cuba's struggle to free itself from U.S. domination and to overcome its underdevelopment.

The same sympathy can be found in almost every other country in the Western Hemisphere, even though their governments have at various times had to succumb to pressures from Washington to cooperate in isolating Cuba economically and politically. All the major Latin American countries have now joined Mexico—which never broke off diplomatic, economic, or cultural ties with Cuba—in normalizing relations with the revolutionary regime of Fidel Castro. Since almost all have been affected by the power of the United States in one way or another, it is not surprising that many, perhaps most, Latin Americans have been sympathetic to Cuba's attempts to solve its problems by means that are anathema to the United States.

What is it that the United States finds so objectionable that it persists in trying to overthrow the revolutionary regime, most obviously through its economic embargo (not supported by any other country in the world save Israel)? It is not so much Cuba's Communist self-identification or the nature of its political regime—the United States has close economic ties with China and is opening up to Vietnam—but rather a question of property rights and unrestricted investment opportunities for U.S. capitalists. Cuba's denial of individual human rights, defined in liberal terms, has been used as a pretext to cover this more fundamental concern. After all, the United States has happily coexisted with a variety of brutal dictatorships, including the Pinochet tyranny in Chile and the Duvalier regime in Haiti. Conversely, it has intransigently opposed any regime, such as that of the Sandinistas in Nicaragua, that has attempted to use collectivist means to redress inequality and oppression when these measures affect or potentially affect U.S. economic interests.

The United States defines the right to ownership of private property in the corporate as well as individual sense as an inalienable right, expressed in the Declaration of Independence, the Fifth Amendment of the Constitution, and various judicial decisions. It implicitly extended this conception of rights to Cuba in the 1902 Platt Amendment, which was attached to the Cuban Constitution in return for the end of the U.S. military occupation. Most recently it has been incorporated in the North American Free Trade Agreement, whose main provisions address the rights of capital with little concern for social rights, in marked contrast to the broader provisions of the Treaty of the European Union.

Given that most Americans conceive of human rights in strictly individualistic and capitalist terms, it is not surprising that they cannot envisage any alternative form of defining and promoting human dignity. Cuba is objectionable because it does pose an alternative conception of human rights. Despite its undoubted denial of human rights conceived in liberal individualistic terms, the Cuban revolutionary regime has demonstrated its commitment to human rights defined in collective social terms. This is most evident with respect to education, health, and culture, which in Cuba are treated as basic rights for everyone instead of as commodities available only to those who can afford them.

Cuba, as is now well known, is currently in a state of crisis that has been exacerbated by the collapse of the Communist camp and the uncontested globalization of capitalism. Its future is uncertain. Will Cuba follow the example of the former Communist countries allied to the Soviet Union, which dismembered most of the social policies established under communism in their sudden embrace of capitalism and market mechanisms? Or will Cuba preserve the best of the revolution's social policies as it implements the badly needed political and economic reforms that are crucial to its future development?

If any revolutionary regime is to survive in Cuba it must learn from its historical experience and rectify the errors that have contributed to a loss of support from the Cuban people. Not all Cuba's problems can be attributed to the U.S. blockade or to global capitalism. Yet its problems have undoubtedly been aggravated by the total ascendancy of conservative worldviews in societies and governments alike. In the mid-1990s there is not a single social democratic, socialist, or even Communist state willing to support Cuba and capable of counterbalancing the power of corporate capitalism, in marked contrast to the situation at the start of the Cuban revolution.

North Americans are as much affected as Cubans by these new conditions. In North America we are living in a time when economic polarization, racism, and violence against women and gays are once again being intensified. We are also living in a world whose economy and culture are being globalized and driven by private profit and the corporate agenda, a world where the rich and the privileged of each country have more in common with their counterparts in other countries than they do with their fellow nationals who are abused and marginalized. It is a world in which human rights, whether defined in classical liberal terms, or in terms of collective social rights, have become much more precarious. For these reasons we should be concerned about the fate of the Cuban revolution. It affects the right of the people living in Cuba, and in the final analysis, the right of all of us, to create an alternative society to the neoliberal order that is currently being imposed under the hegemony of corporate capitalism throughout the world.

A minority of gay people undoubtedly benefit from their identification with the corporate rich, but the majority of gays are deceiving themselves if they do not side with the underprivileged majority. One must be ingenuous as well as oblivious to historical experience to believe that recently acquired gay rights can be secured, let alone expanded, when so many other rights are being trampled upon. For this reason North American gays not only have a legitimate interest in the fate of Cuban gays; we also have a stake in what happens to the Cuban revolution.

This book is an attempt to comprehend Cuba's treatment of homosexuals. It argues that the present situation of gay Cubans can best be understood within a historical perspective that starts several centuries before the Cuban revolution. It also assumes that the current regulation of gender and sex in Cuba must be understood in the context of a poor country's efforts to overcome underdevelopment and dependency in the face of the determination of the United States to prevent the revolution from succeeding at whatever cost. The issue of homosexual oppression, however unacceptable it may be in principle, must be viewed in a broad political and historical context.

Unfortunately, all too many foreign critics have seized upon the issue of oppression and discrimination against gay males as evidence of the singularly oppressive overall character of the Cuban revolutionary regime. Sometimes they are only concerned with the specificity of gay rights, regardless of what happens in other fields. Some sense of perspective is required, however, some recognition of connections and interdependencies. Gay rights would have little meaning if they were enjoyed within a context of social and material oppression in every other respect.

Many people, and no doubt many North American gays, share the contention of Guillermo Cabrera Infante that "those who have suffered most under Castro are the homosexuals . . . expelled from their jobs, forced to marry, put in prison and interned in concentration camps."[2] The longstanding support for gay rights by the acclaimed Cuban writer, who has lived in exile for three decades, should be recognized, but his bitter refusal to recognize any positive changes in Cuba since his departure does not merit the same respect.

For a variety of reasons, the Cuban revolution has long been identified with the persecution of homosexuals, in the manner of Cabrera Infante. The Right, represented by the likes of Armando Valladares, contends "that there have been few examples of repression of homosexuals in history as virulent as in Cuba."[3] On the Left, activists like

Duncan Green, author of one of the best recent books on the underdevelopment of Latin America and the marginalization of its people, seemingly feels obliged to single out the oppression of homosexuals in Cuba, as if this was not a common phenomenon throughout
the region. To write in 1991 that Cuba is "particularly repressive toward gay men . . . and imposes a maximum 20 year sentence for public expression of homosexuality"[4] is very misleading. In like manner,
progressive gay academics such as Jeffrey Weeks and Barry Adam,
who have made comparative historical studies of the regulation of
homosexuality, have too often seemed obliged to make special (albeit
passing) reference to the oppression of Cuban homosexuals without
much effort to relate that oppression to its specific historical and
cultural context.[5] To be sure, some gay activists, such as Allen
Young, have in their time contributed much to the illumination and
documentation of homosexual oppression during the 1960s and
1970s.[6] Though one might have ideological differences with Néstor
Almendros and Orlando Jiménez-Leal, the joint directors of the
documentary film *Improper Conduct,*[7] one should also recognize that
they, too, contributed a great deal to awakening public interest about
the oppressive treatment of Cuban homosexuals prior to the Mariel
exodus in 1980. Their fierce denunciation undoubtedly contributed to modification of Cuba's reactionary policies toward gays and
lesbians.

Unfortunately, there are still too many foreign gays who continue
to recite these criticisms in a simplistic fashion as if nothing had
changed since they were first made more than a decade ago. While
the 1993 *Third Pink Book* of the International Lesbian and Gay Association baldly affirms that in Cuba "homosexual behavior is illegal,"[8] and gay periodicals such as *Lexicon* in Toronto repeat that "homosexuality is illegal" there,[9] it is not surprising that most people,
straight and gay, continue to believe that homosexuals in Cuba are
subject to exceptional oppression and attribute this to the revolutionary regime. This belief has been reinforced by concerns, well-in-
tentioned but typically poorly informed, expressed about Cuba's
AIDS prevention program. When some improvements are grudg-
ingly recognized by glossy magazines targeted at affluent gay readers, such as *The Advocate,* they are deliberately distorted and framed

so as to undermine the significance of any positive change. Thus a 1995 article in *The Advocate* acknowledging the emergence of a more enlightened AIDS policy is replete with malicious falsehoods and headlined "AIDS Crisis in Cuba."[10] Some aspects of Cuba's AIDS prevention program may deserve criticism, but there is hardly a crisis. One wonders what language *The Advocate* editors would use to describe the situation in almost every other Caribbean country, where AIDS crises truly exist.

My study has been written as a contribution to this discourse. To a certain extent it represents a response to the lack of information, to misinformation, and to prejudiced opinions, particularly within the gay communities of North America of which I am a part. My work is also intended to enlighten general readers, including those Leftists who ignore the oppression of homosexuals when they denounce violation of human rights in the Third World.

Many straight male radicals seem completely oblivious of the homophobia within them, which leads them to ignore or trivialize the issue of homosexual oppression. Thus, for example, Sheldon Liss, who professes to share the worldviews of Fidel Castro, uncritically accepts in a one-sentence reference Castro's claim that "he has sought to eliminate discrimination against homosexuality."[11] It is a preposterous statement, doubly so on account of his total failure to substantiate it in terms of Cuba's actual policies. Even in a work as simplistic as that of Liss, his trivialization of an issue that has adversely affected untold numbers of Cubans is unconscionable. Better to say nothing on the subject.

The social revolutions that are so desperately needed in Latin America do not guarantee that either socioeconomic development or gay liberation will occur, but they are indispensable if substantial progress toward either goal is to occur. The belief that homosexuals can experience meaningful liberation when the majority of those who engage in same-sex sex share the poverty, educational deprivation, and ill health that plague much of the rest of the population is as absurd as to believe that the economic problems of the majority of Latin Americans will be solved by the implementation of neoliberal economic policies. How could one possibly believe this of a country such as Mexico, whose recent neoliberal reforms have driven it into bankruptcy and polarized its wealth to such an extent that, according to a recent study prepared for Development Gap, the assets of its richest individual now exceed the total annual income of the poorest 17 million Mexicans?[12] That is why there is an evident tension in this work between the documentation of the oppressive treatment of homosexuals in Cuba and an analysis of the overall revolutionary process that with all its virtues and defects has improved the welfare of the majority of Cubans.

Since I live in Canada I may not avoid making North American assumptions about what constitutes homosexual oppression and liberation (even though at the unconscious level). I have tried to be aware of this danger. I would like to establish at the outset that I do not believe that the dominant model of gay liberation in North America should necessarily establish the criteria by which the situation of homosexuals in Cuba and Latin America should be judged. It is ethnocentric and even an expression of cultural imperialism to believe it should.

To be sure, the gay movement in North America has been at the forefront of the struggles to assert the civil rights, self-expression, and visibility of gays and lesbians. At the same time, however, it has been limited by the self-absorbed individualism, and commodifying consumerism that characterize American culture. Nevertheless, one must also recognize that in the contemporary world, so dominated by American mass culture, North American values and codes of behavior tend to penetrate and to be accepted increasingly by those homosexuals committed to gay liberation in Latin America. Certainly this is true in Mexico and Costa Rica, and it may be becoming more true in Cuba. On the other hand, the concept of a gay identity still has little resonance among most Cuban males who have sex with other males, which is one of the reasons why I have felt ambivalent about using the term "gay," especially in the historical parts of the text. Even when the term is used in Cuba it is not clear that it has the political meaning that it has in North America. That is why I preferred to use "homosexual" instead of "gay" in the Spanish-language drafts of this work that were read by many Cubans over the years. Use of the term "gay" in a text primarily directed to North American readers may obscure rather than illuminate the separate character and perceived needs of gay Cubans, whether or not Cubans themselves have begun to use the term. Moreover, even in North America it may be a transitional term insofar as it is being supplanted by "queer" among many gays who question its adequacy to convey new and diverse definitions of sexual and cultural identity.

The problem of using language and values that respect the sensibilities and experiences of other cultures is not confined to the term "gay"; it also arises with respect to racial references. In particular, I am thinking of how to refer to "racialized" communities in Cuba. For example, is it proper to use the term "mulatto," which has racist origins and is unacceptable in North America but is commonly and unpejoratively used in Cuba? Would it be better to use "mixed racial heritage," even though we now know that all races are "mixed"? Moreover if the term were translated into Spanish literally, it would be meaningless to most Cubans. In place of "mulatto" they might use *mestizo,* a term that is equally problematic since it literally means "mongrel" and in most of Latin America refers (pejoratively) to someone who speaks Spanish but is mostly aboriginal or Indian in origin. The same problem is presented by the use of the term "African Cubans" to refer to Cuban blacks, few of whom politically identify with their African ancestry the way politicized African Americans increasingly do. Instead, they generally refer to themselves as *negros* and *mulatos.* For this reason, it seems artificial to substitute a North American term or terms for those that have meaning in Cuba. As Lourdes Casal (a black Cuban American) noted, there is a problem with "the tendency to apply to the Cuban context formulations derived from the black experience in other contexts, particularly the United States."[13] At the very least continual qualification of the term "African Cuban" would be needed to refer to the color of the individuals concerned because people of mixed racial heritage are considered a distinct racial group in Cuba, even though they are not in North America. I have decided to deal with the issue by using the Cuban term *mulato* in place of "mulatto," which is indeed unacceptable in North America. If and when the Cuban term is rejected and replaced by one more acceptable to those it describes, I will of course use the preferred new term.

Perhaps this is an opportune moment to concede that *Machos,*

*Maricones, and Gays* may be an ambivalent and contradictory work. I do not apologize for this. I do not attempt to offer easy solutions to the issue of reconciling the need for gay liberation with the struggle for national liberation. It is easy to denounce the oppression of homosexuals and that of underdeveloped Third World nations, but it is much harder to demonstrate how both can be overcome in the concrete historical circumstances within which they have originated and persist. The problem is compounded by the fact that I am a gay person who identifies with the national struggles of the Third World as much as to gay liberation within it.

This book offers a historical account of the social construction and regulation of homosexuality in Cuba, particularly in modern times. I hope that I have been fair to the facts, but I am not a disinterested observer. I am emotionally involved in the fate of the revolution and that of homosexuals in particular. This work is inevitably based on participant observation as much as on conventional academic sources. Since 1965 I have spent long periods of time in Cuba as a student, researcher, and visitor. I have always preserved my independence and have never been sponsored by the Cuban government; nor have I cultivated ties with Cuban institutions. Until recently, this would have been counterproductive if not fatal to this kind of study. I have always stayed in small hotels catering mostly to Cubans or in private homes and have lived on a very modest budget. My interpretation of gay oppression in Cuba is influenced by this experience and particularly by my friendships and shared times with gay Cubans. Without such close contacts neither I nor anyone else could do justice to the issue. That is why I have deliberately not addressed the situation of lesbians.

Since virtually nobody is "out" in terms of being willing to be publicly identified as gay in Cuba, I have decided not to give the names of any of the gay people whom I have interviewed. To mention the names of those in elite circles who are understood to be gay would be to accord undue privilege to their opinions, particularly because their experience is not likely to coincide with that of ordinary people.

My final analysis is critical of the regime's politics but still optimistic about the positive consequences for gays that accrue from the changes in Cuban society since 1959. The contradictory conclusions reflect my own ambivalence about the Cuban revolution. Although I continue to support strongly Cuba's right to self-determination, I am also disillusioned and angered by the continued authoritarian aspects of the regime that have harmed gay males and many other Cubans. Still I think that it would be an immense tragedy if the revolution were to be overthrown in a way that undermined, discarded, and ignored its social achievements. They must be preserved as the rightful legacy of the Cuban people and as a beacon of hope for the oppressed people elsewhere in Latin America. Cuba has begun to bring about many reforms. I hope that they will be accelerated and succeed.

# MACHOS, MARICONES, AND GAYS

# ONE

## An Introduction to
## Contemporary Cuba

*MOST VISITORS* who come to Cuba to study the revolution first set foot at José Martí airport in Havana and acquire their initial impressions of the country from the nation's capital. A visit to Havana can be as deceiving today as it was before 1959. Until then Havana lived off the wealth produced in the countryside and enjoyed an immeasurably higher standard of living than did Cuba's rural hinterland. There was a large middle class, which enjoyed many of the amenities associated with the American way of life. The country as a whole suffered from underdevelopment, manifested especially in high unemployment and lack of manufacturing industry, but these problems were less apparent in the capital than in the countryside.

Consumer goods were imported from Florida or were made in Cuba by American branch plants, in exchange for Cuban sugar and tobacco. Havana was an extension of the U.S. domestic market, and American influence was felt everywhere. Advertisements for American products saturated newspapers, billboards, and the television screens that were as ubiquitous in Havana as in Florida. Havana's modern downtown, replete with high-rise apartment buildings and broad thoroughfares, was in many ways more reminiscent of Miami than of Mexico City or San José.

To visitors, then, Havana may have seemed like the capital of a relatively prosperous country, but the rest of Cuba, with few exceptions, belied this impression. Rural society and its economy had long been stagnant. Vast stretches of the countryside had been left untended. The structure of Cuba's agricultural economy, largely based on sugar-cane plantations, huge cattle ranches, and precarious peasant holdings, inhibited the emergence of a vibrant rural culture. There were neither strong *campesino* (peasant or self-employed farming) institutions nor amenities such as schools, hospitals, electricity, and roads. Instead, there was large-scale seasonal unemployment and constant migration to Havana, which was an altogether different world.

In some respects, Havana today continues to be unrepresentative of Cuba. To be sure, the gap in economic and cultural standards has been considerably reduced. The capital does not accurately reflect what has happened during the last three decades precisely because the transformation wrought by the 1959 revolution is most evident in rural Cuba. If Havana was privileged during the prerevolutionary regime, the inverse is true today. Although health and educational facilities have been improved and expanded since the fall of Fulgencio Batista's government, relatively little has otherwise been invested in the physical infrastructure of the city. Provincial capitals are in much better condition.

Physically, Havana now seems quite different from most Latin American capitals. Thirty years ago, its modern hub, Vedado, must have seemed as contemporary as the center of any other Latin American metropolis. No new high-rises have been built there since the early 1960s—the ostentatious new Cohiba Hotel being the most conspicuous exception—and it continues to be dominated by familiar landmarks such as the Habana Libre Hotel and the Focsa Building. Almost every building in Havana now looks run down; most have not had new paint for decades. The stores that distribute rationed food and clothing have become increasingly empty and threadbare. Other goods are virtually unattainable except where customers pay with U.S. dollars. At night street lights are dimmed to save electricity. Power outages are routine. To catch and board one of the capital's jammed buses is a major achievement. Bikes have suddenly become ubiquitous, defying potholes, nighttime darkness, and cars driven oblivious of traffic signs and speed limits.

Walking at night is a major challenge. At any moment you may have to jump out of the way to avoid an untended pothole or a bike hurtling out of nowhere. You place your life in the hands of the gods yet not in the hands of people about to assault you. You can go out on the street almost anywhere during one of Havana's power outages (and many people, including women, have no alternative but to do so) without fear of being raped or assaulted. There has been a recent increase in robbery because of the economic crisis. Nevertheless, the serenity of street life after dark is astonishing in comparison to the eerie, fearful tension that pervades the empty streets of most large U.S. cities and to the social violence that marks the crowded, impoverished barrios of many a Latin American city.

Havana lacks the bustle and noise of traffic, markets, street vendors, and cantinas that you find in places like Mexico City and San José. Until the recent advent of joint ventures with foreign corporations, its billboards have also been strikingly different from others in the hemisphere. Instead of advertisements for Coca Cola and Marlboro cigarettes there are political slogans and educational statements.

The majority of visitors, regardless of their politics, feel ambivalent about Havana's physical appearance. You know that it is the capital of a poor Communist country with different priorities from those of Mexico and Costa Rica. Everywhere you encounter the effects of the American embargo, which is aggravated by the collapse of trade with the former Communist bloc. The empty stores and the ever-present queues evoke unpleasant images for those who associate scarcity and drab monotony with the repressive regimes of the former Communist countries in Europe. People who love it would like to see Havana regain the tropical vivacity (epitomized by the annual carnival) that once made it famous. Aficionados of the city also long for the day when the gorgeous colonial buildings lining the sea-front Malecón and the narrow streets and squares of Old Havana will be restored. Habana Vieja has been designated by the United Nations Educational, Scientific, and Cultural Organization (UNESCO) as a World Heritage site. Though pockets of Old Havana have been restored, the ruined state of much of it confronts you when you walk by its fallen balconies, crumbling buildings, and rubble-strewn sidewalks. You ask yourself if there is time left for Havana to reemerge as the Pearl of the Antilles, surely one of the most beautiful cities in the world.

There is one other major difference between Havana and other Latin American cities, one that is too easily taken for granted. The shops are empty and the food is monotonous and scarce; housing conditions may appall; people may complain about everything; but until very recently impoverished children and mothers begging on the street were nowhere to be found. In their place you see the most obvious fruits of the revolution—children and youths of every color with bodies that radiate health and vitality. They all seem to be in school, and although they bitterly complain about the lack of clothes, overall they are as well dressed and, until the present crisis, certainly better fed than the majority of Latin Americans. Finally, there is a greater mixing and blending of races among all classes than anywhere else in the region.

There are tough working class municipalities, such as Regla and San Miguel del Padrón, in metropolitan Havana and some that remain much more privileged—Vedado or Miramar, for example. Living conditions in much of Habana Vieja and Centro

Habana are often miserable. People in crowded and crumbling tenements are plagued by blackouts and often lack running water and gas. Though their difficulties are in many ways similar to those of the *vecindades* in the heart of Mexico City, it can be argued that Havana's poor are not marginalized as they would be elsewhere in Latin America or in American inner-city ghettoes. To be sure, some truly miserable barrios, largely populated by impoverished, scantily educated blacks, persist—such as Pogolotti and Cocosolo on the outskirts of Marianao (another municipality). They seem worlds apart from the rest of the city and of course are rarely seen by most visitors. Though such exceptional barrios exist, most poor neighborhoods are not bound by class, race, or culture. In almost every block you will find families headed by professionals unable to find better accommodation elsewhere, as well as families in which semiliterate grandmothers live with children and grandchildren who have become doctors and engineers. In less than two generations the extension of health, education, and employment has all but terminated the marginalization of whole sectors of the population. Blacks are integrated into the mainstream of society in a way that would seem inconceivable under present conditions in North America. The new homogeneity of Cuba's people is most apparent in the country's mass culture.

There is undoubtedly much that is problematic about Cuban culture, particularly the fact that until recently much of it has been controlled by a bureaucratic state. The Communist Party retains ultimate control over all the media and cultural outlets ranging from the stultifying newspapers to the bookstores whose shelves are laden with unsought official texts. But such ideological control does not preclude the existence of rich and varied cultural activities. Only when a cultural issue is interpreted by state bureaucrats as representing a direct and serious challenge to the authority and legitimacy of the regime is political censorship exercised. In fact, theater, film, and popular music in Havana are full of satire and criticism of the problems that Cubans confront in everyday life. To be sure, some inequality in access to cultural events inevitably persists. But few countries have done more than Cuba to extend cultural opportunities—theater, music, dance, crafts—to every class and region. Unlike Mexico (and in some respects even Costa Rica), Cuba no longer systematically renders ignorant large sectors of the population through mindless comic books and sensational tabloids. Cubans may be deprived of a wide range of civil rights, but almost all young Cubans can realistically aspire to participate in national culture and public discourse. They may not agree with the regime's policies at home or abroad, and many may fear to criticize them in public, but most Cubans are informed about their major elements. In short, Cuba increasingly enjoys an integrated modern culture capable of applying reasonable solutions to social problems and issues. Nevertheless, newcomers to the country can be taken aback by the persistence of habits, beliefs, and taboos that seem idiosyncratic to outsiders. At times it seems that there is not a single Cuban who, in a crisis, will not resort to making an offering to Ochún (Virgen de la Caridad), Yemayá (Virgen de Regla), or to Babalú Ayé (San Lázaro), or consult a *santero* to divine their future with the aid of coconut, cards, and shells.[1]

Though an abortion or a divorce seems to involve no more than a routine visit to the appropriate office, there are still teenage brides who get married because they cannot imagine a more meaningful way to order their lives. Until the beginning of the 1990s young people who in other respects seemed to be as cosmopolitan as any surprised you by announcing as a matter of fact that only under certain circumstances might you wear shorts or sandals, regardless of the boundless heat and humidity of Havana summers. Until quite recently, universities prohibited students from wearing shorts, and in some provincial towns the police still enforce the number of shirt buttons that may be left undone when men are out at night.

Cuban homophobia is a part of this traditional culture. This homophobia is as much a product of folk prejudices about appropriate masculinity as it is of a conscious need to repress homosexual behavior. Its character is quite different from the fear and rage triggered in Anglo-American culture by males having sex with one another.

There is little malice or hostility in Cuban popular culture. This good nature is something that must be constantly remembered when you try to assess the prejudicial references to minorities that abound in casual Cuban conversations. They are shocking to liberal foreign visitors who have learned to "know better" than to say such things (and less frequently not to feel them). Cubans are different from North Americans in the way they express feelings about race, gender, sexuality, and physical appearance. People commonly refer to others, often to their face, as *fea* (ugly) or *gordo* (fat) without meaning to be unkind. Terms like *maricón,* whose literal translation in a homosexual context is queer or fag, on occasion may be used with underlying affection by heterosexuals in a way that straight North Americans never would, as in, for example, "Tú eres tremendo maricón" (You are a great queen). The same is true of racial references, including verbal ones like *china* (Chinese) and the diminutive *negrito,* as well as physical gestures such as stroking the forearm, which white Cubans nearly always do when they make a critical allusion to a person's blackness. Since racism remains endemic to Cuban society, these actions sometimes reflect hardened racism. But more often they are culturally ingrained expressions and mannerisms whose lack of self-conscious intolerance can be best understood in terms of how whites, *mulatos,* and blacks relate to each other in practice. The fusion of revolutionary values with traditional ones has created a culture that is less alienated in terms of personal connectedness than that of the United States and Canada, which is increasingly dominated by monetary interactions.

Although Havana now looks like no other Latin American capital, its people remain unmistakably Latin. An abundant street and home life is what characterizes Latin America and reveals the soul of its principal cities. In Havana there is a continuous flow of people running errands to the corner, borrowing something from a neighbor, greeting people passing on the sidewalk, kissing visitors as they come and go, or looking for someone with whom to *chismear* (gossip). Cubans tend to be gregarious extroverts who are not put out at all by strangers talking to them in public. This friendliness makes it easier for men who are open to having sex with other men to connect in public places. Those who associate Cuba with homophobic repression would be surprised to know that "homosexuals in Cuba find it much easier to be open and free about conveying sexual desire in the street than they would in Canada" (according to one gay émigré living in Toronto).

The pleasure that Latin Americans take in socializing with each other is manifest in Havana. In spite of all the stress of material and political restrictions on their everyday life, the majority of Cubans still find time for each other. They love partying with friends (and even strangers) whether in an impromptu get-together at home (where they remain oblivious to the effect of their loud music on the neighbors), sharing a bottle of rum on the seafront wall of the Malecón until the early hours of the morning, or in more organized weekend fiestas to which all seem to be invited. Cubans show off their sex appeal everywhere. And yes, it's true, Cuban men are hot and handsome. They enjoy expressing desire and being desired. Gay "attitude" is as rare in Cuba as it is common in Toronto.

The warm-hearted quality of interpersonal relations, most evident in the extended family, is not unique to revolutionary Cuba, of course. It is evident throughout much of Latin America and the Third World in general. That it is not an inherent quality of Cuban or Latin American culture is evident in the banal, addictive materialism embraced by many Cubans in Miami and the emerging middle classes elsewhere in Latin America. If generos-

ity of spirit has remained a feature of Cuban life, and indeed may
have grown stronger in recent times, its survival is surely due to
the collective spirit associated with the Cuban revolution as much
as to the futility of acquisitive materialism in the impoverished
conditions of contemporary Cuba.

The psychic rage and social intolerance that ensue from what
Philip Slater so aptly named "the pursuit of loneliness"[2] are simply not evident in the countenances and behavior of the Cuban
people. Their lives may be increasingly stressful on account of
material shortages and deprivations, and they may be increasingly angry with the shortcomings of the revolution. In fact, the
antigovernment demonstrations in Central Havana in August
1994 may turn into widespread rioting if material conditions do
not soon improve. Still, it seems inconceivable that the huge numbers of young people who gather along the Malecón at night,
many of them bored out of their minds, could engage in the ni-
hilistic rioting that has become an ever more prominent feature
of North American society. Just two recent examples are the Van-
couver riots following the Canucks' 1994 Stanley Cup defeat and
the riots on California beaches that have led to the imposition of
dusk curfews. The lack of such psychic dissatisfaction is one of the
factors that explains why queer baiting and rabid queer bashing,
still an omnipresent threat to most gays and lesbians in North
America, are virtually nonexistent in Cuba, despite its homophobic reputation abroad.

Still, life in Havana is obviously far from idyllic. The inhabitants of the capital are clearly much more restrained and tense
than they were in the 1960s. Does this mean that they are ex-
hausted by struggle, most recently by efforts to survive the current crisis, or is the evident stress simply a reflection of the values
of modernization and development? Whatever the reason, life in
Havana can be very hard and frustrating. As the popular Cuban
expression goes, "No es fácil" (It's not easy).

The shortage of consumer goods is bad enough, but Cubans

also have to endure countless other shortages and inconveniences that are the result of bureaucratic indifference and ideological dogmatism.[3] Although at long last there is starting to be improvement, now that many self-employed tradespeople have been allowed to operate, public services have typically been dreadful. Service and the range of goods have improved in dollar stores, which offer otherwise unavailable goods to tourists, foreign residents, and those Cubans in possession of dollars (legal since 1994), but not in shops run by the state. When Cubans are searching for everyday necessities, trying to repair something, or seeking information from a public official, their efforts are invariably complicated by incredible delays and frustration. Those who staff stores and government offices have had devastating ways of conveying that at best the problems are not their fault and at worst that they could not care less whether customers are satisfied with the service.

It is easy to see why an increasing number of Cubans have begun to question the nature of their regime, for everywhere they are reminded that they live in a bureaucratic one-party state where official institutions and government-controlled mass organizations are never challenged by countervailing private bodies. Though the situation has recently begun to change with respect to cultural organizations, civil society, independent of the state, scarcely exists. The Federation of Cuban Women (FMC) has ostensibly become a nongovernmental organization (NGO), but it hardly represents an independent women's movement. Even if true NGOs did exist, there would be no way for them effectively to challenge government policies since the state ultimately controls all the media, educational institutions, meeting places, and so on. Accordingly, until very recently there has been no place for groups such as AIDS-education organizations, let alone for groups advocating lesbian and gay rights.

These absences, which are the essence of Cuba's one-party state, account for the stultifying lifelessness of public life in Cuba.

Public life is devoid of the clash of competing interests and viewpoints and fails to reflect the diverse human needs and problems of individual Cubans. In this respect, Cuba is the stereotypical Leninist state, which supposedly resolves all issues within the appropriate state organizations.

This political system has increasingly been called into question. The revolution has reached a new stage, one intensified by the economic crisis precipitated by the collapse of the old Communist bloc but a stage that it would have reached regardless of events in Europe. The revolutionary regime has redistributed wealth and income and created the infrastructure for basic social services and for the functioning of a modern economy. The challenge increasingly has become that of generating the economic growth and dynamism necessary to sustain these services. Action is also required to create meaningful employment and fulfilling personal lives for those raised in the postrevolutionary period. There is no way now of knowing whether Cuba could have made progress on these issues if its external environment had not radically changed. What is not in doubt is that the radical change that has occurred has deepened Cuba's crisis while paradoxically offering it a new opportunity to reform its political and economic system.

Almost overnight Cuba was economically and politically cut off from its one-time Communist partners in Europe. It must now find substitutes for the economies that were once its main source of trade and credit. It is hampered by huge debts, lack of foreign exchange, and the malaise caused by the Western hemisphere's worst social and economic crisis since the 1930s. It must find new means of sustaining belief in communism despite its universal rejection elsewhere and the terrible economic crisis within Cuba itself.

The sudden rejection of Marxism-Leninism in Eastern Europe and the former Soviet Union and the collapse of communism at its very core surprised Cubans and had dramatic consequences for them.[4] Some 85 percent of the country's foreign trade was once with the Soviet Union and Eastern Europe. Consequently its ability to import goods has now fallen by 75 percent. There is no oil, factories are shut down, and the GNP may have fallen by 60 percent. Cuba is not only in a social and economic crisis: For the first time, the very survival of the revolution is an issue.

Supposedly, Cuba has been undergoing a process of "rectification" since 1986, a process that, according to its leaders, is not only similar to, but predates, perestroika in the former Soviet Union. Long before Mikhail Gorbachev unleashed the forces that culminated in the fall of the Berlin Wall and of the Kremlin itself, it was evident that events were not unfolding according to plan in Cuba. The response of Fidel Castro was that Cuba was willing to question and to change everything except the fundamental principles of the revolution, which included a commitment to its own version of democracy—that is, one that eschewed conventional party politics. As with so many of his other declarations, his rhetoric was more impressive than the changes it effected. If Cuba had really begun in 1986 to rectify its economic policies, perhaps its current crisis would not have been so severe.

Cuba's leaders, like its people, cannot ignore the magnitude of the nation's crisis. The "special period," as it is called in Cuba, may be temporary, and the major social and structural changes associated with the revolution may survive, but for the moment the viability of the revolutionary project is more in doubt than ever before. Ideologically Cuba is more isolated than at any time since 1959. Some Cubans may still feel committed to the revolutionary transformation of Latin America, but today that metamorphosis is only a dream, given that the revolutionary movements in the region, let alone revolutionary governments, are weaker than they have been for a long time. The United States reigns supreme in the Western Hemisphere, and one country after another in Latin America is following the Canadian example of economic, political, and cultural integration with the United States.

The Cuban American Foundation in Miami and the American Right eagerly anticipate the collapse of Cuban communism and plan the reconstruction of Cuba in their own image. Within Cuba, the crisis has given heart to both reformist and counter-revolutionary critics. They do not have much of an organized base, but their existence can no longer be denied. The bulk of the Cuban people remain at least tacit supporters of the revolution,[5] but a large number wait for a change in the "system," as they call it. People want something to happen. The "survival of the revolution" is no longer sufficient, nor is "saving the country's honor," despite the empty slogans proclaimed on the billboards everywhere.

The most obvious sign of the times is that Cubans no longer rely on the state to meet basic needs such as food. The official food ration now barely meets subsistence needs, so almost everybody has to find ways of supplementing it by scrounging dollars or making deals in _el bisne_ (private business, usually entailing goods stolen from state enterprises, and the black market.) At the same time, the regime's ability to mobilize the support of the population around its own agenda has visibly declined. So has its capacity to ensure that its edicts are respected and implemented whether they relate to the black market, to the functions of the police, to the role of the Committees to Defend the Revolution (CDRs), or to the now endemic corruption. Officials responsible for upholding the law often belong to families who feel they can only survive by breaking the law. So widespread has disparagement of the law become that it is logical to wonder whether the state now turns a blind eye to illegal, once counterrevolutionary activities. One way or another, more and more Cubans, at least in Havana, live different private and public lives. They seek personal ways to resolve their problems and to organize their lives.

The future of the revolution will in large measure be determined

by its success in meeting the expectations of the generation produced by the revolution itself. Cuba's leaders, indeed the whole
generation that made the revolution, are getting on in years—Fidel Castro himself is now approaching seventy—and more than
three-fifths of the population has been born since 1959. The intellectual, cultural, and indeed political expectations of these children of the revolution increasingly differ from those who made
it. More to the point in terms of the present study, they include
the most sexually active group of the population.

Until recently, an impressive number of young Cubans still
shared the altruistic goals of the generation that made the revolution. They may not have been the majority of Cuban youth,
but many still volunteered to participate in agricultural labor
and dreamed of working in Africa or in Nicaragua. Now it has
become evident that the social and political preoccupations of
Cuba's youth are increasingly diverging from those of Cuba's
leaders, who are thirty to forty years older than they are. A young
engineering student who described Fidel Castro as "archaic" to
me in 1989, at a time when almost everybody in Havana was agog
with anticipation of Mikhail Gorbachev's visit to Cuba, simply
showed the conceit typical of youth. Those like him just tune Fidel out. Yet others, even before Cuba's current crisis, indulged in
public ridicule of the Cuban leader when he appeared on television.[6] Though the claim of a young black man that "aquí nadie es
comunista" (nobody is Communist here) may not quite apply to
the older generation, it contains more than a grain of truth with
respect to young Cubans. This is a judgment of youth on Cuba's
Communist regime, but it is not necessarily an accurate judgment
of the revolution's success. For the consciousness of Cuba's youth
is a reflection of both the material and educational advances since
1959 and the current widespread rejection of the regime on other
grounds.

Almost every young Cuban receives at least a ninth-grade education and remains in school until age sixteen. Almost two hun-

dred thousand students are enrolled in advanced postsecondary institutions and an equal number are studying in junior technical colleges. Unlike the rest of Latin America (with the possible exception of Costa Rica), good health care and nutrition have been regarded as indispensable complements to the provision of educational facilities for Cuba's youth. In addition, Cuba is committed to making culture (narrowly defined) available to everyone. This is evident in the low prices and range of theater, dance, and music that are available on stage or in open spaces like the Parque Central in Old Havana. It is evident in the quantity and quality of translated foreign and domestic books that have been published at low prices in huge editions. Finally it is evident in events such as the annual film festival (New Latin American Cinema), which has an impact as great as Toronto's Festival. Until recently the range of foreign films offered in Havana far exceeded that available in most large North American cities.

When you attend a cultural event in Havana you come away as impressed by the informed and critical engagement of the audience as you are by the innovative quality of the performance itself. This involvement is far removed from the commodified nature of so many mainstream cultural events in North America. Ironically, the vitality of Cuban culture has also intensified the anticommunist social and political consciousness of Cuban youth. They have reacted to the regimentation imposed by a Communist regime isolated on a small island by developing an unquenchable thirst for information about what is happening abroad. Despite their exposure to propagandistic, censored media, Cuba's youth tend to be much better informed about the world than their Canadian and American counterparts. Notwithstanding some material and ideological shortcomings (such as being forced to take courses in "scientific socialism" at university), Cubans receive a more rounded education than most North Americans. Their rejection of communism as a political system does not come from ignorant, self-centered chauvinism, as anticommunism so often does in the United States; it springs from knowledge of political developments worldwide as well as from their own experience of Cuba.

Cuba's youth are as much products of the contemporary global youth culture as of their education and upbringing within Cuba. Their aspirations for personal consumption and leisure are not all that different from those of the young people in Mexico City and San José. The problem for Cubans is that while only a minority of (middle-class) Mexicans or Costa Ricans can satisfy their tastes, virtually no Cubans can do so. Cuban young people are sick of being told what conditions were like before the revolution and what they are still like for the majority of people elsewhere in Latin America. Their standard is their own experience of the relatively affluent early 1980s and not the corrupt and unequal conditions of 1958 or the poverty of rural *campesinos* and urban slum dwellers elsewhere in Latin America. Though they may have been reduced to living in Third World conditions, the expectations of young Cubans reflect their privileged adolescence, which had more in common with the First than with the Third World. Their expectations have also been reinforced by the growing number of foreign tourists. Since they have been taught to think of themselves as equal to others, and not as their servants, they naturally want what the tourists have.

Many of the needs and desires of Cuban youth are inspired by American mass culture, to which Cubans have been attracted since they were drawn into the U.S. orbit in the late nineteenth century. Although Cubans cling to Spanish and African influences in their traditional and popular culture, they lean to the United States when it comes to modern culture. Their mass culture is every bit as brash and materialistic as that of the United States. Cubans like individual Americans in a way that would be incomprehensible to most Mexicans, whose traditional culture remains so different from that of the United States. *Yanqui* and *yuma* (a street expression), the Cuban terms for Americans, have a totally different connotation from *gringo,* which is used in Mexico. *Yanqui* is political and focused upon the U.S. government and corporate ruling class; *gringo* includes a pejorative rejection of the materialism and self-preoccupation associated with individual Americans.

Cubans' comfort with American culture stands in marked contrast with their attitude to that of the former Soviet Union. Those who studied or worked in the once Communist countries frequently developed a deep respect for their cultures and people. But within Cuba, most people saw Russians and East Europeans as outsiders, an attitude reinforced by the fact that the visitors were typically housed in separate apartment complexes. Furthermore, unlike Americans, they tended to be stiff and formal. From a Cuban perspective, they also dressed badly and completely lacked sex appeal.

Despite all the Cuba-USSR cultural exchanges over thirty years and the presence of large numbers of Soviet advisers in Cuba, Russians remained as culturally exotic as Martians to most Cubans. They were highly conspicuous in their isolation, whether on the beaches of the Playas del Este or on the streets of Havana. Until the advent of the glasnost new-wave films, Cubans only saw Russian films when obliged to for lack of alternatives. They rarely disturbed the dust on the jackets of the Soviet books that lined the shelves of every bookstore. In short, the Russians came and went without leaving the slightest imprint on Cuban society and culture—partly because they always respected Cuban sovereignty and, unlike the United States, made no attempt to impose themselves on Cuban life.

The addiction to American mass culture, on the other hand, persists despite all the political odds against it. The United States has tried to isolate Cuba from all its goods except counterrevolutionary propaganda. The U.S. government has a long-standing embargo on trade with Cuba and forbids travel by U.S. citizens to Cuba. For its part, the Cuban government has tried to resist the penetration of American culture, particularly the consumerism with which it is associated. Neither side has met its objectives.

The United States has not been able to quarantine Cuba, which now has diplomatic and commercial relations with all the major Latin American countries. In addition, since the collapse of the Communist bloc, Cuba has expanded its trade and investment agreements with an ever-increasing number of corporations from outside the region, notably from Canada and the nations of the European Union. Foreign tourists flock to Cuba from Canada, Western Europe, and Latin America as to any other spot in the Caribbean. For its part, the Cuban government too has failed to convince ordinary Cubans that life in the United States is akin to hell on earth. It sometimes seems as if every inhabitant of Havana has a relative or friend in the United States who keeps in touch by phone, mail, and intermediaries. Furthermore, even before Radio Martí started to beam its anticommunist propaganda from Washington, many Cubans could easily tune in to American radio and some could even pick up television stations. The rest of the population spreads the word in quintessential Cuban fashion.

Cubans continue to want things associated with the American way of life. They see the clothes and gadgets that tourists and visiting Cuban émigrés bring with them. They know the range, quality, and price of the articles that can be bought in Cuba's dollar stores by those who have the greenbacks. They hear advertisements in Spanish on Miami stations. They also watch the latest Hollywood movies on local television and at video centers. Despite the radical shift in Cuba's economic system, trading patterns, and political alignments, much of the country's mass culture remains as Americanized as it was before 1959.

Young people's continuing love affair with U.S. fashions contrasts sharply with their discontent about their prospects in revolutionary Cuba. The regime's restrictions on everyday life have become more intolerable as they are seen as not only repressive but also unnecessary and out of step with the liberalization happening in former Communist countries. Although Cubans recognize that the present crisis was caused by circumstances beyond Cuba's control, such as the collapse of Communism and the ever-tightening U.S. blockade, they also blame the government for its refusal to adjust to new circumstances.

For young people, finding useful work is now at least as great a problem as the rigidity of the communist system. Creating work and leisure outlets that can consume the energy of the young and satisfy their needs has been no easy task. There is already a great deal of open and disguised unemployment, most evident in the overblown and incredibly inefficient service sector. Hundreds of thousands have been laid off in an attempt to increase productivity. Educated youths in Cuba do not want to work in agriculture, where there is a labor shortage, any more than young people do in other countries. Until recently they had the advantage of strong job protection, although promotion prospects were fewer than they had been for their parents' generation. Now most have to submit to dull, oppressive jobs, as in most other countries, and their wages do not offer much incentive to extend themselves at work. To be sure they do not have to save for health care and education, which are taken for granted. On the other hand what most young Cubans earn is almost irrelevant in terms of gaining access to stylish clothes, which are very important to them and which are invariably defined as foreign. The same applies to many of their other leisure interests.

Are the young people in Havana typical of those in the whole country? Havana was once incorrectly equated with the whole country, and the tremendous disparity between living standards in the capital and the provinces was ignored. The inhabitants of the interior, except those in some provincial capitals, were very isolated because of the absence of roads, public transport, schools, and electricity. Since 1959, there has been a leveling of regional disparities. Schools, universities, technical colleges, and cultural centers throughout rural Cuba have brought education and training to everyone. An almost equal number are plugged into television now that almost every Cuban home has electricity.

Havana is much more accessible than it was in the past, and many more of its inhabitants have spent time in rural regions than was the case before 1959. Many of its younger residents have studied, worked, or done military service in the interior. Illiterate and humble *guajiros* (peasants) increasingly belong to the past; their educated children, who may have completed their studies in Havana, are more representative of Cuba's present and future. In addition the tendency toward a standardized mass culture makes Havana much more representative of the whole country than it was before 1959.

Cuban popular culture has always had less regional diversity than that of Mexico or even of Costa Rica. Regional cultural differences undoubtedly persist, particularly those related to race and ethnic origins. You do not have to stray far from Havana to realize how different the life of rural Cuba is from that of the Cuban capital. In Havana itself you hear as many scathing references to the backwardness of the *orientales* (those who live in the eastern half of the country) as you do to the high proportion of blacks who live in the former province of Oriente itself. Nevertheless, Havana's cultural hegemony can only grow stronger. There seems little reason to doubt that the capital—with two and a half million inhabitants, six times more than the population of Santiago, the next largest city, and with a fifth of the country's total population—will continue to dominate Cuba's cultural development for the foreseeable future.

One of the most striking changes in revolutionary Cuba has been the transformation of sexual culture, particularly with respect to the youth. This is not surprising given that Cuban young people increasingly share the values of their counterparts throughout the industrialized West, in which similar changes have taken place since the 1960s. The 1959 revolution in Cuba preceded by only a few years the emergence of the new sexual movements associated with women and gays in North America. Their impact was inevitably felt indirectly in Cuba. Since 1959 young Cubans have become much more open and liberal about sex. They have probably become more sexually active as well. The absence of comparative historical data makes this supposition hard to demonstrate,[7] but changes in values and behavior can be observed and deduced by visitors who have had close contact with Cuba over the last thirty-five years.

Many Cubans become sexually active at a very young age. For example, in 1979 a quarter of Cuba's teenage females were married, living in common-law marriages, or were already separated; no fewer than 587 young girls were actually divorced or separated by the age of 14.[8] Whereas birth rates for most Cuban females dropped impressively in the early seventies, they remained very high among teenagers. By 1981, teenage births represented over a third of total births. Moreover, teenage birth rates would have been even higher were it not for the fact that abortions among teens exceeded live births.[9] In the mid-1970s teenage birth rates were as high as they had been at the turn of the century, despite the fact that there was much greater access to contraception and abortion than in the past. It was also the high rate of abortion rather than a decline in impregnation that led to a reduction in birth rates during the 1980s.[10]

High fertility rates among young women are the product of traditional sexism as well as of active sex lives. A surprising number of young women still regard motherhood as their preferred vocation. Changes in the life choices of young Cubans are as complex as other aspects of the cultural and social shifts since 1959. They are results not only of changes in culture, education, public health, housing, employment, and the economy but also of how young people experience those changes in terms of their class and social background. For many adolescents, becoming pregnant or getting married may seem an escape from domestic, parental confinement. In practice, this is rarely the case since lack of housing forces most teenage mothers, married or otherwise, to continue living with their parents. Machismo[11] as much as sexism causes teenage pregnancy since many young males continue to grow up with the belief that they have to demonstrate their virility as early as possible. It is rare to meet young males who have given much thought to the implications of sex to their partners, or to the parenting responsibilities that might come from failure to use birth control. Until recently men would not use condoms because they diminished penile sensation, and women disliked condoms since they were associated with protection from prostitutes infected by venereal disease. The high incidence of abortion, which is legal and free—in the 1980s there were eighty abortions for every hundred births—suggests that women are still expected to assume personal responsibility for unplanned pregnancies. Homophobia is an indirect cause of pregnancies, because many homosexual males try to mask their sexual orientation by getting their supposed *novias* (girlfriends) and wives pregnant.

There have always been Cubans who were proud of being *caliente* (passionate), but before the revolution there was much more hypocrisy about sex than there is now. At one time only young men were expected to explore their sexuality, while young women were supposed to be virgins until marriage and chaste thereafter. Today, premarital sex is commonplace, whether or not partners are forming a relationship. Few women still believe that they should be virgins upon marriage, and they reject moral judgments about women who have "lost" their virginity before marriage.[12] Young women seem very much at ease with their sexuality.

Most teenage girls become sexually active when they are scarcely beyond puberty. It is quite apparent that most Cuban girls in their early teens are sexually preoccupied, far more so than girls of the same age in Mexico or Costa Rica. Thirteen- and fourteen-year-old girls dress in a sexually provocative way and date outside the home in a way that most girls of the same age would never have been allowed to do before 1959. At an open-air dance I attended in 1988 in Trinidad, a traditional colonial town some two hundred miles from Havana, the carriage of older teenagers appeared almost blasé in comparison to the erotic body language of the younger teens dancing to the music of Madonna.

Women have benefited from the relaxation of sexual mores because double standards are much weaker than before. Homosexual males have also received benefits, but these are largely indirect rather than the result of a state policy intended to change public attitudes toward gay males. More tolerant attitudes come instead from the greater openness and honesty about sexuality among young people in particular. Teenagers are too busy meeting their own sexual needs to worry about the inclinations of others. As one black student athlete said, "Before, people used to get really pissed off by homosexuals. But it's not the same now. Let everyone enjoy themselves as they see fit."

Family restrictions on adolescent sexuality have been considerably weakened because the traditional household has been weakened. There has been a major increase in divorce and family breakdowns. Where parents have remained together, they have often lacked the time and energy to supervise their children as they might have done in the past. Mothers as well as fathers are more likely to be in the labor force. More of the time that they might once have spent at home is taken up by trying to find food and household supplies and by participating in various political activities. Large numbers of students have spent time away from their homes in the schools-in-the-countryside programs and in other boarding schools, which are coed (as is true of all postrevolutionary schools). Finally, military conscription has also offered opportunities for young males to explore their sexuality away from their home environment.

Attitudes about appropriate gender behavior, too, have changed considerably since 1959. Young Cuban men and women still continue to overvalue traditional masculine prerogatives and the commensurate expectations about how young Cuban women should relate to men. For example, young girls typically comply with their brothers' and boyfriends' expectations that females should do chores for them, such as washing their clothes. Most girls and women also remain preoccupied by how men respond to the way they dress and seem emotionally incomplete without a man.

Nevertheless, there have been important changes in women's social roles and in expectations about how they should behave. The 1975 Family Code and Article 35 of the 1976 Constitution, which call for equal male and female responsibility for housework and child care, are a long way from universal acceptance, but progress toward greater gender equality is quite evident within Cuban homes and in society as a whole.

Women's lives have really changed since 1959. They have gained much greater confidence in themselves because of a complete transformation in their education and occupational opportunities. For the first time in Cuban history (prior to the current crisis), women could conceive of being economically self-sufficient and fully-employed for most of their adult lives, and not dependent upon men and their families for their material well-being. Their public behavior increasingly reflects this fact. Most young women seem far more self-assured and less likely to present themselves as mere sexual objects or marital appendages than they did even as late as the 1960s. The "new woman" may be more evident than the "new man" mythologized by Che Guevara. Sexist prejudices persist, but males are having to confront the fact that women are more than their match in virtually every field of postsecondary education and increasingly in the careers that follow. Well over 50 percent of middle- and high-level professionals in science and technology are women.

Young men are not assuming traditional female tasks as rapidly as women are taking on traditional male roles. Women are becoming doctors faster than men are becoming nurses, for example. The employment of men in day-care centers still seems inconceivable to most Cubans. Nevertheless, the *machista* outlook of young males is being undermined and softened. This shift is clearly evident in the matter of male public appearance. Today young males can dress almost as they please and are no longer expected to achieve an invulnerable look. Earrings, artful haircuts, and casual unisex clothing are the fashion as much as they are in North America. Only on social outings do more traditional notions of dress prevail. Then (much as elsewhere in Latin America) young Cubans dress to the hilt if they have the means.

Old habits and prejudices have been undermined by a variety of forces. Cuba is a much more open society than it was before the revolution. Young Cubans are exposed to music and cultural images that are dominated by the U.S. cultural industry almost as much as the youths in any other part of Latin America. In the 1960s the new Cuban government attempted to foist on the young an official culture, which defined appropriate music, clothes, and hairstyles. Government officials banned blue jeans and the Beatles and tried to make Cubans dance to something called the Mozambique! By the mid-1980s there was much less effort to dissuade young people from enjoying the interests of their choice. Ironically, by the late eighties mass culture may have become less distinctively Cuban than it was before the revolution, despite Cuba's political isolation for much of the intervening period. Cuba's attachment to American mass culture, which has shifted the popular representation of sexual and gender identities in recent times, continues despite all the political odds against it.

Foreign tourism has also begun to affect attitudes to self-presentation. The annual number of foreign tourists already far exceeds that of prerevolutionary times and is expected to reach two million by the year 2000. Their presence is beginning to have a profound influence on Cubans. Tourist facilities were once restricted to Havana and Varadero, but today they are found throughout Cuba. Charter groups are still the norm, but more and more foreigners now travel on their own using local hotels and private homes for accommodation. This is because visiting families attracted by cheap charter packages to the Caribbean have in recent years been joined by an increasing number of more adventuresome young Europeans whose dress and behavior, although initially shocking to some, are likely to serve as models for Cuban youth. Nude sunbathing is taken for granted by many European tourists in Varadero. How long can Cuban conventions and authorities dissuade intrepid youths from doing likewise? A few of the more daring are already following the European example. Even in the Playas del Este outside Havana, a handful of Cubans had joined foreigners taking sun in the buff by the summer of 1994.

Though the extent of cultural change to date is limited, its direction is quite clear. Traditional *machista* values are being gradually undermined. In this context, there is far more social space than formerly where homosexuals can spread their wings.[13] Although there may be fewer ostentatious *locas* (queens) about, the number of more or less visible gay males (depending on the sensibility of the observer) is as great, if not greater, in Havana than in other large Latin American cities. The renewed visibility of homosexuals has created a new awareness of homosexuality among young people that weakens the traditional stereotypes that were reinforced by the homophobic campaigns of the sixties and seventies. Homosexuality is no longer something essentially private and personal (in the sense that its existence is not validated in public). A series of events, starting with the public denunciations in the 1960s, and then proceeding to the homophobic resolutions of the 1971 Congress on Education and Culture, the 1980 Mariel exodus (which included large numbers of homosexuals), and the AIDS epidemic in the 1980s contributed to a growing recognition that homosexuality is integral to contemporary Cuban society. So did the 1993 release of the acclaimed Cuban film *Fresa y chocolate* (Strawberry and chocolate), which addressed homosexual oppression in Cuba. This recognition, however, has not brought legitimacy. The lives of gay males in Cuba continue to be conditioned by the machismo that has pervaded Cuban culture for generations and that the present government has not done enough to challenge.

# TWO

# Machismo and Homosexuality
# before the Revolution

*THE OPPRESSION* of homosexuals in contemporary Cuba cannot be fully understood without relating it to the ways in which male sexuality and gender identity were constructed prior to the revolution. These are linked to the way in which male and female relations were historically organized. For the overall character of a patriarchal society will determine how men relate to each other as much as it determines how they will relate to women. In general, there is a correlation between the oppression of women and the oppression of homosexuals. Still there is no necessary correlation between the latter and the incidence of same-sex sex or homosexuality. The celebration of conventionally masculine values extends to the way in which sexuality is experienced. The right of masculine males to enjoy their sexuality as they see fit matches the power they have in society as a whole. The greater their power, whether in terms of gender, class, or race, the more likely they are to exercise it. Accordingly, before 1959 masculine ostensibly heterosexual males were able to satisfy some of their sexual needs with "nonmasculine" males while simultaneously oppressing them in other ways. In this respect there was not much difference between how they treated homosexuals and how they treated women. These patriarchal relations evolved in a society that was conditioned by its Spanish, Catholic, and African origins and by the way in which the cultural values that were brought to Cuba were modified over time in a new context.

This chapter will begin by examining the character and incidence of same-sex sex and then review the place of women in Cuban society on the eve of the 1959 revolution. Dominant values about homosexuals and women were affected by the fact that Cuba had been a Spanish colony for four hundred years and then retained close cultural ties with Spain subsequent to its independence in 1901. Catholicism is a central component of Spanish culture and of the values that the Spaniards brought with them to the Western Hemisphere. After reviewing the place of Catholicism and its values in Cuban culture, particularly with respect to its attitude toward homosexuality, I will examine the other great historical factor in Cuban society, the culture of the Africans brought to Cuba as slaves. Afro-Cubans have been crucial to the formation of Cuba in terms of their role in a plantation economy, and their sheer numerical presence has led to the insertion of African values into Cuban culture and influenced the values of the dominant whites. The chapter will conclude with a reminder that the history of modern Cuba revolves around its relationship to the United States just as its relationship to Spain was central during the colonial period. The machismo of its revolutionary culture, particularly that of its leaders, has to be related to Cuba's long struggle to free itself from its domination by the Colossus of the North.

Historically, machismo, the Latin American variant of patriarchal sexism, has been more socially punitive toward deviations from traditional male appearance and manners than toward homosexual behavior in itself. In Cuba, it was assumed that males whose comportment appeared effeminate and deviated from stereotypical masculinity would be homosexual. They were called *maricones,* a word also used to denote cowardice.[1] Seen as the antithesis of masculinity, *maricones* encountered repugnance and ridicule from most Cubans. Discreet homosexuals who presented themselves in a more conventionally masculine manner were more likely to be tolerated (albeit despised) by the public. They were called *entendidos,* as in "entendido pero no dicho" (understood but not declared).

By making certain mannerisms unacceptable, machismo ensured that homosexuals who could neither fit traditional male roles nor conceal their erotic attraction to other men would act in a way that confirmed the *machista* assumption that no homosexual could possibly be "un hombre de verdad" (a real man). Not only did Cuban *maricones* often incorporate stereotypical feminine traits, they also tended to idealize machos—ostentatiously masculine men. The belief that homosexuality involves gender inversion even led many to think of themselves as "women" who could only be attracted to their opposites, "real" men. The effeminate personality and the macho personality would then be seen to complement each other, as did heterosexual women and men who behaved in conventional ways. If the effeminate men were not really men, they could then become objects of desire for "real" men. (In practice, of course, actual sexual behavior did not necessarily coincide with the public image of who was *activo* [inserter] and who was *pasivo* [insertee].) Surely, there must have been a considerable number of "real" men who passed as *hombres hombres* (another term for "real" men) but who used *maricones* as occasional or even regular outlets to satisfy their sexual appetites.[2] They were known as *bugarrones* by the homosexuals with whom they had sex.[3] *Locas* (the preferred gay term for *maricones*) were very unlikely to relate sexually to each other. According to the late gay Cuban novelist Reinaldo Arenas, "It was not the norm for one queer to go to bed with another queer; 'she' would look for a man to fuck 'her' who would feel as much pleasure as the homosexual being fucked."[4] Many *entendidos* rejected such apparently self-oppressive behavior. But according to one older homosexual, others understood and even envied the freedom of the *locas* to be themselves, for "curiously enough although they were the most rejected, they were not the most repressed. For *locas* did what they wanted to do. They put on make-up, they did the work they wanted to do, and they took pride in having *bugarrones* as lovers."

Prior to the revolution, discourse about sexuality was repressed in a way that was common to much of Latin America but that had reached extreme proportions in Cuba. The Spanish belief in *pudor* prohibited any public discussion or education regarding sexuality.[5] Males bragged about their potency in informal situations, but sex was never mentioned in polite conversation. Furthermore, the body's relation to both sex and reproduction was mystified and obscured. This was one of the reasons why women who were pregnant were kept under wraps, hidden from public view. *Pudor* also dictated that men should refrain from exposing more of their body in public than was strictly necessary.[6] There was thus enormous naïveté regarding the basic "facts of life."

Despite this ignorance, Cubans had strong convictions about the sexual behavior that was appropriate to males and females. Men were supposed to be particularly passionate, full of lust and ardor. According to Mirta Mulhare de la Torre, author of one of the very few studies of prerevolutionary sexuality, Cubans assumed that "the dominant mode of behavior for *el macho,* the male, [was] the *sexual imperative.* . . . A man's supercharged sexual physiology [placed] him on the brink of sexual desire at all times and at all places."[7] Although this hypersexuality was strongly channeled toward women by Cuban culture, particularly women seen as sexually available, an aroused man might also be expected to "lose control of himself and ignore the boundaries of 'honor and decency.' "[8]

According to Mulhare's study of the idealized attributes of masculinity, the sexual preoccupations and drives of typical males were so great that:

ordinary, "straight" intercourse does not easily satisfy him. His insatiable appetite for sexual pleasures makes him prone to explore any form of sexual satisfaction which in some men may lead to "vicious" sexual habits, such as voyeurism, the use of other means of sexual satisfaction with a woman than direct intercourse, homosexuality and even bestiality.[9]

Consequently, despite their repugnance toward homosexually identified people—that is, effeminate men—Cubans were more able than North Americans to conceive that males in certain circumstances could desire other males as outlets for their sexual drives. For this reason, homophobia, insofar as it implies fear of same-sex sex, is a problematic term to apply to Cuban (and Latin American) machismo.[10] In fact, until quite recently the term was scarcely used in Cuba. It acquired some popular currency after the institutionalized oppression of homosexuals in the 1960s and 1970s. Through the widening public discourse initiated by the U.S. gay liberation movement, the term eventually acquired its current meaning in Cuba—scorn and repugnance of individuals identified as homosexuals.

Homosexuals were socially rejected much more in the countryside than in Havana, but until the mid-1960s this did not preclude homosexual acts from taking place. Rural Cuba's sexual culture was repressive for women, but it left space for all sorts of sexual adventures between men. It allowed homosexuals surreptitiously to conquer supposedly "real" men in private. It even allowed them to flirt with "horny" machos in bars catering to their respective needs, which could be found in many provincial cities until the mid-1960s. Sexual desire outweighed *machista* postures, provided always that the *activo*'s image was respected. Reinaldo Arenas's rich personal experience in these matters allowed him to conclude that in the countryside "it is a rare man who has not had sexual relations with another man."[11] Still, rural values made life hard for males who were publicly identified as homosexuals. Arenas, who had "fooled around" with other teenage *campesinos,* would soon realize that it was one thing to have sex with other males and another thing to be labeled as a homosexual. To be known as a *maricón* in rural Cuba was "one of the worst disasters that could ever happen to anyone."[12] For this reason, many homosexuals migrated to Havana hoping to submerge themselves in the relative anonymity of the capital.

Havana included a quarter of Cuba's population and was by far the largest city in the Caribbean, with more than ten times the population of any other city. Most of the country's wealth was produced in the agricultural interior of the island, but Havana was the center of commerce as well the port through which most of Cuba's foreign trade was funneled. In addition, the Cuban capital was a playground for large numbers of American tourists who came in search of the unbeatable combination of money, sin, and sex. Before 1959, almost anything that was prohibited on the puritanical mainland of North America became possible in Havana.

Havana's domination by American money, brothels, crime lords, and tourists undoubtedly endowed the city with a seamy, exploitative side. Still, Cuba's capital was an environment where sex with other men could be secured more easily than in the countryside. That is why Virgilio Piñera, who would go on to become Cuba's most famous playwright, fled to Havana from Cárdenas, a dreary provincial town, knowing that in the capital he could realize his dreams: "throwing myself into the arms of the first available man, I could at last experience sex in the way that I understood it."[13]

Habana Vieja and Centro Habana, the old colonial sections of the city, offered spaces where homosexuals, particularly those who were poor, could be themselves. There were countless bars, such as Dirty Dick, Johnny's Bar, and the Barrilito, where they could hang out day and night. The *ambiente* of the Colón barrio in Centro Habana attracted some American tourists just as it did *gente decente* from the middle-class neighborhoods on the other side of the city. But the majority of the bar patrons were locals, many struggling to make ends meet. Organized crime and American tourism were prominent in prerevolutionary Havana, but they were much more likely to be associated with the larger cabarets, casinos, and hotels that had sprung up in Vedado, the newer part of the city. Male brothels such as the Lucero, which catered to tourists, were the exception, and unlike female brothels were not really part of the *ambiente* of the barrio Colón. There were many cinemas like the Rialto, the Verdun, and the Campoamor to which, according to an old homosexual, "you could go and immediately pick up a young guy. Many had their first experience there. There was a lot of sex in those cinemas." There was also a rich street life in which you could always find someone with whom to pass the time of day. At carnival time, some *comparsas* (bands) such as the Sultana were famous for their contingent of homosexual cross-dressers parading as the sultan's harem.[14]

The fact that many of Old Havana's bars and brothels may have been associated with crime and prostitution would surely have been incidental to the homosexual migrants from the countryside. More important was the fact that they created employment opportunities, such as bar and brothel tending, just as red-light districts have traditionally done for sexual outcasts throughout Latin America. Other jobs, such as hairstyling and dressmaking, which required traditionally feminine skills, were also more numerous than in the interior. These would have been important considerations for those homosexuals who had absorbed beliefs that homosexuals are as frail as the stereotypical woman. For them, physically demanding agricultural work would be doubly hard.

Havana's homosexual cruising areas, such as the Prado and the Parque Central, were well known for over a hundred years. The male prostitutes who frequented them were so common by the late nineteenth century that they had evoked a controversy in the press about who was more reprehensible, the *maricón pasivo* or the *pederasta activo*.[15] Havana's notoriety was similar to that of other port cities such as Marseilles and New Orleans. Havana was also the capital of a grossly misdeveloped (as much as underdeveloped) country. Beautiful though it was, it exhibited all the defects of a society that conjoined political graft, speculation, and comprador spoliation. As the capital of a profoundly dependent country it exuded all the worst symptoms of colonial provincialism. Although Virgilio Piñera's description of Cuba's prerevolutionary culture is scathing—he describes Havana as a large city but not a great city, the "provincial capital of a perfectly provincial state"[16]—Havana's size and relative social diversity allowed him and other gifted homosexuals such as José Lezama Lima to express their creative talents as much as the times would allow.[17] It does an injustice to many groups, including homosexuals, to portray prerevolutionary Havana as no more than a "lumpenized" sexual cesspool. In fact, it was the home (albeit intermittently for some) of acclaimed writers and artists such as Nicolás Guillén, Fernando Ortiz, Alejo Carpentier, Amelia Pelaez, Wifredo Lam, and René Portocarrero, to name but a few besides Lezama and Piñera.

Its intellectual life was not much inferior to that of another profoundly colonized but impeccably virtuous city, "Toronto the good." Havana had a very large middle class, as is evident in the extensive, affluent suburbs of Miramar and Vedado. Much as elsewhere, middle-class *entendidos* had to live very private sexual lives. They might occasionally and discreetly visit bars in the *ambiente* of Centro Habana and Habana Vieja, but for the most part their socializing with other homosexuals was conducted in private. They also spent much time with their family and social peers, going to supposedly "normal" cabarets like the Montmartre and the Tropicana. This group included doctors, journalists, actors, police officers, and priests. Many of them may have sought sex with "heterosexual machos from the lower strata of the population,"[18] but such cross-class sexual contacts were not unique to Cuba nor necessarily symptomatic of a decadent society or exploitative sexuality. Such contacts were commonplace throughout much of Latin America and indeed not unknown elsewhere. Middle-class Cuban *entendidos* were not puritanical about their sexual fantasies, though they may have been less than honest. Not many of them would have disagreed with the reminiscences of an old homosexual whom I interviewed in 1989 about the *ambiente* of prerevolutionary Havana. "The lower classes had much more *sabor* (flavor). Decent people had no *sabor,* no spice. . . . Did we often pay for sex? Of course we did. And we paid well."

There were also more settled homosexual relations than might be supposed by their relative invisibility. Just as no mother who knew that her son was gay ever admitted this in public, provided that he also refrained from doing so, so too lovers were accepted by some families with the tacit understanding that the relationship would not be made explicit to anyone. Instead, they would be introduced to outsiders as best friends, brothers, or relatives. There were also other relationships that might have been considered too blatant except for the fact that they conformed to traditional *machista* conventions. In poorer barrios (according to the previous source) you might find two men living as a "husband and wife . . . as if they were married. She was the lady of the house. She didn't work. She was the housewife."

Why was homophobic machismo so powerful in Cuba prior to the revolution? It should be noted that Cuban machismo differs only in degree from that found elsewhere in Latin America. Mexicans, Costa Ricans, and Argentines all exhibit their own brands of oppressive masculinity. Moreover, the fact that a Spanish term has been coined to describe overbearing masculinity should not obscure the fact that Canadian and American males share many of the gender attributes of Latin American males. In fact, in Anglo-American culture, homophobia, expressed either as fear of intimacy with other men or as hatred of homosexuals, is much more powerful than it is in Cuba. Be that as it may, it is still true that domination of females and contempt for males perceived to be effeminate, the two essential elements in machismo, had reached extreme proportions in Cuba by the time of the revolution's triumph.

Contemporary machismo has deep roots in Cuba's traditional culture, which allotted men economic power, custody of their families, and sexual dominion over women. In rural Cuba, men once entirely dominated the paid labor force. In the cities, women's labor outside the family home was typically limited to domestic service, clerical and factory work, and —not least—prostitution. On the eve of the revolution only 13.7 percent of adult females had gainful employment.[19] Women were bound to the home by housework, child care, and by men's fear that their women might be seduced or corrupted outside it. "The ideal woman [was] a subservient figure, not only chaste, but preferably sexually innocent."[20] In reality, this applied more to upper-class women than to the urban poor. The latter were more independent given that they were more likely to have some sort of work outside the home and to have less stable spousal relations.

The celebration of women's chastity fueled machismo since the pursuit and conquest of women demonstrated men's sexual virility, while the "protection" of chaste women gave them the excuse to assert control, a central prerogative of machismo. Mariana Ravenet Ramírez et al. provide a horrifying portrayal of the life of a typical rural woman before the revolution.

> [She met her boyfriend] when she was fourteen and he was nineteen. Two years later they began a courtship that lasted nine years. They went to few fiestas, because Rosa's father didn't approve. . . . Nor could they go to the beach because formerly "they used to say that women who went to the beach were bad." Rosa had few friends. When she became engaged she went out a bit, but he was very jealous. They fought for a whole year because she had once gone shopping in the local

town without telling him. . . . [Her entire life] had consisted of housework with little relief from the social isolation imposed first by her parents, then by her fiancé . . . and later within her marriage, as a means of control.[21]

Conversely, women themselves expected men to assert their machismo. Since they were rendered powerless in so many other respects, many women enjoyed, indeed exploited, their power to attract men. The exhibitionist bent of popular culture in Cuba was reflected in the public behavior of many women. Contradictory though it might sound, Cuban women were expected to be both chaste and provocative. This was reflected in the extravagant dress of many women and in the way they courted and then rebuffed *piropos*.[22]

In fact, the situation of women in prerevolutionary Cuba was contradictory in more ways than this. Though they were excluded from virtually all but the least prestigious and lowest paid occupations, they were better educated than men. The only exception applied to postsecondary education. And even there a third of university graduates were female. Double sexual standards were evident with respect to adultery and divorce (as was the case in other Latin American countries whose civil codes had been patterned after that of Spain). Whereas adultery on the part of a wife entitled the husband to an automatic divorce, in his case it was overlooked unless it caused a "public scandal" or entailed the neglect of his wife. Still, by Latin American standards Cuban women had gained considerable legal rights before 1959.[23] Divorce had been legal since 1918, half a century before it was legalized in such major countries as Brazil and Argentina. (Chile has yet to do so.) Married women could own property in their own right, and in the event of divorce and remarriage they were no longer restricted with respect to custody of their children. Nevertheless, the social and familial dominance of men largely remained intact. From a public perspective, what really mattered was the reputation of men, not that of their women. One reason wives were not allowed to work outside the home was that their labor reflected poorly on their husbands' ability to provide for them. From early years, husbands, sons, and brothers preened themselves in public oblivious to the fact that their freedom, health, and looks had been procured by the labor of women confined to home and child care.

Many traditional beliefs about sex and gender roles had no doubt begun to weaken long before the revolution. It seems scarcely credible that most parents in 1959 still believed that "little boys should not be given the opportunity to be alone with little girls to prevent 'instincts' from taking over."[24] Yet in the mid-1980s, comparable worries were still being voiced in official manuals for parents. Cuban mothers were being warned not to undress in front of their sons, nor allow them to touch their breasts or kiss them on their mouths, for fear of arousing them.[25] Young children in day-care centers were separated according to sex, and different codes were still enforced about children's nudity. Even today, only girls are expected to help their mothers with work around the home, and young girls are rarely seen playing in public. It is considered unseemly for them to do so.

Even now, when most young women work as equals with men in a wide range of previously male-dominated occupations, viewpoints still appear that unwittingly reveal outdated paternalistic attitudes. For example, the *Manual de Educación Formal* (published by the Education Ministry) insists that "there should be great emphasis upon courtesy and respect; in particular, excessive intimacy, incorrect and bossy language should be avoided . . . [men should] rise to greet women, make way for women, give them their seats and offer them help with heavy loads, to descend steps or get out of a vehicle."[26]

Male *piropos* remain commonplace on the streets and beaches of Havana. The *Manual de Educación Formal,* which is so strict in other aspects of correct public behavior, merely insists that *piropos* should be in good taste. It has simply escaped the authors that such archaic gallantry is a symptom of the *macho*'s need to control relations between the sexes. The textbook encourages the new Cuban male to be sensitive to the supposed vulnerability of women without addressing the causes of the imputed dependence that stem from the character of Cuban machismo itself.

Cuban sexism, embodying the *machista* subjugation of women and homosexuals alike, epitomizes quintessential Spanish values. This is not surprising since Cuba was a Spanish colony for four hundred years and gained its independence long after Mexico and Costa Rica had attained theirs. Not only was Cuba subject to Spanish colonial laws and administration until the turn of the last century, but it also continued to receive a flow of Spanish immigrants, most recently during the Spanish Civil War.[27] Once in Cuba, they typically retained their Spanish cultural ties, for example through membership in Spanish mutual-benefit societies based upon regional ancestries. There was considerable travel back and forth from Spain for work and education. Spain remained home, *madre patria,* for many of Cuba's white inhabitants in a literal way that it wasn't for Mexicans or even Costa Ricans. Throughout the long colonial rule, Spanish citizens enjoyed privileges over Cuban-born citizens. Even as late as 1934, children born of Spanish parents retained their parents' citizenship unless they chose Cuban citizenship at the age of twenty-one.

Although a majority of Cubans now have the mixed racial heritage that is typical of much of the Caribbean, their nation's hegemonic culture is clearly Hispanic. The Spanish model of sex and gender has essentially remained unchallenged by other cultures. Native Indian customs are absent because the small indigenous population that survived the initial conquest was soon racially overwhelmed. Unlike Mexico, Cuba's pre-Columbian indigenous origins have been completely expunged from the country's identity. The African presence in Cuba is, however, striking. As late as the mid-nineteenth century, blacks, largely slaves, constituted more than half of Cuba's entire population. (Slavery was not abolished until 1886.)

African influence has been particularly noticeable in music, dance, and religious customs, but it is also reflected in food and speech patterns. Afro-Cuban culture, however, has been devalued by its association with slavery and with impoverished black Cubans who have been historically marginalized and subject to prejudice in countless ways. Although blacks have been subject to discrimination throughout Cuban history, racism has never assumed the proportions of that of the United States. There have always been many Afro-Cubans who have formally enjoyed status almost equal to whites. For example, Antonio Maceo, a *mulato* who led the military struggle for independence against Spain, is a national hero whose stature is only exceeded by that of José Martí.

Unlike Spanish citizens, whose numbers and culture were constantly replenished by migration from Spain, Cubans of slave descent were torn from their various African backgrounds and must have lost much of their indigenous culture in the process. Only 13,000 individuals were defined as Africans in Cuba's 1899 census, while in the 1931 census most of the 670,000 people defined as foreign whites must have been Spanish. As Esteban Montejo, the maroon or runaway slave who lived to see the triumph of the revolution, told his biographer, by the mid-1960s no Africans remained in Cuba.[28] This was true only in the sense that, unlike Spaniards, Cuban blacks were denied their national heritage. Accordingly, African influence on Cuba's dominant culture is not proportionate to the numbers of people of African descent in the country's population. Although the Spanish descendants have "had to adjust to the presence of non-whites" it is the "colored person, whether slave or free, [who has been forced at every point] to shape his behavior in accordance with the actions and expectations of the dominant white sector."[29]

Attempts to establish a race-conscious Afro-Cuban movement have not been able to overcome the legacy of the suppression of the Partido de los Independientes de Color and the ensuing "nation-wide extermination of blacks of quasi-genocidal proportions" in the 1912 war.[30] Afro-Cuban nationalism has also been subsumed by the broader nationalism associated with anticolonial struggles. Fidel Castro, himself the progeny of Spanish parents, made scarcely a reference to the particular needs of Afro-Cubans, let alone to racial discrimination, in his initial denunciations of prerevolutionary Cuba.[31] In short, unlike in the United States, blacks have not been able to assert a distinct identity and are not seen as embodying a legitimate culture. Cuba is not socially and culturally polarized in the same way as the United States. Afro-Cubans may be stereotyped by Cuban whites as particularly "sensual," but they, too, have their own share of tropical exuberance, not to mention the African element which is commonly present in their own make-up. As the Cuban saying goes, "Si no tiene de Congo tiene de Carabalí" (If you haven't some Congo blood in you, you have some Carabalí).

Despite the historical presence of so many blacks and *mulatos* in Cuba, African culture did not significantly impinge upon the Spanish model of relationships between the sexes. Cubans may be less austere and more extroverted than the Spanish, but patriarchal masculinity still prevails. The conquest, extended colonial rule, and Spanish cultural hegemony during the Republican period explain many of the archaic sexual values that persisted for so long in Cuba. Despite the seeming renaissance that Spain enjoyed in the late fifteenth century, the values of the Spanish crown, nobility, and Church remained the most reactionary and decadent in Europe. Spain's conquest of much of the Western Hemisphere bolstered these atrophied ideals. Spain's Catholic Church, home of the Inquisition, became ever more intolerant and myopic, while the country itself, imbued by feudal preoccupations, slumbered more and more at the margins of Europe, which was beginning to enjoy a religious, political, and commercial expansion.

It is initially surprising that the most Spanish of Spain's col-

onies offers so little evidence of the Church's role in Hispanic culture. Unlike Mexico and many parts of Central America, where
cities and towns are dominated by magnificent cathedrals and
churches, in Cuba religious buildings are conspicuous by their
absence, particularly in the countryside. Colonial towns like
Trinidad are the exception. Churches and popular Catholic festi-
vals in Cuba are scarce because the mission of Catholicism in most
of Latin America was the spiritual colonization of the native population geared to the exploitation of natural resources, particularly gold and silver. Unlike Mesoamerica's Catholic Church,
Cuba's had neither the need nor opportunity to legitimize itself
by appropriating indigenous rites and traditions. In Cuba, there
were neither precious metals nor surviving natives to be exploited
by the Spanish colonizers in alliance with the Church.

The influence of the Catholic Church in Cuba has not been
nearly as great as it has been in other parts of Latin America with
respect to the regulation of male and female sex roles. There is no
Cuban equivalent of Mexico's Virgin of Guadalupe to subjugate the
people, women in particular. The Virgen de la Caridad is but one
of the triad of the most popular Catholic saints linked to *Santero*
deities in Cuba. And strong-willed Cuban women do not fit well
with the image of the self-abnegating woman associated with the
cults of the Virgin Mary and the Virgen de Guadalupe in Mexico.
*Hembrismo* as much as *marianismo* characterizes Cuban women.[32]

In Cuba, the majority of the population considers itself Christian and even more so Catholic, but not everybody who professes
such beliefs practices them in an orthodox fashion. Cubans have
historically been casual and individualistic about their religious
observances. This fact has enabled Afro-Cuban religions to manifest themselves through the attribution of the qualities of
Orisha or Yoruba deities to Catholic saints. Many Cubans who
practice informal Catholicism, removed from the Church and its
dogmas, make vows to Catholic saints who have taken on the personalities of Yoruba deities. They make this transfer without con-

sciously identifying themselves with Afro-Cuban religions of Yoruba or Congo origin. In fact, as the bishop of Cuba, Juan del Castillo, noted in the sixteenth century, the Cuban people are the "most incorrigible and free, and least responsive to the commandments of the Church in the whole of the Indies."[33]

The influence of the Church was weakened by its political support for the Spanish colonial regime, accentuated by the fact that many priests came directly to Cuba from Spain. When the struggle for independence began to take shape in the late nineteenth century most of the priesthood, particularly the hierarchy, sided with the colonial power. This option increased the Church's isolation from the majority of the population whose needs it was supposed to serve. The Church's official standing was further undermined through the separation of church and state that was promulgated in 1901, after independence was achieved. State subsidies were terminated and religious instruction was forbidden in the newly secularized schools. As the Church became more and more isolated, its congregations became increasingly composed of women and members of the upper classes. By 1959, only seven hundred priests, almost all of them Spanish, remained in Cuba. As in the struggle for independence, most priests had sided with the ancien régime, a choice that further weakened the Church's credibility.

Today, the Church has so little influence on people's personal lives that virtually no one bothers to be married in church. For that matter, fewer than three out of five Cuban couples bother to get married at all. Unlike Catholicism in Costa Rica (where it has become a secular ideology as much as a theology), or Mexico (where the Church hierarchy derives its sociopolitical authority from Catholicism's mystical hold on the impoverished, uneducated majority), Cuban Catholicism lacks a belief system that would make it a cohesive social force. The individual's relation to saints such as the Virgen de la Caridad/Ochún is highly personal. Although the Church's capacity for political interventions may have increased lately because of the weakening legitimacy of the Communist regime, its ability to influence public attitudes on issues such as abortion, contraception, and homosexuality is insignificant. Indeed, rather than being perceived as a bastion of homophobia, as in Mexico and Costa Rica, the Church has a certain popularity among gays because of its opposition to the regime.

Currently, the Cuban Catholic Church may be the weakest in all of Latin America and Cuba may have a Communist regime that officially espouses a materialist view of the world; nevertheless, in some respects, the Catholic Church has a privileged status. The revolutionary government has retained diplomatic relations with the Vatican, and papal policies, even those of the present obsessively anti-Communist pope, are rarely criticized. In fact, for a while during the late 1980s, Cuba even went so far as to extend an invitation to Pope John Paul II to visit Cuba, despite the possibility that he might have exploited the visit for political ends, as he did in Nicaragua during the Sandinista regime. It is clear that Cuba's Communist regime is preoccupied about how people, and especially Latin Americans, perceive its relationship to Christianity.[34] Christmas and Easter may not be official holidays in Cuba, but the government has had to come to terms with Cuba's Catholic heritage in other ways, most recently by allowing religious believers to become members of the Communist Party.[35]

Although the spiritual authority of the Church has been weak, secularized Catholic values nonetheless are rooted in Cuban culture. Condemnation of sodomy and subsequently of homosexuality, along with repressive mystification of women's sexuality, have long been at the core of Spanish Catholic dogmas regarding sexuality. In the Middle Ages, sodomy was regarded as the ultimate crime, uniting sin, physical degradation, and unmasculine behavior. In Spain, sodomy was exceeded as an offense only by heresy and crimes against the king. There was competition between the Inquisition and the secular courts about who should have authority to exorcise it from the body politic. Penalties ranged from castration to live incineration.[36]

The Spaniards brought their rabid opposition to sodomy with them to Cuba. There is much speculation about the incidence of homosexual activity between Cuba's indigenous people, as there is with respect to other parts of the New World. Whatever its true extent, it was used as a pretext for Spain to enslave natives on the grounds that they were not fully human. The hysterical reports of priests such as Fray Tomás Ortiz about the sodomitic practices of the Carib Indians, which according to him rendered them "like beastly animals," was crucial to this end.[37] Scandalized by the sexuality of many Indians, the Spanish colonists castrated some of them and even forced them to eat their own testicles encrusted with dirt.[38] Toward the colonizers themselves, the Inquisition seems to have been more moderate in Cuba than in other parts of the Spanish empire. There were no cases of auto-da-fé against Jewish heretics; nevertheless, at least on one occasion, eighteen "effeminate" men were put on trial in Havana's Plaza de Armas late in the seventeenth century.[39]

As if to deny the responsibility of Spanish Catholicism, some Cubans (including Fidel Castro) have argued that Cuba's homophobic machismo is derived from the Moorish influence upon Spain. "Dreadful ideas about sexuality"[40] have been attributed to Islam and Arab civilization. By contemporary Western feminist standards there can be no dispute about the oppression of women within Islamic culture. However, although Muslim customs may have been misogynist and sexist, they were nevertheless sex-positive and more tolerant regarding Christianity's "unspeakable sin" than medieval Spain.[41] In fact, the Spaniards' obsession with sodomy stemmed from their desire to expunge Moorish cultural influence from Spain, which they associated, among other things, with homosexual and cross-dressing behavior.

Although the Koran condemned homosexual behavior, particularly when it was adulterous, Moslem culture celebrated sexual pleasure, in marked contrast to the repressive values of Judeo-Christian civilization. The Spaniards were as opposed to heterosexual as they were to homosexual anal intercourse, but "in Moslem teaching, the lawfulness of sexual pleasure was never connected with procreation."[42] Although sex between males was formally proscribed, it was in fact widely (though discreetly) practiced, being integrated into the "general framework of sexual life without taboos and, it would appear without problems."[43] According to sex historian Vern Bullough, male "homosexuality seems a natural outgrowth of a sex-positive sexually segregating religion [Islam], in which women had little status or value."[44] In short, the homophobia implanted within Cuban culture stemmed more from the resurgent Catholicism of a superstitious culture than it did from any Moorish influence in Spanish culture.

And what about the African contribution to Cuban sexual values?[45] To be sure, some of the tribes from whom the Cuban slaves originated, such as the Ibos in southern Nigeria, had strong *machista* values.

> They taught their daughters to obey and serve men, and taught their sons to look down upon women. Consequently close friendships were restricted to their own sex. Their friends and not their wives became their intimate associates and mentors. The only woman in whom an Ibo or Ibibio man would have confidence was his mother, who would retain the love and respect of her sons.[46]

Clearly, there were no basic differences between such values and those of the Spanish with respect to gender roles. Furthermore, women's sexuality did not have much importance for Ibo men except insofar as it provided pleasure for them, whereas their own sexual organs were fetishized. (They said their prayers before phallic altars.)

The Ibos were part of the Carabalí culture, which after the Yorubas and Bantus supplied the largest number of African slaves. Over time their values became transculturized in Cuba.

Descendants of the Carabalí slaves became the nucleus of the secret religious organization known as Abakuá. Its contemporary members, known as *ñañigos,* continue to emphasize the values of virility, bravery, and masculine pride, along with discrimination against women. Neither women nor effeminate men (seen as homosexuals) are allowed to be initiated in their religion. Although only a very small number of Cubans now are associated with Abakuá, it is reasonable to assume that many more have incorporated some of the values that the Carabalíes brought with them to Cuba.

On the other hand, Santería, the Cuban manifestation of the religion of the Yorubas or Lucumíes in Africa, is both more widespread and much more tolerant of gender deviation than Abakuá. *Santero* fiestas, which feature sensual music and dances, are reputedly very popular with homosexuals. Furthermore, the gender of the spirit or *orisha* who possesses the *santeros* during the festivities is not fixed. *Santero* initiates are known as *iyabós,* the Yoruba word for bride, regardless of their actual sex. Nevertheless, the attraction of Santería rituals for homosexuals probably derives as much from the relaxation of sanctions against nonmasculine behavior as it does from the performance of explicitly erotic acts that could be interpreted as homosexual. In fact, neither homosexuals nor women are allowed to become *babalaos* or high priests.

Caution is advisable when attempting generalizations about what can be attributed to specific African cultures. Afro-Cuban culture has not been validated or studied in Cuba to the extent its diffusion merits, even subsequent to a revolution that has committed itself to erasing racial discrimination. Although countless Cubans share superstitions with African origins, many deny it and attribute backwardness to those who believe in them. Even Fernando Ortiz, Cuba's most renowned ethnologist, in his early writings referred to the religious creeds of Afro-Cubans as "witchcraft" and to their sexual practices as "corrupt."[47] Like-

wise, Fidel Castro, who was educated by Jesuits, distances himself from the superstitions of Santería, as if Catholic rituals were
any less superstitious.[48]

Whether Ortiz had homosexuality in mind in his reference to
corrupt sexual practices among Afro-Cubans is not clear. Certainly, sex did happen between African male slaves in the early
colonial epoch. This "sodomy" was used, as it was with indigenous Indians, to justify slavery since it was considered proof that
the Africans had no soul.[49] Overall, however, there is not sufficient evidence available to make a strong generalization about
how contemporary sexual values and practices can be traced back
to African roots.

Though the cultural origins of the homophobic prejudices
within contemporary Cuban culture may be a complex matter,
the material forces that have reinforced machismo during the last
two centuries are easier to detect. These factors are the political
economy of slavery and the economic role of women after emancipation in 1886, particularly in the rural economy. Slavery started in the colony's earliest days when the Spaniards sought to
replace the depleted indigenous source of cheap labor. At first, the
number of slaves was small because Cuba's lack of the precious
metals and agricultural products wanted in Europe caused it to
stagnate economically. It was only after the liberalization of trade
(including that of slaves) and the opening of American markets
for coffee and sugar in the late eighteenth century that Cuba began to expand rapidly. It had taken over two hundred years for
Cuba's population to double prior to 1730, but then it redoubled
within the mere twenty-five years from 1792 to 1817. Imported
slaves were a major component of this increase.

The expansion of sugar production, and of agriculture in general, fueled the demand for slaves. As a rule the Spaniards did not
set out to breed slaves within Cuba and discouraged the import of
females because they realized women and children were less suitable for work with sugar cane than with some other crops, like

cotton. Male slaves outnumbered females by almost two to one. Slaves were frequently housed in *barracones* or barracks on isolated sugar-cane plantations, which often excluded women on the grounds that their presence would be disruptive. The inevitable consequence, according to a prominent nineteenth-century theologian José Agustín Caballero, was that "in the absence of black females with whom to marry, all blacks [became] masturbators, sinners and sodomites."[50] Without sharing Fernando Ortiz's beliefs about the "uncontrollable sensuality" of the slaves' "African psyche,"[51] it is quite possible that sex between males may have been widespread within the *barracones* because there were no other sources of affection or pleasure.[52]

As Julio Le Riverend, Cuba's leading economic historian reminds us, the development of Cuba, particularly since the eighteenth century, cannot be understood without recognizing the pivotal impact of slavery as a mode of production on all social relations, including domestic ones.[53] Homosexuality among slaves occurred in a context—that is, a country whose dominant culture was both racist and homophobic.[54] Sexual relations that were apparently tolerated and institutionalized within the *barracones* were viewed in hypocritical *machista* terms outside the world of the *barracones*. Although Esteban Montejo, the former slave whose life was recorded by Miguel Barnet, only defined slaves who looked after their *maridos* (husbands) as "sodomites," his description of these relationships does not suggest that "sodomites" were particularly stigmatized. According to Montejo, it was only "after slavery that that word *afeminado* [effeminate, i.e., homosexual] appeared."[55]

Even if blacks continued to engage in same-sex sex, after emancipation, they would have had every reason to project a particularly virile image in public. They already had social disadvantages within a sexual order that placed black women at the service of white men and undermined black men's ability to exercise the traditional male prerogative of guarding women's "honor." It also encouraged "their own laxity in matters of sexual conduct."[56] Demeaning sexual stereotypes of blacks became integral to the racial hierarchy that arose from the plantation economy. The contemporary Cuban put-down of black homosexuals reflects the double prejudice they have had to endure: "Negro y maricón," an insult that says that someone is not only black but has the effrontery to be unmasculine (homosexual) as well.

Although Esteban Montejo recalled that former slaves continued their homosexual relations subsequent to emancipation, we do not know how widespread same-sex sex was within the black community.[57] The majority of black homosexuals have understandably been particularly reticent about public revelation of their sexual orientation. Exploitation, discrimination, and marginalization of blacks within a *machista* society has thus contributed to the emergence of a black gender identity that publicly appears more *machista* and homophobic than it may be in private. Cubans expect blacks to be "symbols of virility,"[58] and many blacks apparently feel obliged to fit this supervirile mold. The revolution's failure to address the persistence of racial prejudice (as opposed to institutionalized discrimination) and to validate the multifaceted identity of blacks (among many other groups) may have reinforced the need for such public stances.

Discrimination against homosexuals has also been bolstered by the *machista* devaluation of women. This link is evident in the fact that normally only males who are perceived as effeminate are labeled homosexual. Isabel Larguía and John Dumoulin have demonstrated how Cuba's political economy before the revolution contributed to the depreciation of women. The vast majority of women had no independent income or work outside of the home that could validate their social worth. They only cooked, cleaned house, and raised children. In the countryside, women were particularly dependent upon men, since men constituted 99 percent of agricultural wage earners. Furthermore, rural women were almost unique in Latin America since they neither "made ceramics, nor wove textiles, nor made basket-ware, nor worked with leather," nor made other commodities.[59] The wives of Cuban peasants who owned or cultivated their own land were exceptions, but they were a small percentage of the rural population. Most rural workers were landless and as such attached to the sugar-cane and coffee plantations, which along with cattle ranches monopolized the majority of the land.

Large-scale unemployment made men insecure about their employment and led them to propagate beliefs about the innately masculine character of agricultural labor. In fact, cane-cutting is a particularly grueling activity but certainly one that many women could also have endured, as demonstrated by the record of women who volunteered for cane-cutting in the early years of the revolution. Before 1959, however, only young boys were initiated in the ritual of using a *machete,* the symbol of masculinity in rural Cuba, and allowed to sling it from their belts. Conversely, the confinement of most women to the vicinity of their homes, where they were restricted to housekeeping and child-rearing tasks, reinforced beliefs about the biological destiny of women as wives and mothers. In these circumstances, "taboos based upon the notion of the physical and mental inferiority of women reached extreme proportions,"[60] thus justifying men's monopoly of paid labor and public life.

It is possible that the *machista* devaluation of women's work was also accompanied by the eroticization of male companionship. Cuban men have historically spent an unusual amount of time apart from women. Many men worked as seasonal migrant laborers, spending months apart from their families, living and working almost exclusively in the company of other men. Because so many young women migrated to Havana and other cities in search of domestic employment, single men outnumbered available women in most provinces. In the rural area of Camagüey (a province, according to some, that is famous for its homosexuality), for example, the ratio of single men to single women in 1943 was as high as 1.6 to 1.[61]

One way or another males have outnumbered females, in certain population categories by extraordinary proportions, for most of Cuba's modern history. Apart from the predominance of males among imported African slaves, males also constituted the vast majority of the 124,000 indentured Chinese coolies who were imported in the mid-nineteenth century (e.g., only 66 women were listed among the 40,261 Asians in the 1871 census). Since Chinese males were not allowed to marry Afro-Cubans, it is hardly surprising that they acquired a reputation for being homosexual.[62] Males outnumbered women in the more recent Spanish immigration. In all, 1.3 million immigrants came to Cuba between 1902 to 1934. Not only were the majority male, but they were also in the most sexually active age group of fifteen to forty-five. By 1931 there were 113 males for every 100 females in Cuba.[63] In these circumstances it would not be surprising if Cuban machos had not enjoyed the possibility of having greater access to men while simultaneously despising those with whom they had sex for not being sufficiently masculine.

The final factor contributing to the denigration of *maricones* was their association with cowardice—*maricón* means coward as well as homosexual—in a country that has had to fight hard and long for its national liberation. The exaltation of physical bravado, so evident in Cuban machismo, is striking in comparison to its relative absence in Costa Rica, a country that has been involved in far fewer military struggles. In fact, a central plank of Cuba's revolutionary strategy, the role of guerrilla warfare in the countryside, was firmly planted in these beliefs. Castro long maintained that if other Latin American countries did not follow the Cuban example, it was because their ostensibly revolutionary leaders lacked the will, and implicitly the courage, to initiate armed struggle in the countryside. For some Cuban machos who shared his outlook there is no place within a revolution for males who don't reflect the values of an "ultra-virile country, with its army of men." As Samuel Feijoo, one of Cuba's most prominent intellectuals at the outset of the revolution, added with unparal-

leled bluntness, "no homosexual [can represent] the revolution,
which is a matter for men, of fists and not of feathers, of courage
and not of trembling."[64]

In actual fact, Cuba has been engaged in violent struggle of one
sort or another for much of the last hundred years. Cuba's Ten
Years War for independence from Spain ended in 1878 only to be
reinitiated in 1895. The second war was even more violent than
the first. American intervention in 1898 robbed Cubans of the full
independence they had fought to attain. The country subsequently endured U.S. military occupation from 1898 to 1902, and
again in 1906-9. Another repetition of military intervention was
threatened in 1917.

In addition to suffering military occupation, Cuba has been
brutalized by two of the most vicious dictatorships in Latin
American history. Neither the regime of Gerardo Machado in the
late 1920s, nor that of Fulgencio Batista in the 1950s, could have
survived without U.S. support. It is no wonder that violence fig-
ured so prominently in the *machista* culture that Cuba inherited
after the triumph of the revolution. It also goes without saying
that the Cuban revolution would probably not have occurred, at
least not as a radical transformation, without the reckless bravery
of a handful of men. Nor would the revolution have survived
without constant military mobilization as a top priority because
of the long-standing U.S. determination to overthrow it.

# THREE

# Institutionalized
# Homophobia

*AT THE OUTSET* of the Cuban revolution, machismo was deeply ingrained in the fabric of Cuban society. Gender roles were clearly identified and sharply differentiated. Men were expected to be strong, dominant, and sexually compulsive. Women were expected to be vulnerable and chaste. Because of this, many women were forced to lead domesticated lives within patriarchal family structures, finding fulfillment as wives and mothers and at best living in the reflected glory of their menfolk's social status.

The family was typically the most important institution in prerevolutionary Cuba. It was an extraordinarily strong one[1] with an influence reinforced by the weakness—indeed absence, in the case of most of rural Cuba—of other institutions, such as churches and schools, and of indigenous communal organizations that could play a major role in the inculcation of cultural values. The economic precariousness of many Cubans, in a society where more than a quarter of the population was frequently out of work and where there was no social security, ensured that the family would become the indispensable safety net for most people. Any member of the family who lost a job or fell on hard times could expect financial support from other members. In Cuba to this day, welfare payments to the unemployed, the sick, and the elderly are only paid out if they have no family to support them. Furthermore, Cubans are legally responsible for the economic support not only of their children but also of their parents and grandparents. This may not seem as onerous to most Cubans as it might to many North Americans because attachment to families is so strongly ingrained in most people's consciousness. For Cubans, someone who does not "have *sentimiento* [affection] toward his own *familiares* is not to be trusted by anyone. . . . It is in the expression of *sentimiento* toward his *familiares* that a person reflects the essence of his humanity."[2] Accordingly, it is very rare to encounter anyone who is critical of his family, including those whose decision to emigrate has been partly motivated by the belief that their families were insuperable obstacles to the full realization of their homosexuality within Cuba.

The only extramarital relationships that were recognized by Cuban culture were the sexual affairs of husbands, which were tolerated so long as the preeminence of wives over other women was affirmed in public. Within this context there was little social space for emotional relationships to develop between males who were sexually involved with each other. Where such intimacy could not be denied by their families, it would almost invariably be treated as platonic friendship. As far as the general public was concerned, such relationships remained virtually invisible. In the case of upper-class families, homosexual sons were sometimes shipped abroad to avoid social disgrace for the family. Public manifestations of homosexual gender identity were thus confined to effeminate *locas* who parodied stereotypical female mannerisms for lack of alternative ways of defining themselves and making their sexual orientation visible.

For those who were unable or unwilling to deny their perceived effeminacy, life was hard. Shut out of access to most occupations and respectable social institutions, they naturally gravitated toward bars, brothels, and neighborhoods where their sexual orientation was accepted or inconsequential. In conditions of prolonged economic stagnation they had to live by their wits and lead lives whose social contribution was seen as minimal. Regardless of their work, they became identified with indecent or antisocial activities.[3]

*Redadas* or *recogidas* (police raids or mass arrests) were part and parcel of the experience of homosexuals, prostitutes, and other street people who lived in such notorious barrios as that of Colón in Centro Habana. Newspapers like *El Mundo* and *Prensa Libre* periodically demanded that the barrios be cleaned up.[4] Still, most *entendidos* could enjoy their personal life as they saw fit. And although *maricones* and *locas* were often harassed by the police, they were not systematically persecuted. In reality, police raids of bars and other homosexual hangouts were motivated by corruption rather than by institutionalized policies meant to uproot homosexuality from Cuban society. The latter goal would have been unrealistic before 1959 in any case, because the Batista government was not effective enough to be able to regulate personal behavior. It was much more concerned with the acquisition and division of spoils. The police, in particular, were more interested in tithing the people in their power than with controlling those whose personal behavior contravened conventional morality. All this would change subsequent to the overthrow of the Batista regime.

The onset of the revolution allowed the contradictory social and moral concerns of many Cubans to be addressed. The revolutionary regime was able to mobilize public support on moral issues because its policies reflected the latent needs and preoccupations of most Cubans. Above all, there was a desire to recuperate the national dignity, which was felt to have been lost under Batista as Havana became ever more a playground for American gangsters and "decadent" tourists. The fact that ten to fifteen thousand women had resorted to prostitution in order to survive seemed to reflect everything that was wrong with prerevolutionary Cuba. In fact, one of the first programs of the revolutionary government was to train female prostitutes as seamstresses. Its main publicly stated objective was to offer the women alternative employment, but there was also a moralistic desire to make them "decent" women. Many Cubans felt the same way about homosexuals, particularly ostentatious *maricones* and *locas*—that is, that they should be socially redeemed and turned into "real" men.

Despite their association with prostitution in such neighborhoods as the Colón, homosexuals were initially left to themselves. Theaters like the Shangai and the Pacífico, which were notorious for their pornographic shows, were closed down. But this measure was dictated more by their scandalous reputation than because of any specific association with homosexuality. In any case, their shows were essentially heterosexual, and most of their clients passed as "normal" people. The majority of bars patronized by homosexuals remained open for several years.

Nevertheless, in 1961 many homosexuals were arrested in a massive *redada* in the Colón. The round-up of "pederasts, prostitutes, and pimps"—Operation Three P's[5]—was primarily driven by a moralistic desire to sanitize the streets in general. Although *redadas* directed specifically against homosexuals would not become characteristic of Cuba until several years later, Operation Three P's was seen by many as an ominous portent of what lay ahead. In the past, homosexuals might have been stigmatized, mocked, or even individually exploited by the police. But according to Carlos Franqui, one-time editor of *Revolución,* the organ of the July 26 Movement that had led the struggle to overthrow the prerevolutionary regime, now they were beginning to be treated as a class of antisocial pariahs in the "first massive socialist raid" of the revolution.[6]

Operation P did not take place in a moral vacuum, however. Although many Cubans might be amused by the transvestites and *pájaras locas* (outrageous queens) who were prominent in events such as the annual carnival, in which the barrio Colón's Sultana *comparsa* included many cross-dressers, the majority of Cubans remained contemptuous of men whose (perceived) effeminacy was displayed on other occasions. That is why the police had been able to exploit them with impunity. Moreover, Cuba was becoming an ever more socially conscious society as it confronted the social ills that had festered in prerevolutionary society— large-scale unemployment, poverty, an impoverished countryside, lack of decent health care for much of the population, a corrupt educational system, and so forth. Most of these problems did not directly relate to the regulation of sexuality and gender. Still, the growing U.S. opposition to the revolution, allied with antirevolutionary forces within Cuba itself, tended to frame all issues, including those relating to gender "deviance," in terms of identification with the revolution. This atmosphere was also conducive to the abuse of authority by "power-mad machistas," as Carlos Franqui has retrospectively labeled them.[7]

One example of such abuse was the arrest in 1961 of Virgilio Piñera, Cuba's most famous playwright, in his house in Guanabo on the outskirts of Havana, seemingly on no other grounds than that he was a mouthy *maricón.* He was detained for only a few hours, but the incident shocked the homosexual artistic community, which like the rest of Havana was addicted to *bolas* (rumors). His detention was outrageous, but it was unfortunately perfectly consistent with other steps taken against intellectuals who were considered provocative nonconformists. For example, the closure of *Lunes,* the sparkling literary supplement of *Revolución,* reinforced the apprehension of homosexual intellectuals. Although the closing was motivated by the ideological nonconformity of the magazine, the weekly was also known as a haven for homosexuals. Later, Antón Arrufat, another playwright known to be homosexual, was dismissed as editor of *Casa de las Américas,* in part because he had included a homosexual poem in the journal.[8]

In the main, those who were then in power did not consciously set out to persecute homosexuals. Rather, it was a question of a lack of respect. They could not conceive how homosexual intellectuals could be valued in their own terms as intellectuals or as positive contributors to the revolutionary transformation of Cuba. Che Guevara, admired by so many for his commitment to the creation of the "new man," was apparently among those unable to conceive that *maricones* could have any redeeming qualities. He demanded to know "which asshole reads this *maricón?*" when he saw the work of Virgilio Piñera on display in the Cuban embassy in Algiers.[9] At a more popular level, weekly magazines such as *Palante* instigated homophobia among the general population by ridiculing anyone whose appearance or cultural interests deviated from the most brutish expressions of traditional machismo. They were labeled *enfermos* (sick), a term that soon rivaled *anti-social* as an epithet for homosexual in the revolutionary lexicon.

The reinforced "masculinization" of public life was furthered by the fact that, unlike the Sandinistas in Nicaragua, the vast majority of those directly involved in Cuba's guerrilla struggle had been male. The revolution also happened before the advent of the contemporary women's movement, which would challenge traditional expectations about women's roles. Less recognition was given to Cuban women's roles in the urban struggle (which was linked to the guerrilla insurgence in the countryside) than would subsequently be accorded to women's participation in the mass insurgency that toppled the Somoza regime in Nicaragua and in the long struggle in El Salvador. Accordingly, the mythologized martyrs and *comandantes* were almost all men, as had been true of heroic figures throughout Cuba's history. Relatively few women occupied conspicuous positions in the regime after 1959, and most of those who did, such as Celia Sánchez, Fidel Castro's secretary and personal aide, Vilma Espín, head of the Cuban Federation of Women (FMC), and Haydée Santamaría, director of the Casa de las Américas, occupied positions that befitted traditional expectations of women. The lesbians who had played important roles in the clandestine urban struggle tended to be *machista* themselves and consequently did not identify with the oppression experienced by *maricones*. Cuba was also led by Fidel Castro, whose public persona was the incarnation of machismo. Revolutionary Cuba, he had said, "needed strong men to fight wars, sportsmen, men who had no psychological weaknesses."[10] The traditional Cuban image of homosexuals hardly fit this paradigm of revolutionary attributes.

Another aspect of revolutionary Cuba that would soon begin to affect the lives of homosexuals was the relative efficiency of the new state. Previously the Cuban government had been corrupt and inefficient, but the new revolutionary regime began to develop an administrative apparatus that increasingly had the capacity to conceive and implement social policies that could affect the private lives of the entire population. The public service was cleansed and expanded, and mass organizations such as the Committees to Defend the Revolution (CDRs) were created. The mass media became an extension of the state. So did the educational system, rationalized and expanded. The state now had the capacity to reach and mobilize most people on behalf of specific social goals.

As the revolutionary struggle intensified and became increasingly polarized, the presumption that those not identifying themselves as its opponents were supporters of the revolution gradually gave way to a demand for unqualified commitment. There is nothing unusual about that. All revolutions tend to become all-encompassing experiences that seek to transform the individual as well as society itself. The distinction between personal needs and social obligations becomes obscured. However, individuals who attach a great deal of importance to their private lives because of the social prejudice they have experienced naturally tend to feel much more threatened by regimes based on mass mobilization.

The response of males who had sex with other males to the revolution would in part depend upon the relationship of their sexuality to their private and public identities. When their homosexuality was quite evident they would tend to be very threatened. But this need not have been the case for the majority. Sex, for many, was compartmentalized from other dimensions of their lives, particularly from their home life. Given the place of the family in Cuban culture, it was very difficult to prioritize the satisfaction of psychosexual needs in opposition to the relational (and material) needs that were met within the family. Many males whose sexuality was predominantly homosexual were nonetheless very close to their families and placed these relations ahead of the satisfaction of their sexual needs. For a variety of reasons, their sexuality would have been less likely to have been experienced as the core of their identities and to have determined their response to the revolution than would have been the case with marginalized *locas*. Thus, if *locas* would initially have been the most affected by the revolution, those males who had sex with other males but who did not identify themselves as homosexual would have been the least directly affected. Nevertheless, they had reason to be concerned because the regime had already begun to use the accusation of homosexuality to enforce social cohesion and repression.

Fears about the repercussions of the revolution upon the private lives of homosexuals intensified and spread along with the institutionalization of the revolution. Social space—the *ambiente* available to them—also began to diminish. For example, bars patronized by homosexuals began to close because of state intervention, emigration of their owners, or unprofitability due to declining patronage. Cruising and sex became more difficult in traditional venues such as the Campoamor, Negrete, and Duplex cinemas on account of increased police surveillance. There was less room for homosexuals to socialize or even to "pass" and therefore all the more reason for *entendidos* to be protective of their private lives. Even private homosexuality, of course, would have been anathema to many people who passionately identified with the revolution and who insisted that others should support it in like manner. In an atmosphere where more and more people felt constrained to demonstrate their revolutionary credentials on every possible occasion, even the most revolutionary *entendidos* began to feel that their careers might crumble at their feet if their homosexuality became public knowledge.

A more important factor, particularly in terms of its implications for the future political direction of the revolution, was the decision of Fidel Castro in 1961 to adopt Marxism-Leninism as the revolution's official ideology and to fuse the July 26 Movement with the Communist Party, at that time still known as the Popular Socialist Party (PSP). There has been much conjecture with regard to the motives that impelled Fidel Castro to embrace communism and to ally himself with a party that had opposed his revolutionary strategy until the final stages of the overthrow of the Batista regime. There must have been ambivalence on both parts, given that it took several years and two major purges before the new Communist Party was clearly unified behind the official ideology expounded by the revolution's "Maximum Leader" in the mid-1960s.

Until then the policies of the revolutionary government had been largely open minded and humanistic, dictated as much by its determination to transform radically the structure of Cuban society and free its economy from American domination as by any a priori commitment to a specific revolutionary blueprint. The speed of its expropriation of foreign investments, major industries, and large landholdings—mostly in response to American threats and imposition of economic sanctions and trade embargoes—left the government unprepared to administer a publicly owned economy. Nor was it ready to deal with the fact that in a very short time the Soviet Union had replaced the United States as its major ally and trading partner. Only the cadres of the "old" Communist Party would have the political experience to fill the vacuum created by the fact that, as Castro put it, Cuba had made a "socialist revolution without socialists."[11]

The primary concern of Fidel himself was to protect the integrity of the revolution by deepening the revolutionary consciousness of the Cuban people in preparation for the long struggle ahead. He was as much concerned with instilling a new socialist *conciencia* among the masses, particularly the new generation of Cuban youth, as he was with extirpating the vestiges of petit-bourgeois values in Cuban culture. This overriding preoccupation, which no doubt owed much to the influence of Che Guevara, underlay the authoritarian pursuit of idealistic goals that has characterized the Cuban revolution to the present day.

By temperament, Fidel Castro has little time for those who do not share his vision, even though realpolitik has often forced him to make accommodation with external forces beyond his control. For him, "the ideal thing in politics is unity of opinion, unity of doctrine, unity of forces and unity of command as in war."[12] He had no empathy for those Cubans, particularly youths, whose personal values contradicted his goal of developing a radically "new man." The effeminate image of homosexuals would certainly have been anathema to him. Nevertheless, although he probably shared the *machista* values of his generation, there is not much to suggest that the repression of homosexuality itself was a particular concern of Castro's. (In fact, one of his closest friends dating back to his student days is Alfredo Guevara, the head of ICAIC, the Cuban film institute, and a member of the Central Committee of the Communist Party, who is widely known to be homosexual.)

The chemistry of the fusion between the "old" Communist Party and the July 26 Movement is in many ways more relevant than Castro's personal attitude to the issue.[13] The doctrinaire rigidity of communism, at that time still essentially defined by Moscow, provided many ready-made answers for questions still unasked within the formerly populist July 26 Movement. One

Stalinist ideological tenet was that homosexuality was a decadent bourgeois phenomenon. Within the Soviet Union itself, homosexuality was made illegal in 1934, and severe penalties were imposed upon anyone convicted of engaging in homosexual acts. Much of the public image of homosexuality in prerevolutionary Cuba, as perceived by its new leaders, would have supported the Soviet belief that it represented "moral degeneration," a legacy of capitalism that could not be "tolerated in a socialist society."[14] The fact that homosexuality had initially been decriminalized by the Bolsheviks was an aspect of Soviet history the Cuban leaders ignored (as would be true of so many other aspects of the pre-Stalinist era).[15] These Stalinist dogmas found fertile ground in Cuba, given its own traditional prejudices and the universal belief of Cuban doctors, psychiatrists, and lawyers that homosexuality entailed crime and social delinquency as much as gender inversion and medical disease.[16] Moreover, like so many Leftists from other countries who visited the Soviet Union after the Bolshevik revolution, many of the new Cuban converts to socialism accepted Soviet claims at face value. Following an extensive visit to the Soviet Union, Samuel Feijoo, who from the outset of the revolution had led a campaign against homosexuals in the pages of *El Mundo,* made the ridiculous claim that homosexuality did not exist there, a fact he attributed to the capacity of socialism to cure vices and restore people's health.[17]

This was the background to a plan that emerged in 1965 to rehabilitate individuals whose attitudes and behavior were perceived as being nonconformist, self-indulgent, and unproductive—in short, nonrevolutionary by the standards of the revolution. The Military Units to Aid Production (UMAP), according to the sober account of José Yglesias, author of a very sympathetic book about revolutionary Cuba, were instituted: "to take care of young men of military age whose incorporation into the Army for military training was considered unfeasible. Young men known to avoid work and study were candidates; so were known

counter-revolutionaries; and also immoralists, a category that included homosexuals."[18]

The camps also served another purpose. They provided cheap
regimented labor for the province of Camagüey, within which
they were all located. At the time there was an acute shortage of
labor in the province, which was converting large tracts of ranch
land into cane fields. In reality the UMAP involved forced labor,
since their inmates were paid seven pesos a month, much less
than other agricultural workers, and could only leave the camps
under military escort in their spare time.[19]

Homosexuals were among those most affected by the UMAP
camps, but there is no evidence that these were created with
homosexuals exclusively in mind. Together with homosexuals
the camps contained such sexually incompatible companions as
Jehovah's Witnesses and Seventh Day Adventists, conscientious
objectors to military service whose religious faiths are notoriously
homophobic. In addition there were many other young men who
would have been perceived as counterrevolutionary on account of
their refusal to toe the line on correct public behavior. Since
Cubans have inherited that most Spanish of all qualities—stub-
born individualism, or being *conflictivo,* as they say in Cuba—
there were probably many Cubans who adopted a "fuck you" attitude when told how to dress, how to walk, what music to listen
to, and how generally to behave in public. Their nonconformist
behavior was as provocative to those preoccupied with the "revolutionary hygiene"[20] of the new Cuba as was the gender identity
of homosexual males.

Virgilio Piñera claimed that sixty thousand homosexuals were
taken to the camps,[21] but other estimates suggest that the total
number of all inmates was much lower. Furthermore, it would
appear that the majority of the camps' occupants were not homosexual but heterosexual. Given that many of those who spent
time in the UMAP camps had been accused of victimless crimes,
it is possible that many of them were there as a result of the

personal prejudices of local leaders of mass organizations, such as the CDRs, who were entrusted with reporting "antisocial behavior."

If they were inconsistent with Fidel Castro's beliefs about moral persuasion, the UMAP camps were quite consistent with other policies being implemented within Cuba at the time. From the outset of the revolution, Fidel Castro had stressed the redeeming quality of the countryside and of agricultural work carried out by city people alongside rural inhabitants. Apparently, he believed that *maricones* could not emanate from the harsh conditions that had spawned Cuba's virile *campesinos.* The revolutionary regime had also quickly demonstrated its *machista* preoccupation by publicly purging anyone suspected of being homosexual from its new polytechnic schools. It forced students to undergo endurance tests such as climbing the Pico Turquino, Cuba's highest peak, before they were allowed to graduate, as a means of demonstrating their fitness and commitment to working in the countryside after graduation.

The young men who were sent to the UMAP camps were forced to perform agricultural labor instead of participating in the regular activities of military conscripts. The motivation was largely punitive, but there was also an expectation that such work would transform them into "real" men. At the time, everybody was being coerced by one means or another to do manual work for very similar reasons. Regular military conscripts were required to do agricultural work for much of the time. In fact, all healthy males and young women were expected to do some farm work. It was usually called "voluntary labor," but the work was extracted from people through sociopolitical coercion as much as through persuasion. Some people worked for weeks at a time in the sugar-cane harvest, while others assisted only on weekends. Schoolchildren, too, were expected to help in agriculture, by picking coffee beans, for example. It was also about this time that the decision was made to combine work and study at all levels of

Cuba's educational system. Boarding schools for secondary school students were constructed throughout the countryside for ideological as much as for economic reasons. The intention was to break the dislike for agricultural work that has plagued urban Cuba for so long.

The moralistic rigidity that partially accounts for the decision to establish the UMAP camps was a reflection of the revolutionary voluntarism to which Cuba had committed itself by this time. "Sanitizing" the environment politically and socially was part of the "revolutionary offensive" that led to political purges and to the closure of the state lottery, all bars, cafes, and remaining private businesses in 1968. The Cuban leaders were castigating other Latin American Communists for being "pseudorevolutionaries" and for lacking the will and courage to make revolutions elsewhere in the region. The debate regarding the use of moral versus material incentives as the primary motivations of the Cuban labor force was being resolved in favor of the former. It was the time of intransigent commitment to the "new man" in Cuba and to "One, two, three, many Vietnams" abroad. Ultrarevolutionary ideas about the "simultaneous construction of socialism and communism" were crystallizing and provoking considerable tension with Cuba's Soviet and East European allies, without whose enormous economic support the revolution could scarcely have survived. Despite this the Cuban leaders self-righteously denounced the bourgeois tendencies and weakening revolutionary commitment that they discerned in Yugoslavia, Czechoslovakia, and by implication the Soviet Union itself. As true believers and recent converts to revolutionary socialism, they were also at loggerheads with Mao's China (over Vietnam), which in many ways embodied ideals about the redeeming value of agricultural labor that were similar to Cuba's aspirations.

Even allowing for understandable exaggeration, there is every reason to believe that conditions in the UMAP camps were very harsh. Ernesto Cardenal, who would become Minister of Culture in Nicaragua's Sandinista government, included a description of these conditions in his book on Cuba. According to his informant, "work is hard because it is nearly always in the sun. We work eleven hours a day [cutting marble in a quarry], from seven in the morning to seven at night, with one hour's lunch break." In another camp conditions were even worse: "We worked 12 to 16 hours a day . . . [and] were surrounded by a barbed wire fence that was two and a half meters high."[22] Homosexuals frequently (but not invariably) suffered more than other inmates, particularly those whose flamboyant personalities were offensive to the *machista* guards.[23] Still, conditions varied from camp to camp. Although some camps were reserved exclusively for homosexuals, overall conditions in such camps were not necessarily worse than in other camps in which homosexuals were a minority. In some respects, they might have even been better as a result of the collective efforts of their inmates to humanize their environment by adding a gay touch to their barracks and camp life.[24]

Nevertheless, much as homosexuals suffered during this period, it is misleading to equate their treatment to that of the Jews in Germany, even in terms of being scapegoats for the revolution, as has been suggested in oft-repeated remarks attributed to Jean-Paul Sartre. The extermination of Jews in Germany was a monstrous and unique operation that was nevertheless consistent with the Nazis' racist ideology. In contrast, the persecution of homosexuals and other minorities in Cuba completely contradicted the humanist and liberating values that had motivated the revolution. In any event, it should not be compared with one of history's great human catastrophes. In this respect, the film *Improper Conduct* is particularly misleading in its use of emotive analogies to Pinochet's Chile, Nazi Germany, and Stalin's Russia. Allen Young, author of *Gays under the Cuban Revolution,* who could hardly be said to underestimate Cuban oppression of homosexuals, concludes that "the emphasis [within the UMAP camps] was clearly on hard labor."[25] Yet surely almost the same

could be said about many other activities that were simultaneously being conducted in Cuba, not least of which was the back-
breaking work of the sugar-cane harvest. Successful sugar har-
vests were crucial to Cuba's economic survival, especially because
of the economic blockade and Cuba's isolation within the Western Hemisphere. This fact does not excuse the barbaric treatment
suffered by the inmates; conditions were so severe that some people committed suicide. Some camps were apparently so notorious
that their military commanders were actually charged and convicted of brutalizing inmates.[26]

The UMAP units were a temporary phenomenon, but the
official attitudes that they reflected and the persecution of homosexuals that was associated with them, persisted for many more
years. These were terrifying times for many homosexuals, particularly those in entertainment, culture, and education. As one
leading designer recalled, they carried within them the "ever-
present fear that at any moment there might be a knock on the
door to report for an interrogation, or simply to be perfunctorily
shipped out by truck-load to the countryside."

The explanation for the camps' closure in 1968 is not clear, in
part because their existence has never been publicized in Cuba.
One factor may have been the criticism they evoked from members of the Cuban Union of Writers and Artists (UNEAC), reinforced by the denunciations of intellectuals in Mexico and Europe
who had once been supporters of the revolution. The intervention
of Raquel Revuelta, a prominent actress with impeccable political credentials (she had been a PSP member even before 1959),
may have been decisive. Her theater group, Teatro Estudio, had
been shut down because so many of its members were gay. She
was shocked by what she came to learn about the UMAP camps
from friends and colleagues alike. She succeeded in persuading
Comandante René Vallejo, Fidel Castro's personal aide and
physician, that the camps were a terrible abuse of human rights.
Although Castro responded by declaring that the camps would be

closed (in the only public and indirect reference to their existence), they were not eliminated for another year. To be sure, conditions soon began to improve under the supervision of Captain Quintín Pino Machado, who had been personally commissioned by the Cuban leader to oversee their eradication. But they could not be immediately shut down because by then their regimented labor had become irreplaceable in the short run. Moreover, the decision to close the camps in no way reflected an official admission that there was anything wrong with the persecution of homosexuals and nonconformists in general.[27]

In the second half of the 1960s systematic purges of homosexuals in the arts, theater, and universities became institutionalized. Resolución Número 3 of the Consejo de Cultura (which administered cultural affairs prior to the creation of the Ministry of Culture in 1976), the edict used to fire homosexual artists from their jobs and force them to do manual labor, became an infamous symbol of the regime's homophobia. The "revolutionary social hygiene" for which Samuel Feijoo had called was now being put into practice, cleansing the arts of "fraudulent sodomitic" writers and "sick effeminate" dancers. Brilliant painters like Servando Cabrera Moreno and Raúl Martínez were purged from Cubanacán, the art school, on no grounds other than that they were homosexual, regardless of whether they had lent their craft to the revolution in other substantial ways.[28] It was not just a question of purging "ostentatious" homosexual students from places like the University of Havana, since by then no such person could possibly have been admitted as a student. They would have lacked the appropriate political credentials and character references from organizations such as the CDRs that were necessary for admission.

By this time even relatively closeted *entendidos* were at risk of being publicly grilled in a manner reminiscent of the Cultural Revolution in China. Countless *recogidas* in the streets struck terror in the hearts of homosexuals. As in Mao's China, those with long hair were shorn of their locks by the police and given conventional masculine cuts. Countless *locas* were also being entrapped by the police and arrested for their "scandalous" public behavior. Once again, they were not alone, being joined by others who had been defined as "lumpen" and "scum" elements. Furthermore, as exiled Cuban novelist Guillermo Cabrera Infante reminds us, the persecution of homosexuals was due more to their nonconformist public identity and refusal to endorse the political dogmas of the regime with appropriate enthusiasm than to their sexual orientation per se.[29] For the Cuban leaders could not tolerate any form of opposition, even if it was merely implicit rather than overtly counterrevolutionary. The need to "contain any form of deviance among youth" would be declared an integral part of the commitment to "preserve the monolithic ideological unity" of the Cuban people.[30] Such motives explain why writers were also being imprisoned, often on the most flimsy grounds, such as in the notorious case of Heberto Padilla, who was pressured into making a humiliating public confession of his "errors" shortly after winning an important Cuban literary prize in 1968 for his book of poems, *Fuera del juego* (Out of the game).

The gifted young writer Reinaldo Arenas provoked the regime on two accounts. Not only was he open about his homosexuality but he also challenged the right of the Cuban state to control the publications of Cuban writers. His second novel, *El mundo alucinante* (published in English as *The Ill-Fated Peregrinations of Fray Servando*), was rejected for publication by UNEAC, even though the union had already reluctantly acknowledged the novel's merits in its annual competition. In fact, the then-president of the Imprenta Nacional de Cuba, Rolando Rodríguez, told Arenas that he would be willing to allow publication of the novel so long as he eliminated its "homosexual" chapters. Arenas replied ironically that he was not prepared to do so since it would demonstrate to foreign readers that there was censorship in Cuba.[31] Arenas proceeded to smuggle the novel abroad, where it eventually became a great success. As a result Arenas was placed under surveillance by state security and later jailed for alleged homosexual crimes.

The obsession with homosexuals would become even more intense. Now the "danger of social contact" was publicized by Abel Prieto Morales (who was to become Vice Minister of Education) in an article in *Bohemia,* Cuba's most widely read magazine, as was the need to control "*a compulsive activity that includes the tendency to form groups of followers and propagandists bent on seducing new practitioners*" (emphasis in original).[32] Homosexuality was to become a major concern at the first National Congress on Education and Culture, which took place in 1971. After it had examined the "antisocial" character of homosexuality and had recognized its "sociopathological" nature, the Congress resolved "that all manifestations of homosexual deviation" were to be firmly rejected and prevented from spreading. Specifically, the Congress resolved that "notorious homosexuals" should be denied employment in any institution that had an influence upon youth. It further resolved that homosexuals should not be allowed to represent Cuba in cultural activities abroad. Finally, it was agreed that severe penalties should be applied to those responsible for corrupting the morals of minors, to "depraved repeat offenders," and to "irremediable antisocial elements."[33]

In Cuba, conferences such as the Congress on Education and Culture are not mere routine meetings of academics, teachers, writers, and so forth because civil society does not exist separate from the state. Spirited debates may occur in closed sessions and in private among conference participants.[34] Nevertheless, these conferences have an ideological orientation that is determined by the Communist Party, and their objectives are always political in the broadest sense, regardless of the matter under discussion. Their conclusions, particularly if they are presided over by Fidel Castro, are invariably highly publicized by the mass media and set the tone and parameters of public discourse for a considerable time. After such a conference public figures will make approving references to its resolutions, while there is no public outlet whatsoever for an alternative viewpoint. The Party and mass organizations will devote study sessions to its conclusions in every neighborhood and work center. In time, resolutions may be forgotten and contradicted by practice, but for a while they legitimize certain viewpoints, in this case the homophobic *machista* prejudices that have always been endemic in Cuban society.

The homophobic repression that was unleashed by the Congress on Education and Culture was associated with a more generalized attack upon intellectual and cultural nonconformists. The breadth of its scope was reflected in Castro's denunciations of foreign intellectuals such Jean-Paul Sartre who dared to question the direction of the revolution. Even more extreme, indeed paranoid, denunciations were directed at the European Marxist K. S. Karol, who had previously been invited to visit Cuba and write a book on the revolution. The repression of any form of dissent was conjoined with the broader economic reforms that followed the debacle of the 1970 sugar-cane harvest. The Cuban leaders had put themselves out on a limb by promising that the goal of ten million tons would be fulfilled at whatever cost. When they were unable to achieve the target, despite massive disruption of the rest of the economy, they had no alternative but to admit the failure and collective responsibility of the leadership. The ensuing economic reforms had to be counterbalanced, at least in terms of the preservation of political power, by the reaffirmation of the regime's ideological commitments.

Accordingly, after the 1971 Congress on Education and Culture more homosexuals, or even people supposed to be homosexual, were systematically fired from their jobs according to the prejudices of those who were responsible for carrying out the Congress resolutions. Ana María Simo, a Cuban writer exiled in New York, was perfectly right when she argued that although Cuba had always been a homophobic society, this was the first time that such prejudice had been institutionally legitimized.[35] Moreover, individuals who were subject to such officially legitimized prejudice became particularly vulnerable because the postrevolutionary state was based on mass mobilization. Their personal lives were exposed to the public, and they also found it extremely difficult to obtain alternative employment suited to their qualifications.

Nevertheless, the very size and diversity of Cuba's increasingly modern state also allowed some degree of autonomy to its various components. Institutions such as the Ministry of Culture and the Casa de las Américas, which were directed by such well-established humanists as Armando Hart and Haydée Santamaría, could be more flexible with regard to the enforcement of certain policies. Less severe resolutions of the Congress on Education and Culture—such as that which noted that although homosexuality required attention, "it should not be considered a central problem or a fundamental one in [Cuban] society"—could be used to sanction more liberal treatment of homosexuals. During the course of the Congress, Fidel had been seen to put his arm ostentatiously around Alfredo Guevara, as if to give a clear signal that the resolutions need not apply to important homosexuals who had otherwise demonstrated their revolutionary commitment at work—provided that in public they uncritically accepted the homophobic policies that had now been legitimated by the Congress.

Other departments, like the Ministry of the Interior (police) administered by the notoriously homophobic Ramiro Valdés, were provided with plenty of ammunition to persecute homosexuals, however. In effect they were given carte blanche to hound anyone who indulged in "extravagant," "exhibitionist," or "foreign" behavior. Bizarre and pathetic as it may seem that the regime could feel threatened by the nonconformity of what at that time amounted to an insignificant minority of young Cubans, the government even went so far as to establish an agency to define dress codes.

The lives of "ostentatious" homosexuals were damaged and frequently ravaged. Hard as it was for Cuban homosexuals to develop a career in the first place, their self-confidence and creativity, not to mention their sexuality, were crippled by the discrimination they suffered during this period. Regardless of their commitment to study and work, they were defined as "antisocial" beings whose very presence in a revolutionary milieu was intolerable. It did not matter whether they had participated in the 1961 literacy campaign or had tried to prove their "manhood" by doing voluntary work in agriculture. Once they were defined as ostentatious homosexuals, their presence among voluntary work contingents was prohibited on the grounds that it was provocative. They were also rejected for military service. Purges from the universities and exclusion from military service effectively ensured that they were denied any further opportunity to develop their talents. Their *expediente* or file would follow them to whatever job or college they applied for thereafter. Nor were they accepted for programs to study or work abroad, opportunities especially coveted since they represented the only way to travel outside the island. For many, the most painful and humiliating repercussions involved their immediate families and neighbors. They were "outed" in a break with a long-standing Cuban convention that respected the needs of parents and sons alike. Through this convention homosexual sons could retain their places in the family, provided that they did not, so to speak, "come out." It is understandable that many became embittered and disaffected from the revolution. As an exiled, gifted artist in his mid-forties explains:

> Of course I am bitter. I could have been a brilliant architect. I was the most outstanding student in the Faculty of Architecture when I was expelled in 1965. They prevented me from pursuing an alternative program in the National School of Design. Nor could I study art at the Cubanacán. So I took up ballet. Then when I was to get a job in the Teatro Lírico in 1967,

it coincided with a mass purge of all the theaters, which ruled that out as well. I was detained by the police in 1968 because of my haircut, and again in 1977 during a private party for being in possession of two pornographic magazines. I then spent three days in jail in 1982 for alleged "ostentatious" behavior. If it hadn't been for my gutsy sister, who was married to a colonel in the Ministry of Interior and who defended me in court, I would have spent six months in jail. But she wasn't able to prevent them from devastating my mother, who had little education and provincial values since she came from Las Villas. I love Cuba, but they forced me to leave. There was nothing else I could do.[36]

Eventually, in the mid-1970s, the mass purges of writers and intellectuals would cease. Resolución Número 3 was squashed by order of the Tribunal Suprema (Supreme Court) in 1975, and many of those who had been purged earlier were financially compensated. Upon Armando Hart's assumption of the Ministry of Culture in 1976, conditions began to improve for homosexuals in the arts. Oppression of homosexuals would become more and more similar to what had occurred informally in most other Latin American countries, including liberal democratic ones such as Costa Rica. Instead of incarceration, *recogidas,* and systemic purges, there was more emphasis on regulating the type of contact that open homoscxuals could have with the rest of society. Entry into certain professions was impeded—occasionally by official edict, such as the 1971 Labor Code in the case of education, medicine, and sports—but more typically by the use of informal selection procedures. If someone escaped the net on entry to a profession, he could be denied promotion or recognition of his merits on other grounds. It was of course very difficult for homosexuals to demonstrate that they had been subject to official discrimination, particularly once formal prohibitions, such as the ban on employment of homosexuals in education, had been allowed to lapse. Furthermore, very few homosexuals would have been prepared to contest their discriminatory treatment since it would only have drawn further attention to their homosexuality. The consequences at work and in other aspects of their lives could have been too detrimental to them in the long term. There were no civil rights organizations to fall back on for moral and political support. They would have had no access to the media. And needless to say, it would be impossible to raise the broader issue of discrimination within the Party and state institutions given their bureaucratic character and indifference to individual human rights.

Understandably, the vast majority of homosexuals remained embittered and completely alienated from the revolution. They were reluctant to accept the possibility that a reevaluation of state policy toward homosexuals might have begun in the late 1970s. They were skeptical that the creation of the National Working Group on Sexual Education in 1977 might have signaled a new departure.

The occupation of the Peruvian Embassy by would-be émigrés and the subsequent exodus of over one hundred thousand Cubans from Mariel in 1980 were associated with the last gasp of *institutionally* promoted homophobia. There are varying estimates of the number of gays who seized the opportunity to get out of Cuba at the time of Mariel. They were numerous enough to be singled out as targets in the mass demonstrations directed against those who had opted to leave. Such political events cannot take place in Cuba without the state's tacit support and usually unofficial organization. There is also evidence to suggest that media coverage, such as in the documentary *Escoria* (Scum), deliberately drew attention to the homosexuals who were seeking to leave Cuba.[37] *Granma,* the organ of the Communist Party, featured the story of one seventeen-year-old boy who had been taken to the Peruvian embassy by his parents. When he saw that he would be among "homosexuals, dandies and delinquents," enemies of the revolution, he was said to have realized that he himself could not be anything but a revolutionary.[38] *Granma* followed this story with a cartoon that referred to revolutionaries having "genes and hearts" in the right places.[39] Officially, the regime dealt with the issue in the following *Granma* editorial: "Even though in our country homosexuals are not persecuted or harassed, . . . there were quite a few of them in the Peruvian embassy, in addition to all those involved in gambling and drugs who find it difficult to satisfy their vices here."[40]

Few homosexuals were taken in by this denial of prejudice. The majority were understandably more impressed by the fact that the government had once again sought to discredit them by publicly linking them with criminals, delinquents, and drug addicts, as well as mocking their dress, mannerisms, and language. They could hardly remain impervious to the mass demonstrations in the streets in which they were branded as "scum," "lumpen," and "antisocial elements" for wanting to leave Cuba. They would also have been aware that the government had actually pressured some of the more extravagant *locas* to board boats to Miami, along with the common criminals who were sent packing to the United States.

Cuban homosexuals' feelings about the revolution surely came out when so many grasped the opportunity to leave Cuba at the time of Mariel. The homophobic character of the regime is also evident in the fact that many homosexuals were pressured into leaving. An article in the Mexican liberal newspaper *Uno Más Uno,* citing a joint statement by lesbian and gay socialists denouncing the Cuban measures, made a telling point:

> If it is true that all the refugees are criminals, bums and homosexuals, we should wonder how it is that after twenty years of revolution and in a country that defines itself as socialist, homosexuality is persecuted as a crime to the extent of forcing those who practice it to leave in exile, and how and why there could exist so many bums and criminals, particularly among the young, the children of the revolution.[41]

Still, it is significant that since the time of Mariel, there have been no further explicitly homophobic campaigns by the government or in the mass media.[42] This may not amount to much, but in the context of the Cuban past and in relation to the homophobia that was initially unleashed by the AIDS epidemic even in such liberal countries as Costa Rica, it must be acknowledged as an advance. In fact, although Cuba and its government remain homophobic, there is little evidence to support the contention that the *persecution* of homosexuals remains a matter of state policy. On the contrary, there is considerable evidence to suggest that the government is now seeking to devise a much less repressive way of regulating homosexuality.[43] Most homosexuals stress, however, that although there may be more tolerance, there is still no respect or support accorded to them by a government that claims to represent the whole population.

# FOUR

# Homosexuality
# and the Law

*MEMORIES OF* the systematic oppression of homosexuals during the period of the Military Units to Aid Production (UMAP) and then during much of the 1970s still color many older homosexuals' perceptions of the Cuban state. The major milestone of this repressive era was the 1971 Congress on Education and Culture, which adopted a number of homophobic resolutions. Younger gays are much less affected by events that in some cases occurred before they were born. Still, the history serves as an ever-present reminder of their vulnerability in an authoritarian regime that has never validated their existence and social contributions, let alone tried to make amends for the immense harm that was done to specific individuals. Nevertheless, it is important to acknowledge that the overall situation of gay males has improved considerably over the past decade, though it still varies from sector to sector. Their civil status may not have changed all that much, but there is far more social space available to them than there once was.

As is the case of Mexico and Costa Rica, homosexuality is not a criminal offense in Cuba. The 1979 Penal Code decriminalized homosexuality per se. It is therefore perfectly legal for consenting adults to engage in homosexual acts in private. Nevertheless, until the Penal Code was revised in 1987, it prohibited "public ostentation" of a homosexual "condition" and penalized private homosexual acts inadvertantly seen by third parties. Homosexual males who had sex with minors were also penalized much more severely than males who had sex with underage females.

The Penal Code enforced in Cuba until 1979 was basically the same as the 1938 prerevolutionary Social Defense Code, which in turn derived from Spanish law. The latter was characterized by its discriminatory treatment of homosexuals and other "deviants."[1] For example, in Spain the Ley de Vagos y Maleantes (Law against Malefactors and Vagrants)—and more recently, the Ley de Peligrosidad (Law of Dangerousness) enacted in 1970—made homosexuals subject to preventive detention.[2] Moreover, in Cuba Article 490 of the 1938 code imposed a prison sentence of up to six months or an equivalent fine upon anyone who "habitually engaged in homosexual acts," who "sexually propositioned someone," or who created a "public scandal" by "flaunting" his homosexuality in public.

Although Cuba has been rightly criticized for its prejudicial treatment of homosexuals, especially considering its publicly proclaimed goal of social justice for all, its criminal code's treatment of homosexuals is by no means unique in the Western Hemisphere. The majority of Latin American countries may not mention homosexuality in their criminal codes, but a few, such as Chile and Ecuador, criminalize even private homosexual acts. Many Latin American codes contain prohibitions similar to Costa Rica's, which in the name of public decency penalizes "scandalous homosexuality" albeit as a misdemeanor rather than a crime.[3] Police regulations and city by-laws in Mexico, Argentina, Brazil, the Dominican Republic, and Peru, as in Cuba,[4] are also used to victimize homosexuals for the sake of "public decency." In fact, police throughout the region exercise informal authority to enforce taboos and social prejudices against public expressions of homo-sexual orientation.

The 1988 *Second Pink Book* of the International Lesbian and Gay Association (ILGA), which documents homosexual repres-sion throughout the world, points to the fact that the section of Cuba's criminal code dealing with "estado peligroso," commonly known as the Ley de Peligrosidad Social (Law of Social Danger-ousness), was used to persecute homosexuals who deviate from "prevailing (socialist) morality." It contends that Articles 76 to 94 of the 1979 Penal Code "are often used to arrest homosexuals and imprison them usually for 4 years."[5] Whether the last statement is true or not,[6] Cuba was not unique in having such laws. Even liberal states such as Costa Rica have laws relating to public secur-ity that permit preventive detention of homosexuals perceived to be a threat to the social order.[7]

Although the section of the current Penal Code that regulates "social dangerousness" does not specifically mention homosexual acts among the types of behavior that the law is designed to curb, it is clear that homosexuality falls within the general category of "the exploitation or practice of socially reprehensible vice" and "antisocial conduct" (Article 73). In Cuba, *antisocial* has been a code word for allegedly ostentatious homosexuality, among other "deviant" forms of behavior. Whether homosexuality is the chief target of the law, as has been suggested by some North American gay critics, is quite another matter. The section applies to drunk-ards and drug addicts as much as to homosexuals. Still, it is in-disputably reactionary in its relegitimation of archaic laws that contradict concepts of human rights that are increasingly hon-ored in theory, if not in practice, throughout the world.[8]

The Law of Social Dangerousness is both sweeping and vague. It is designed to control not only the potentially dangerous be-havior of drunkards and drug addicts but also any conduct that could be considered "antisocial"—that is, in open conflict with "the norms of socialist morality" (Article 73). Its control extends

even further through its applicability to anyone who does not fit
into one of the already-named categories but who associates with
those who do. In this case the person in question is merely warned
(with the warning recorded in police files) of the possibility of
transgressions against "the social, economic and political order of
the socialist State" (Article 75).

The laws specifically regulating homosexuality are grouped
together in the section of the Penal Code that deals with "Crimes
against the Normal[9] Development of Sexual Relations." Underlying the code's provisions about homosexuality is the consistent
assumption that it is a contagious condition that prompts those afflicted by it to seduce young children. Accordingly, Article 317
permanently bars from teaching or from any other jurisdiction
over children anybody who has been convicted of a sexual crime,
even an insistent homosexual proposition to another *adult*. It also
contains a strong assumption that homosexuality is restricted to
males, despite the reference to a minor of either sex being corrupted by a homosexual (Article 310).

Although the provision of the 1979 code that penalized "ostentatious" displays of a "person's homosexual condition" was
deleted from the 1987 code, homosexual behavior that causes a
"public scandal," either because it contravenes public decency or
because it entails sexually importuning another person (in the
sense of molestation), may still be penalized by prison sentences
of three to twelve months, or a fine of between one and three hundred *cuotas* (a *cuota* is equivalent to a day's minimum wage) (Article 303). In fact, in 1987 the maximum sentence was *raised* by
three months compared to the 1979 code. Yet it is a mistake to interpret the "public scandal" provision as a prohibition of harmless
homosexual behavior such as persistent verbal cruising, an error
made in the *Third Pink Book* of the ILGA. To be sure, Article 303
is homophobic, but it is also quite consistent with traditional
Cuban (indeed, Latin American) preoccupations with regulating
public behavior. If sexually propositioning another male were in

reality penalized, the jails of Cuba would be packed with men who had sought to have sex with other men!

Penalization of homosexuality involving young Cubans is both homophobic and oppressive in that it denies any possibility of choice on the part of the minors in question. An adult who "induces" someone under sixteen years of age to engage in homosexuality may be sentenced to up to five years in prison (Article 310).[10] In the case of "active pederasty" with someone under fourteen, the sentence may be up to twenty years or even death (Article 299). Significantly, the age of consent is sixteen years for males to engage in homosexual acts, while it is only twelve for females to participate in heterosexual sex. If females have engaged in homosexual (lesbian) acts, however, the age of consent is raised to sixteen (Article 310). The provision restricting males under sixteen from having sex with other males is oppressive since it disregards the fact that many Cubans are sexually active long before then, frequently by the age of fourteen. They are further repressed by the penal stipulation that the custodians of youths under sixteen years of age who engage in homosexual acts are compelled to report the youths to the state, even if they might believe in and support their children's sexual maturity (Article 311).

The homophobic (and sexist)[11] bias of the current Cuban Penal Code is thus beyond doubt, doubly so because the 1987 revisions to the 1979 code followed lengthy study and debate at the highest levels of the Party and National Assembly. Discriminatory penalties for much homosexual behavior remained on the books despite the fact that the goal of the Penal Code revision was to make it less repressive.[12] Over seventy offenses were removed from the code, and thousands of prisoners were released in a retroactive application of the new code. If certain homosexual behavior has remained a criminal offense, it must be because Cuban authorities believe that it should be included among those "acts that cause considerable social harm or which cannot be contained by other means."[13]

Many individuals claim that they were subjected to the "public scandal" and "social dangerousness" provisions of the Cuban criminal code. Official denials by Fidel Castro and others that they were ever applied in an arbitrary, repressive manner are not plausible. Until recently, it was not "gay paranoia" to fear the law in Cuba, as was implied by Lourdes Arguelles and Ruby Rich in a controversial and influential article for which I otherwise have considerable sympathy.[14] The Penal Code remains a central element in the homophobic environment that has confronted Cuban homosexuals for much of the last three decades. The fact that some homophobic strictures have remained in the criminal code (and that a few were even strengthened in 1987) indicates that they exist because they serve the purposes of the Cuban state. Their purpose is to intimidate homosexuals and to contain homosexuality within a heterosexist if not *machista* social order. It would be ingenuous to believe otherwise. In short, while statements such as those made by Debra Evenson that "consensual homosexual relations in Cuba have been freed from the reach of criminal law" may be theoretically correct, it is a travesty for her to suggest that in practice "homosexuals are no longer subject to official harassment for simply being identified as homosexuals."[15] In Cuba, as in all other homophobic societies, the criminal code and police regulations will always be used to harass and oppress gays until the state removes all discriminatory references to same-sex sex in the criminal and civil codes and commits itself to combating the residues of homophobia in society and state institutions alike.

Cuban homosexuals have long remained alert to the possibility of being detained by the police in a *redada* precisely because they understand the law's conscious intent. Although, to be sure, *redadas* and *recogidas* have markedly declined,[16] questioning and sometimes detention of individual homosexuals (among other marginalized groups, such as poor blacks) are still common occurrences. Minor infractions, such as not carrying an identity card, are used as a pretext for detention and cross-examination in a police station. Harassment of "street" homosexuals, particularly cross-dressing *"travestis,"* who socialize in downtown parks and street corners, and of couples who embrace or kiss in public is commonplace, just as it is throughout Latin America (including Costa Rica and Mexico).

The integration of the police force and the judicial system within a one-party state, where there is no effective civil society to monitor its function, has also facilitated the repression of homosexuals. Knowledge of this fact has had a marked effect upon how most homosexuals behave in public. Whoever doubts this has simply not shared nor been exposed to the daily life of ordinary gay males in Cuba. Until recently few Cubans have been willing to challenge arbitrary behavior by officials, gays and lesbians least of all. Few Cuban gays who have any familiarity with street life in Havana would be surprised by the experience of an acquaintance of mine who was detained and fined half a month's wage for kissing his lover on the cheek on a park bench in San Miguel del Padrón. Nor would they be surprised that he would not risk questioning the legitimacy of the fine or the police officer's tirade about *"maricones* making out in public."

Laws regulating public morality and standards of decency in every country are affected by material changes as well as by shifts in the way those in power interpret the standards. The way these statutes are interpreted and enforced also varies since "moral" offenses are more susceptible to subjective evaluation than many other kinds of infractions. This generalization certainly applies to the antihomosexual provisions of Cuba's Penal Code. As Luis Salas, a Cuban émigré criminologist, has noted, "statutory prohibitions do not give an adequate picture of the homosexual's legal status [in Cuba]. The attitudes of judges and prosecutors vary widely and are especially influenced by their own biases and beliefs."[17] The fact that Cuba's court system provides for lay judges to serve alongside (and outnumber) professional judges on each panel is not necessarily reassuring in this respect, given the *machista* nature of Cuban society. The possibility that homosexuals are subject to discriminatory treatment in Cuba's courts (as in courts elsewhere) has to be considered seriously. Yet by the early 1990s, sensational reports of such cases had ceased to be a feature of gay life in Havana, which was certainly not the case even in the late 1980s.

The same applies to the treatment of homosexuals within Cuban prisons. It is difficult to ascertain how many people have been charged and imprisoned on grounds relating to homosexuality or to generalize about their treatment. There are conflicting reports about conditions in Cuban prisons,[18] and it is difficult to determine whether they are any worse than those of other underdeveloped countries. (Given Cuba's socialist aspirations they should be better.) Allowance must be made for the fact that Cuba has been under a constant state of siege. Armando Valladares's claim that "there have been few examples of repression of homosexuals as virulent as in Cuba," particularly his account of the treatment of homosexuals in prison, must be treated with some skepticism even though Reinaldo Arenas's account of conditions in El Morro prison seems to substantiate the contention.[19] But so must claims by Fidel Castro that there has never been a "single case of someone tortured" or subject to inhumane prison conditions within Cuba.[20] Considering the society's historically ingrained homophobia, it would be surprising if prison guards treated *maricones* in a particularly humane way.

At least two of my gay friends have spent time in prison, in the Combinado del Este outside Havana. Neither of them claims that discrimination occurred there because of their homosexuality, but the conditions of their detention were to say the least callous. The most reprehensible feature of their imprisonment was deprivation of exercise and access to open air, particularly in the case of one of them, a middle-aged artist who was there for two months on a trumped-up charge. He was quite *obvio* (clearly gay) and yet not mistreated on that account. Nor does he claim to have been subject to harassment by the other prisoners. Perhaps this was because of his age. The other friend was jailed for having assaulted (under provocation) an undercover police officer. He was brutally beaten up in the police station and jail, but not on account of his homosexuality since he looked typically *macho*. (His skull was so badly fractured—it remains severely indented to this day—that he was hospitalized prior to being jailed.) Since he was young and extremely good-looking, he was in danger from his fellow prisoners, but the guards did nothing to protect him. Fortunately, since he had been a martial arts juvenile champion, he was able to fend off other prisoners' attempts to rape him.

Fidel Castro is clearly as dishonest about the treatment of homosexuals as he is evasive about prison conditions. Despite his disclaimers, there is every reason to believe that he, most Communist Party leaders, and other top officials are as *machista* as their generation as a whole. It strains credulity to accept the contention that the UMAP camps and the purges of the late 1960s and early 1970s could have happened without the knowledge and consent of the Cuban leaders. Nor could the revisions to the 1979 Criminal Code, which were discussed for three years before their 1987 promulgation, have been formulated without their support. Despite this indisputable record, and its continuing self-righteousness, Cuba's leadership cannot remain ignorant of the more liberal ways of understanding and regulating homosexuality now beginning to spread beyond the boundaries of the "decadent" capitalist countries. Cuba's leaders cannot have been unaware of developments that were beginning to take place within Eastern Europe prior to the collapse of communism. They must also have known about attitudes toward homosexuality within Nicaragua's Sandinista regime, a government that had close ties with Cuba. The Sandinista regime, even in a much more Catholic country than Cuba, that was in a state of war, had much more progressive sexual policies than Cuba's. Is it overly optimistic still to give credence to Fidel Castro's 1965 statement that "Traditions and customs can clash somewhat with new social realities, and the problems of sexual relations in youth will require more scientific attention.... I believe that new realities, social, economic and cultural will determine new conditions and new concepts of human relations"?[21]

The new realities are present. A new culture is already emerging in Cuba, but whether the Cuban government will embrace it is a question still unanswered. People who want to believe that the regime can change, perhaps particularly those who are straight, attach too much significance to any sign of the government promising to make life easier for gays.[22]

Nevertheless, the situation of homosexuals is improving. The demotion in 1985 of Ramiro Valdés, a long-time Minister of the Interior who was notoriously homophobic, seemed a good omen for Cuban homosexuals. Once one of the most powerful figures in Cuba, he was dropped from the Politburo of the Communist Party and reduced to mere Central Committee membership in the mid-1980s. Homosexuals whom I spoke to in 1986 were jubilant that he was gone from this key ministry (of police). There was widespread belief that more tolerant police behavior, particularly liberal enforcement of the Law of Social Dangerousness, was associated with the departure of Valdés.

Although there is no record of the views on homosexuality of his successor, José Abrantes (eventually charged and imprisoned in relation to the Ochoa drug scandal),[23] Abrantes appeared to have had a far more liberal approach to the repressive function of the state than Valdés. Abrantes insisted that its function was to "prevent in order not to repress." Speaking of the revisions to the Penal Code, he declared:

> This rectification implies thorough ideological work, a change in mentality. Not only in our police organizations, but also in nearly all our country's institutions, and in the population itself, a general tendency to repress has developed, to look for so-

lution for faults, problems, misdemeanors, and infractions by means of the intervention of the police. We have to struggle to change that repressive outlook.[24]

The Ministry of Interior internal manual issued in 1988, which indicates how police regulations are to be enforced, also reflects this new outlook. Significantly, the only clause in the new regulations that might have special implications for homosexuals is the archaic and rather quaint prohibition of "lewd behavior" that contravenes "public decency." Even then, the fine for such behavior is less than that imposed on those caught "peeping" into private homes.[25]

An indication of this new outlook may be reflected in the lessened penalization of homosexuality in places such as public toilets, cinemas, and parks. Until 1987, the Penal Code was quite clear that anyone who engaged in "homosexual acts in public places or in private ones where they might be involuntarily seen by other people" should be charged (Article 359). It imposed a three-to-nine-month sentence on people convicted of such acts. The 1987 revised code omitted this provision (while retaining the "public decency" clause), hopefully in recognition of the fact that Cuban gays resort to "public" sex to the same extent and for the same reasons as gays do in most other Latin American countries—that is, lack of access to private spaces within a homophobic society.

In the past, during the worst period of homosexual oppression—from about 1965 to 1975—there were many cases of homosexuals being entrapped in places like universities, secondary schools, and military camps. Some of these incidents may have occurred because of the initiative of low-level police officers. Yet it is much more likely that the police were generally acting in response to policy directives from the top about how Article 359 (Public Scandal) should be enforced. In recent years, however, policies regarding "public" sex have seemingly reverted to the more permissive attitudes toward male sexuality characteristic of most of Latin America and of prerevolutionary Cuba. Police rarely patrol parks and public toilets with the specific intention of entrapping homosexuals. This is not to say that homosexuals are not occasionally caught having sex in "public." When this happens, police are likely to regard the incident as a misdemeanor that merits a fine rather than one that warrants a formal charge entailing possible imprisonment (Article 303).

Still, much remains to the discretion of individual police. Some have been known merely to lecture gays when they are "caught in the act," so to speak. At the other extreme, some have been known to assault gays brutally and others to have propositioned them in a way very similar to what frequently happens in Mexico. In some cases, probably rare given the low incidence of sexual assault in Cuba, attractive young gays have even been raped by the police. Such was the case of one young man whom I interviewed in 1994. He had been detained by two police officers late at night and taken handcuffed in a cruiser to the Parque Almendares. After being consecutively raped he was released, the officers knowing full well that his word would never count against theirs.

When gays are charged, their reaction and disposition to fight back in the police station or in court varies a great deal. Some, such as one friend of mine who was caught receiving a "blow job" in a dark alleyway late at night, become paralyzed with fear of the possible consequences if the incident becomes publicized—that is, of being ostracized by family and friends alike. Others, who react in much more assertive ways, may well have as much chance of being excused as they would in Canada. The outcome depends on the specific circumstances, including the person's social and political background and the attitudes of all involved, including that of the person charged.

Even in the late 1960s there was less preoccupation with same-sex sexual acts in marginal public places than with the overall character of institutions responsible for forging the next generation of "new men." The primary concern of the Cuban state was to control possible homosexual influence on the gender identity of the ultramasculine, macho men they were seeking to create in schools, universities, and military institutions. Repressing homosexual acts per se was a relatively minor concern. This contrast is even more evident today. In the absence of a specific policy directive to repress "public" sex, Cuban police action probably reflects the attitudes of the public as a whole. "Indecent" sexual acts are tolerated as often as not if they are discreet and do not directly challenge the macho identity of anyone who is involved or who witnesses them. Their treatment is also affected by the integrity of individual police, a factor that becomes increasingly important with the resurgence of corruption in the police force and in other Cuban public institutions.

Police harassment of gay males, however, is only the most direct and visible aspect of homosexual oppression in Cuba, as it also is in most other countries. Still, there is a crucial difference between the role of the repressive apparatus in a Communist state and in a liberal capitalist state. In the former, the ordinary citizen has little or no way to contest or expose arbitrary punitive acts by the state because the state controls all the means of communication and organization. Even in authoritarian regimes like that of Mexico there is some possibility of publicizing and resisting illegal police actions. There is even more possibility of doing so in a liberal democratic state such as Costa Rica.

A typical Cuban homosexual's life is far more likely to be constrained by the state's political-ideological structure than by the repressive apparatus itself. He will be seriously affected in two ways. First, he will normally be denied admission to the Communist Party, particularly if his masculinity deviates significantly from conventional machismo. There is no explicit prohibition to this effect, but as Fidel Castro admitted in 1965, Cuba's leaders could "never come to believe that a homosexual could embody the conditions and requirements of conduct that would enable us to consider him a true Revolutionary, a true Communist militant."[26]

It is clear that only closeted homosexuals, or those who are willing to be public apologists for the regime with regard to the regulation of homosexuality, could escape the net intended to sift out those who do not meet the required moral, social and political criteria for Party membership.[27] Although nonmembership in the Party does not necessarily block professional advancement, it nevertheless remains true that appointment and promotion above a certain level are usually affected by personal political history. Requirements for admission to the Young Communist League (UJC) are not as stringent, so that it is much more common for discreet homosexuals to be members. Secondly, until recently homosexuals were explicitly excluded from the military, an exclusion that constituted a blot on their political credentials and occupational prospects thereafter.

Those who are known as homosexuals could normally expect to play only a minimal role in mass organizations such as the Committees to Defend the Revolution (CDRs).[28] The same would apply to the Poder Popular (popular assemblies at the municipal, provincial, and national levels). Homosexuals could hypothetically raise issues relating to the human or civil rights of homosexuals in mass organizations or local government institutions, but at present it is inconceivable that they would risk doing so. Nor could they directly raise in the press any issue related to their interests or rights. (Nevertheless, for the first time newspapers have begun to report demands for greater acceptance of homosexuals who have established their revolutionary credentials in other respects.)[29] Cuban homosexuals are therefore second-class citizens in a country where almost all public life is politicized.

Discrimination and political marginalization start at an early age. Teenagers suspected of being homosexual may find it difficult to gain admission to many educational institutions, particularly those that train students for elite careers. Even if homosexual students are admitted to the schools or colleges of their choice,[30] they are then taught by instructors who until very recently went out of their way, because of ingrained *machismso* to devalue any personal traits or behavior that could be interpreted as effeminate and therefore homosexual.[31] This can only be detrimental to their self-esteem and future development as full citizens and workers. Although there are no doubt many closeted teachers in the school system, they have to be very discreet about anything relating to sexual education.

Furthermore, until the late 1980s the regime (and not a student's academic record) determined eligibility for university graduation. Diplomas were given only to students who could demonstrate that they met the criteria set for professionals in a socialist state. Students had to present a supportive statement from their work center in order to graduate. It is not surprising that even today homosexual students in law and medicine, more so than students in such fields as modern languages and fine arts, remain scared of being identified.

# FIVE

# Homosexuality and
# Sexual Education in the 1980s

*THE INSTITUTIONALIZED* homophobia of the 1960s and 1970—when the policies and actions of the Cuban government seemed designed to incite the prejudice against homosexuals already deeply rooted in Cuban culture—is much diminished today. Still, the Cuban regime's cultural and ideological preoccupations have come in waves, and there is no guarantee that increased official tolerance (*not support*) of homosexuals cannot be reversed. Certainly there is no institutional protection for homosexuality because of the real power structure in Cuba (that is, Fidel Castro and those in his trust), as opposed to the formal organization of People's Power (Poder Popular) and even of the Communist Party itself.

There is good reason to believe that the present leadership remains instinctively homophobic, though now it may be intellectually more open to the possibility that homosexuality is not "pathological" and that homosexuals are not by their very nature diseased child molesters. It would be jejune to believe otherwise because of the current leaders' ages—sixty or seventy-odd years of age—their cultural background, and their ideological conversion to Soviet-style communism.

Despite his assertions to the contrary, Fidel Castro's prejudices became evident in a much publicized (abroad, not in Cuba) interview by former Sandinista Minister of the Interior Tomás Borge. Noting that "the prevailing opinion . . . is that there is sex discrimination in Cuba," Borge asked Castro about his views on homosexuality and lesbianism. His reply is worth quoting at length.

> I told you that we have eradicated sexual discrimination. To be more precise I would say that we have done the maximum that a government, that a state could do, to eradicate sexual discrimination against women.
>
> More to the point we could refer to a long struggle, which has been successful, which has achieved great results, with respect to discrimination against women. But we cannot make absolute claims in that respect. There is still machismo in our people, I believe at a much lower level than in any other people in Latin America, but there is machismo. That has been part of the idiosyncrasy of our people for centuries, and it has multiple origins, from the Arab influence in Spain to other influences from the Spaniards themselves, because we absorbed machismo from the conquerors, just as we absorbed many other bad habits.
>
> That was a historical legacy, in some countries more than in others, but in none of them was there a greater struggle than in our own, and I believe that in none of them were more practical and tangible successes achieved than in our own. That is real, that we can see, you can still see it, and above all, you can see it in our youth. But we can't say that there has been a total eradication, an absolute eradication of sexual discrimination, nor can we let our guard down. We have to carry on struggling in that respect because it is an ancient, historical legacy; we have made progress and there have been achievements, but we have to keep on struggling.

I won't deny that, at a certain time, this *machista* thing also influenced the attitude toward homosexuality. I personally, you are asking me my personal opinion—I don't suffer from that type of phobia against homosexuals. Really, that has never formed part of my make-up, and I have never been in favor of, nor promoted, nor supported any policy against homosexuals. That corresponded, I would say, to a particular stage and is very much associated with that legacy, with machismo. I try to have a more humane explanation, a more scientific explanation of the problem. Very often it becomes converted into a tragedy, because you have to see how the parents think; they include some parents who have a homosexual son and it becomes a tragedy for them, and you can only feel sorry that such a situation should occur and that it should also become a tragedy for the individual.

I don't see homosexuality as a type of degeneracy, rather I see it in other ways. My view is of another type: a more rational approach, seeing it in terms of human tendencies and natural factors which simply have to be respected. That is the philosophy with which I see these problems. I believe that it would be better to have consideration for the family that suffers these situations. I wish that families themselves had another mentality, that they had another approach when something like that happens. And I am absolutely opposed to all forms of repression, of contempt, of scorn or discrimination with respect to homosexuals. That is what I think.

*Borge:* Can a homosexual become a member of the Communist Party?

I would say to you that there has been quite a lot of prejudice with respect to that, that is the truth, I will not deny it; but there were other types of prejudices against which we chose to focus our struggles.[1]

At first sight, the expressed sympathy for homosexuals appears to be an advance upon the blunt homophobia expressed in Castro's 1965 statement that homosexuals could never embody the qualities of a true revolutionary. However, his lack of interest in the issue and by extension his tacit acceptance of discrimination against homosexuals remain abundantly clear, particularly on the issue of homosexual membership in the Communist Party. His disinterest in the lot of Cuban homosexuals must be placed in the context of his repeated denials that gays are oppressed in Cuba. His machismo is evident in his disregard of the reference to lesbianism that is contained in Borge's question. This interview was a rare opportunity for Castro to make a supportive statement to a broad audience at home and abroad—very rare, because no Cuban journalist would dare to pose such a question let alone write a column that examined and challenged Cuba's treatment of homosexuals.[2] Still, Castro had nothing positive to say about homosexuals or about the need to combat the homophobia that impairs the quality of life of a sizeable minority of Cubans. Consequently, given his refusal to acknowledge the appalling treatment of homosexuals in the late 1960s and 1970s, and the Cuban government's continuing failure to rectify the institutionalized discrimination to which gays continue to be subject, few of them have been won over by this sudden expression of supposed sympathy for their situation.

Cuban leaders may have learned not to make explicitly homophobic statements in public, but every now and then their true feelings become crystal clear. To borrow a Latin American expression about inadvertently revealing your homosexuality, "se les ven las plumas" (their feathers are showing). In the case of Fidel Castro, his "feathers" showed when he went on television and denounced Ramses del Pino—the otherwise inconsequential son of General Rafael del Pino, who had fled with his father to Miami in 1987 in a stolen aircraft—for being a "queer" as well as a traitor.

It is quite understandable that many, perhaps most, Cuban gay males should harbor resentments against Fidel Castro and other leaders on account of their homophobia. In the long run, however, public policies coupled with social change, rather than the personal sentiments of the leaders, will determine the place of ho-

mosexuals in Cuban society. Though Fidel Castro is anything but
a liberal or social democrat, he is not immune to the influence of
cultural and demographic shifts within Cuba and to a lesser extent to political pressures from abroad. He would not have retained for so long the public support that he undoubtedly has had
if this were not the case.

To be sure, the organization and expression of public (as opposed to private) opinion is tightly controlled in Cuba. Furthermore, the absence of an effective gay and lesbian organization or
movement has undoubtedly enhanced the regime's ability to sup-
press public discourse about the situation of homosexuals in
Cuba. Nevertheless, there has been a shift in public perception of
homosexuals and an erosion in traditional machismo. Official attitudes to homosexuality may be beginning to change in Cuba,
just as they are in most other places, although more slowly than
in comparable countries—for example, former Communist allies
like East Germany, Poland, and Hungary, or underdeveloped
countries such as Mexico and Costa Rica.

Despite the resurgence of homophobic sentiments precipitated
by the AIDS epidemic, homosexuals have begun to enjoy
a degree of tolerance in many countries that was unimaginable at the start of the Cuban revolution. In 1959, the New
York Stonewall riots had not yet happened, for example; the
Wolfenden Report had not been released in Britain, homosexual
acts had not been partially decriminalized in Canada, and East
Germany had not yet legalized homosexuality. By the 1970s,
however, the gay liberation movement had become an important
social movement in North America and Western Europe. A
decade later the struggle for gay liberation was launched in Mexico, Costa Rica, and other parts of Latin America. Gays began to
come out in the streets, press, theater, and airwaves.

For the most part, the Latin American gay movements were
not able to replicate the North American advances in establishing
gay political organizations, social centers, and support services.

Gay couple living in the Bahía *beca* (student residence) of the University of Havana.

El Cayito, the gay strip of the Playas del Este outside Havana.

Entrance to gay disco at El Mejunje community center in Santa Clara.

El Mejunje. Who says Cuban gays don't have attitude?

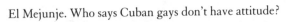

Late-night scene outside the Yara cinema, opposite the Coppelia ice cream parlor in Vedado.

Police checking identity cards, a common occurrence among those black and gay people who hang out on the street.

Sara, a popular *travesti*
performer and activist.

Celebrating the success of the Gunila *travesti* gala outside the Teatro
Rita Montaner (América) on February 28, 1995.

Queen of the ball at a Santa Clara *fiesta de cinco pesos*.

*Fiesta de diez pesos* in Havana.

Los Cocos AIDS sanatorium in Santiago de las Vegas outside Havana.

Inside a Los Cocos residence.

But in cultural matters there was more convergence of interests among gay and lesbian people throughout the hemisphere. Latin American intellectuals, artists, and middle-class youth became increasingly aware of the new visibility and status of gays and lesbians in North America. Cuba was no exception. Although state control of communication and all forms of organization prevented any duplication of these gay initiatives outside Cuba, there were nevertheless cultural repercussions. The Cuban public keeps well informed, one way or another, about cultural developments in North America, and it was exposed to these new sexual values. Cuban youth, both gay and heterosexual, began to exhibit the new attitudes to homosexuality. Artists and intellectuals who traveled abroad helped to circulate the new ideas informally. State officials became sensitive to the fact that the issue of homosexual oppression was now a part of the contemporary discourse about human rights and required some Cuban response. Cuba is still far from supporting lesbian and gay rights as many North American (and increasingly East European and Latin American) activists would understand them, but government policies indicate a much greater awareness than they formerly did of the political costs of oppressing homosexuals.

If the Cuban leadership was still bent on making homosexuals scapegoats for the economic and social problems that bedevil Cuba, as many Cuban exiles and foreign gay critics have implied, then surely there was no better opportunity to do so than during the current AIDS epidemic, which has coincided with a severe economic crisis in Cuba. It is possible to disagree with aspects of Cuba's AIDS-prevention program (as I certainly do with its policy of quarantining people with AIDS and those who have tested positive to HIV antibodies), but allegations that the handling of the AIDS issue has been designed to reinforce or incite prejudice against homosexuals are made without regard for the evidence.

Another indicator of the direction of change was the establishment in 1977 of the National Working Group on Sexual

Education (GNTES) (since renamed the National Center of Sexual Education, CNES). Objections can be raised to the heterosexist assumptions that underlie the sex-education program and the literature on sexuality published under its imprimatur, but it is simplistic to deny the organization's overall significance in beginning to undermine traditional prejudices and taboos about sexuality. The largely nonhomophobic handling of the AIDS issue in Cuba is partly attributable to the insistence of GNTES (CNES).[3]

Marvin Leiner notes in *Sexual Politics in Cuba* that "those who initiated sex education in Cuban society clearly saw it as a revolutionary project."[4] It was indeed revolutionary in the sense that sexual education had been nonexistent in Cuba before its initiation by GNTES. Cuba was not unique in this respect. Informed public discourse about sexuality has been entirely absent throughout most of Latin America. Sexuality has been a taboo subject in educational institutions as much as in society as a whole. The Catholic Church has ensured that sex education, other than in the most vacuous, formal, and moralistic terms, will not be accessible to young people. The extent of the Church's influence can be gauged by its success in blocking the incorporation of sex education into the curriculum of the Costa Rican school system, which in many respects is the most progressive in Latin America.[5] Although Catholic Church representatives participated in the commission that created a sex education manual for Costa Rica's secondary schools, conservatives within the hierarchy were still able repeatedly to block the manual's use. They did this in 1992 regardless of the fact that their move involved an enormous waste of public resources (the manual had already been printed and was ready for use in the schools). By then the Costa Rican government had become open to the adoption of much more enlightened policies on sexual education for gays and bisexuals because their marginalization is a major factor in Costa Rica with respect to the practice of unsafe sex. Still, there were no references to homosexuality in the aborted manual. Within this regional context of sex regulation the groundbreaking character of Cuban sexual education initiatives becomes clear. The GNTES directors' caution about the treatment of homosexuality in their sexual education program also becomes more comprehensible.

It was important that Cuba chose East Germany as a collaborator in its new sexual education program because East Germany had the most tolerant attitude toward homosexuality among all the Communist countries.[6] Indeed, one could go further and argue that some of the policies implemented there were as enlightened as any found elsewhere. For example, in 1989 East Germany equalized the age of consent—only fourteen years of age—for homosexual and heterosexual acts in its penal code.[7] It would have been preferable for Cuba to have undertaken its own research into the situation of Cuban homosexuals and the relation of homosexual oppression to the still largely unchallenged *machista* values prevalent in Cuban society. Yet it is also true that the initiation of policies that would begin to call into question Cuba's age-old homophobia, and implicitly the homophobic values of its leaders, could be made more acceptable by reference to the experience of a more developed Communist country.[8] Given this assumption, there could be no better choice than East Germany.

Taken as a whole, the translated versions of the East German books published in Cuba since 1979 make a strong argument against antihomosexual discrimination and in favor of toleration and the full integration of homosexuals into society, but these books are also unquestionably heterosexist in their assumptions. Since all these texts have been edited by the GNTES staff to reflect their interpretation of Cuban needs and conditions, GNTES must assume full responsibility for the editorial content. Celestino Alvarez Lajonchére, the foremost sexologist in Cuba and joint director of the center, has admitted that there was nothing to prevent Cubans from being "more liberal if necessary" in their adaptation of the original German texts.[9] It is also significant that the

Cuban media (to which the GNTES staff had access) disseminated a great deal of information about the culture of East European countries before the collapse of communism but not about the rights and lives of gays in those countries, particularly those of East Germany. Indeed, argument can be made that positive information was being deliberately censored.

*The Sexual Education of the Young Generation,* a manual written in 1985 for the Young Communist League, the UJC, with the collaboration of Lajonchére, offers a striking example of the heterosexism of Cuba's current sexual education policies.[10] So does a later publication, *Let Us Speak Frankly about Love,* which claims to reflect and respond to adolescent preoccupations about sex and relationships.[11] Both are completely oblivious to the needs and problems of Cuba's homosexual youth and also omit any information about the homosexual component of sexual desire and behavior of young males and females in general. This is a glaring omission since, as the Cuban translations of the East German texts themselves remark, up to 40 percent of young males have had homosexual impulses and experiences of varying intensity.[12]

This omission is critical given the fact that the only two references to homosexuality in the UJC manual are a mention of diseases sexually transmitted by "people with socially disturbed behavior, such as homosexuals" and a reference to Article 354 of the 1979 Penal Code, which criminalized "active pederasty" with a partner under sixteen years of age.[13] The mention of this law in the UJC manual, taken out of context, along with a footnote explaining that "pederasty" means homosexual acts between a man and a *child,*[14] could only reinforce homophobic stereotypes. It is disturbing that the manual was prepared to help the cadres of the UJC undertake sexual education among their members. Most of them were highly unlikely to have been exposed to the more positive views about homosexuality contained in internal position papers written by East Germans, such as Kurt Bach and

Siegfried Schnabl, that were used by the GNTES (CNES) staff in the formulation of their sex education programs.[15]

In the context of the historical oppression of homosexuals and absence of any informed public discourse on sexuality that included homosexuality, it was nevertheless significant, as Stephen Risch and Randolph Wills recognized in the *Gay Insurgent,* that at least one officially endorsed publication had "very clearly stated that homosexuals should have equal rights, respect and recognition, and that any kind of social discrimination is reprehensible."[16] Schnabl's book, *The Intimate Life of Males and Females,* to which Risch and Wills referred, has aroused most interest abroad with respect to Cuba's new sexual education policies. It may be the most influential theoretical publication since it is the basis of much of the educational work carried out by the GNTES staff in medical schools and pedagogical colleges.

On the other hand, the Cuban editions of other East German books, such as Heinrich Brückner's *Are You Beginning to Think about Love?* (published in 1981, two years after Schnabl's text), are much more ambivalent about homosexuality. The Cuban edition of Brückner's book was intended for a broad audience and therefore had a much larger printing than Schnabl's book. It reinforced myths about homosexual corruption of youth and concluded that although homosexuals were able to function in society as well as other people, "in reality they can't be as happy as married people."[17] Monika Krause, who was responsible for the GNTES sexual education program, has admitted that chapter 12 of the Cuban edition of Brückner's book, which deals with "sexual deviations," was edited (*and then some*) in response to criticism that Schnabl's book was too positive toward gays.

Chapter 12 of the Cuban edition—which was revised in accordance with suggestions made by GNTES, along with the Permanent Commission of the National Assembly of Poder Popular (People's Power) dealing with "the Care of Infants and Equal Rights for Women," and a commission from the Ministry of

Education—completely distorts Brückner's more sympathetic treatment of homosexuality. It is a travesty of the original text. Although these revisions are acknowledged in small print, there is no indication of the extent to which the substance of the original text has been altered in the Cuban edition. For example, the original German text states that a homosexual couple can be just as happy as a heterosexual one; the Cuban version denies this. The German text makes a passing reference to the possibility and criminality of a male adult seducing a minor; the Cuban text uses unnecessarily emotive language (e.g., references to abnormal and degrading practices, serious psychic traumas) in its lengthy discussion of cross-generational sex. The German text clearly states that society as a whole is responsible for neurotic behavior on the part of homosexuals and that they are capable of making social contributions equal to those of heterosexuals; the Cuban text implies that homosexuals invite rejection and discrimination by their "scandalous and anti-social behavior."[18] The alterations can only be described as homophobic since they imply that gay males are neurotically driven to commit antisocial acts and that they can never be fully happy.

The second edition of *Are You Beginning to Think about Love?* however, promises to be much more progressive in its treatment of homosexuality. Its publication, which was originally intended to have a mass printing of 250,000 copies, has been delayed for economic rather than ideological reasons. The editorial changes made by Monika Krause, which I have examined in the National Center for Sexual Education, now stress that sexual violation of minors has no causal relationship to sexual orientation; dismiss theories of seduction into homosexuality; and emphasize that since no one is responsible for their sexual orientation, homosexuals have as much right as anyone else to be respected and to enjoy their sexuality.

The chapter on homosexuality in the second edition of Schnabl's *The Intimate Life of Males and Females,* published in 1989, is also a vast improvement on the first edition, as was the publication of the Cuban edition of Masters and Johnson's *Human Sexuality*.[19] Schnabl says that he knows of no "cures" for homosexuality and that homosexuals are not even sick in any way; therefore they should not be criticized or pressured into changing their sexual orientation. On the contrary, they should get the support they need to have full and happy lives. This cannot happen unless homophobic values in society as a whole are transformed. He concludes that the repeal of penal sanctions against homosexuality is a formality without real consequences as long as homosexuals are still subject to social prejudice and institutionalized discrimination.[20]

Except for the release of publications such as the second edition of Schnabl's textbook and that of Masters and Johnson (for the most part restricted to use in institutions such as teachers' colleges and medical schools), little has been done to combat traditional prejudices about the nature of homosexuality either in the schools or among the wider public. Changes in state policy have been slow and grudging. The textbooks on sexual education that are actually used in schools still make no mention of homosexuality. I have yet to meet any Cuban youth who can recall being exposed to gay-positive information at school.

The Cuban rationale is that deep-rooted taboos and prejudices cannot be eliminated overnight. Since "neither parents, nor teachers, nor specialists in different branches of medicine, psychology and pedagogy were equipped" to undertake sexual education in the past, according to Monika Krause, "a careful and systematic" effort has been required to inform teachers first so that they in turn could prepare future generations.[21] She also asserted that if GNTES had attempted a direct confrontation with the issue of homophobia in schools and among the public, it would have lost all credibility.[22] This position meshed with that of the Cuban authorities, who are loath to draw attention to the specific needs of any minority given the regime's commitment to inclusive unity as one of the fundamental principles of the revolution. GNTES (CNES) staff contend that sex education cannot be divorced from the broader issue of preparing people for life in a socialist society with all the mutual social obligations that it entails. In an interview in 1989, Krause explained that what was required was:

> a deep, systematic and above all very careful program to achieve our objective, which is the assimilation of homosexuals in the whole population; not mere toleration, but assimilation of homosexuals as equals, as citizens with the same rights and duties as everyone else. That is to say, no one should be measured, be it a man or a woman, by their sexual orientation. What is important is their attitudes toward work and society and not their sexual preference.[23]

Although the approach Krause outlines contains much that sounds like a rationalization for inaction—at least in terms of responding with a sense of urgency to prejudice and discrimination—it is a legitimate strategy toward gay emancipation, despite its differences from the widely accepted approach in North America, where more emphasis has been placed on trying to secure formal recognition for the needs and rights of specific minorities. Certainly, Cuba's policy is a variant of the strategy pursued in the Netherlands, which has helped to create a society that many gay foreigners find enviable.[24] It also consistent with the organic, communal character of Cuban (and Latin American) political culture. A similar strategy pursued in East Germany helped to create a society that some Cuban gays found very attractive when visiting there on a work-study program. According to one of them, who eventually gained refugee status in Canada: "Being gay is not a problem in East Germany. Germans are much more civilized and tolerant than Cubans when it comes to homosexuality. Consequently, gays are much more integrated into society as a whole. I had lots of straight friends, and I was always accepted by the rest of the staff when I visited my lover at his work-center." Another Cuban gay now living in Toronto added: "It is much harder to tell who is straight and who is gay because [East] Germans are very relaxed and free in their behavior. When you went to a tavern people were very warm and physically spontaneous with you regardless of whether they were straight or gay. The same was true of the beaches, many of which are nudist." As applied to Cuba, however, an assimilationist strategy that disregards sexual orientation perpetuates a heterosexist bias. As Monika Krause herself repeatedly stated, "in our society we understand sexual education to mean preparing the younger generation for love, marriage and the family."[25]

Sporadic information about AIDS (which admittedly does not exploit homophobic prejudices) and an occasional article about gays abroad are the only bits of information about homosexuals offered by Cuba's sexual education program. There has not been a single informative reference to homosexuality as experienced in Cuba in the pages of Cuban newspapers or on Cuban television.[26] Most striking is the fact that although the sex education column in *Juventud Rebelde* (mainly intended for younger readers) has dealt with a wide range of issues ranging from premarital sex to venereal disease, it has not found space for a single feature dealing with homosexuality in general or with problems that are of specific interest to Cuban homosexuals. The same is true of *Somos Jóvenes* and *Muchachas,* monthly magazines for teenagers and other young people. Monika Krause's claim that GNTES could not "use the means of mass communication to demand rights for homosexuals because the population would reject it"[27] is hardly persuasive. How is it that the Cuban public is more prepared to deal with the erosion of age-old taboos regarding women's premarital virginity and not with the increasing visibility of gay males? Surely there can be only one explanation for this lacuna in awareness: the Communist Party leadership, which is responsible for the ideological content of all media, would prefer not to acknowledge or legitimize the presence of homosexuals in Cuba.

Moreover, because of the bureaucratic nature of the Cuban state, organizations such as the Federation of Cuban Women (FMC) and the National Center of Sexual Education (CNES), which could have done much to publicize the needs of lesbians and gays, are in the final analysis conservative bodies whose leaders are more adept at accommodating themselves to the system than in effectively representing the interests of homosexuals. They are not prepared to take any risks or make any intervention in public discourse that might be construed as controversial. It is not a question of homophobia or lack of good will toward gays on the part of the CNES staff members. They act the way they do because they are products of a state system within which the Party, with all its influence in the media, education, and culture, nevertheless "prefers the absence of any debate—even one that is under its own control."[28]

The intervention of Vilma Espín, head of the FMC for thirty-five years, correcting the homophobic remarks by a delegate to the 1992 UJC Congress, could conceivably be a "significant representation of the changing ideas of the Cuban leadership."[29] She emphasized, somewhat patronizingly, that since effeminacy had a congenital basis, homosexuals could not be changed. "If you try to force them to change you will be doing more damage. What you have to do is to accept them, and teach them how to live in this society, and educate people in this society to accept them as they are."[30] Unfortunately, the only sexologist that she cited to support her intervention was Gunter Dorner, an East German who gained notoriety in the 1970s on account of his studies of the "homosexual" behavior of rats and the conclusions he drew from them with respect to the biological origins of "diseased" and "unhappy" homosexual people. In any event, Vilma Espín's remarks are not to be confused with any desire to promote public debate about the extent and consequences of homophobia in Cuba. If

combating homophobia were a significant priority for her or the
FMC, she would presumably have seen to it that her intervention
was publicized in the Cuban press (which was not the case) or that
the issue was aired subsequently.

To be sure the FMC invited a delegation from Queers for Cuba,
based in San Francisco, to visit Cuba in July 1994. Since their visit
was not publicized within Cuba, it is reasonable to conclude that it
had more to do with trying to influence foreign rather than Cuban
opinion regarding homosexuality in Cuba. Even when she had an
opportunity to demonstrate leadership on the issue before a restricted audience in the November 1994 Latin American Congress
of Sexology and Sexual Education in Havana, Vilma Espín expressed only vacuous platitudes. When asked whether homosexuality—not homophobia—should be considered a social "problem,"
she replied:

> We must still continue struggling in our society to ensure that
> it should not be so, given that to discriminate against anyone
> with respect to race, color, ethnicity, religion, sex or sexual ori-
> entation, is profoundly unjust and is not acceptable in a society
> such as ours that has advanced applying genuinely humanistic
> principles.[31]

That was all she had to say about homosexual discrimination in
an interview designed to inform the foreign delegates about sexual issues and education in Cuba. Her remarks would scarcely deserve repeating but for the fact that nobody else, particularly gays
and lesbians, has had the opportunity to publicize an opinion on
the subject.

The same avoidance of publicly expressed concern for or interest in the situation of homosexuals is evident at the National
Center of Sexual Education. It has not reached out to homosexuals in any systematic way, either to solicit information about their
needs or to invite their cooperation in the preparation of position
papers dealing with contemporary sexuality in Cuba. To be sure,

one or two gay doctors may have been involved in the Center's work, but not necessarily to represent homosexuals as a whole. Moreover, they would be unlikely to retain such positions for long if they were to publicly challenge state and CNES policies regarding the gay content of sexual education. The only access that Cuban gays have to such organizations is informal—for example, by using the good offices of foreign gays visiting Cuba under the auspices of Queers for Cuba or the Center for Cuban Studies in New York, who act on their behalf. The FMC has made it clear that it will not recognize the formal existence of any gay Cuban organization.[32]

The 1994 Latin American Congress on Sexology, which incorporated the first Cuban Congress on Sexual Education, Orientation and Therapy, was organized by CNES. Despite the undoubted interest abroad in the situation of homosexuals in Cuba, particularly among those with a special interest in sexology and sexual education, the organizers did not see fit to include presentations by Cuban gays. The Congress included presentations related to homosexuality in Chile, Argentina, and Mexico, but Cuban gays who wanted to discuss homosexuality in Cuba were relegated to the margins of the Congress. They were only allowed to present wall posters outlining their research and conclusions. It was only after mounting criticism from the foreign participants in the conference, many of them undoubtedly feminists and gay males, that the organizers reluctantly made provision for a special forum to discuss the Cuban film *Fresa y chocolate,* which deals with homosexual oppression in Cuba.[33]

Evidently, the Cuban state, to which all public organizations are ideologically accountable, is not prepared to have the situation of homosexuals in Cuba discussed in any situation it does not completely control, such as in interviews with Fidel Castro typically conducted by deferential foreign visitors. Nor is the Party willing to consider the possibility that Cubans are personally hurt by the repression of homosexuality. Although Monika Krause herself freely acknowledged the fundamental role of sex as a source of creative pleasure, sex education in Cuba has little to say about the pleasurable aspects of sex per se. Such a statement might seem unnecessary, given Cuban young people's enthusiastic pursuit of sex. Yet if the Cuban government shared Monika Krause's belief that sex is a source of pleasure and energy, one to which people are entitled so long as their sexual activity does not harm nonparticipants, then it should have felt obliged to combat taboos against homosexuality actively since these prohibitions restrict individual self-fulfillment.

The censorship of any positive information about homosexuality has many repercussions. Young males who want to relate sexually to each other suffer needlessly—not only because they continue to be subject to social prejudice and discrimination but also because the state denies them any positive images and information that could improve their sense of themselves. (Needless to say, the possibility of homosexuals collectively developing and publishing such information themselves is out of the question, given the state's monopoly of all means of public communication.) This image making is vital because of the homophobic environment that surrounds Cuban gays. Consequently, young gays grow up ignorant of the fact that Cuba's greatest composer, novelist, playwright, and modern painter were all gay, not to mention the many outstanding artists and intellectuals who are still living.[34]

Having recognized the limitations of Cuba's sex education program with respect to improving the situation of gays, one should also admit that overt state repression has diminished. There is increasing tacit tolerance toward homosexuals. I deliberately apply the term "tolerance" to current Cuban state policies toward homosexuals. There is little evidence to suggest that the Cuban state is about to take any positive steps, at least in terms of explicit sexual education, to combat the homophobia that is shared by much of the population and that affects the day-to-day lives of homosexuals in countless ways.

Nevertheless, significant changes in the structure and nature of Cuban society are happening that herald an erosion of homosexual oppression. Traditional *machista* and homophobic beliefs are being undermined by the growing emancipation of women in the labor force and in their lessening marital dependence on men. Taboos and traditional stereotypes about gender are being questioned by youth in particular as a result of the educational and cultural opportunities that have been offered to them since 1959 and of their exposure to the more open values associated with the global youth culture.

# SIX

# The Erosion of
# Traditional Machismo

*THE OPPRESSION* of homosexuals in Cuba has its origins in
a patriarchal culture that celebrates conventional masculinity at
the expense of women and of men whose public behavior is perceived as unmasculine. "Effeminate" men who do not exhibit the
required traits of masculinity are labeled *maricones*. Homosexuals whose gender identity more closely resembles that associated
with heterosexual males suffer less discrimination, but in the final analysis they too are considered to be *maricones*. Effeminacy
will be projected onto them even if it is not apparent in their behavior. The hegemony of *machista* values—and by extension homophobia—is weakened to the extent that male privilege in social relations is challenged by women at work and in the home. It
is also undermined by cultural changes which question traditional stereotypes of masculinity and legitimate alternative forms
of sexual expression.

Despite a formal commitment to equality for women that
dates back to the earliest years of the revolution, and that was for-
malized in both the 1975 Family Code and the 1976 Constitution,

sexism remains a powerful ideological force in Cuba. Its effects on how men and women behave toward each other are most starkly revealed in the private sphere.

It is understandably difficult to transform domestic relations among older Cubans, whose family gender roles are as resistant to change as they would be in any other country, revolution or no revolution. Still, more rapid progress could surely have been made in the cultivation of different behavior among younger Cubans. Girls continue to be raised with the expectation that they will do the bulk of the housework, and boys have corresponding expectations about their right to more leisure time than women.[1] Young women seem inordinately preoccupied by and emotionally dependent on men. It is common to see men with other men enjoying plazas, beaches, sports, and cultural events, but most women are accompanied by men when they do so. Even more important is the fact that many traditional gender values have been implanted in young Cubans from the earliest age by parents and teachers. Until recently, girls and boys were treated differently in day care centers and by most parents at home with respect to toys, household tasks, and expectations about future sexual behavior.[2] However, conscious efforts are now being made to change age-old customs. For example, more fathers can be seen carrying babies in public, a sight that was very rare in the past.

It is not that Cuban leaders have been unconcerned about the emancipation of women. The speed of women's incorporation into professional education and into the labor force on an increasingly equal basis with men—equal pay for equal work is the norm—is both a cause and a result of their improved status in Cuban society. For years, too, there has been official concern about discrimination against women's participation in political life. Fidel Castro has repeatedly drawn attention to their underrepresentation in all political bodies ranging from the Communist Party to the various levels of Poder Popular (elected popular assemblies).[3] Despite this, only 3 women were elected to the

16-member Politburo and 37 to the 225-member Central Committee of the Communist Party during its Fourth Congress in October 1991.

At the local level, where the election of women to municipal assemblies might seem more likely, their percentages are even lower.[4] The contradiction between Cuba's official commitment to the empowerment of women and their continued de facto subordination shows how difficult it is to transform traditional sexism at the interpersonal level. Of course, Cuba is not unique in this respect, but the Cuban state's bureaucratic character does not make it any easier to change gender values. Instead it inhibits the autonomous, self-directed struggles that are needed to complement exhortations from the top. Gender relations cannot be transformed without such politics at the personal level. But this kind of politicization, whether it involves gender, race, or sexual orientation, is problematic for the regime since it may increase militancy at the grassroots level and threaten the state's ability to contain social struggles within a framework defined at the top. Women's striking underrepresentation in municipal assemblies reflects the continuing force of machismo in Cuba. Male demands that women give priority to housework and child care have proved major impediments to the latter's fuller involvement in political life. Worse still, Cuban males have insisted on applying different moral standards to male and female candidates for public office. In more extreme cases, their husbands simply did not permit their wives' political participation.[5]

Much of the regime's concern about the personal relationship of males to females has been articulated in terms best described as "heterosexist gallantry,"[6] a vocabulary more appropriate to the values of our grandparents than to contemporary discourse.[7] According to Fidel Castro, "if there is to be any privilege in human society, if there is to be any inequality in human society, there should be some little privileges and little inequalities in favor of women."[8]

Castro's paternalism, which is incarnated in his public persona, is even more apparent in a speech to the Fourth Congress of the Cuban Federation of Women.[9] After acknowledging the extent of sexism in Cuba, he actually went on to argue:

> We must go on educating, creating an awareness not just among men but also—and I would dare say above all—among women. I believe that men in our country have shown some progress in overcoming their prejudices, and in this connection, when it comes to prejudices against women, they may have progressed more than women.[10]

This is an incredible statement to make in a society where recent surveys indicate that women do almost all household chores and that 50 percent more women than men are dissatisfied with their marriages.[11] In fact, apart from complaining about the latter's failure to share housework, Cuban women fault men for drinking too much, for wasting money, and for not spending enough time with them. According to Sara and Cristina Robaina of the Centro de Estudios sobre la Juventud (Center for the Study of Youth) in Havana, the males' response remains as *machista* as ever. They accuse their partners of being disorganized around the house, of not wanting to prepare meals, and of spending too much time out in the street.[12] The fact that half of all marriages end in divorce must have some relationship to women's perceptions of their relationships with men. The statement that women's consciousness of their own rights has developed less rapidly than men's sense of women's rights is implausible, especially because of women's accelerated rate of participation in advanced education and their employment in scientific and technical fields. If there is no collective feminist consciousness, this lack may be a product of the tight controls that Cuba's authoritarian and bureaucratic state keeps on the articulation of feminist viewpoints. Until the mid-1990s there were no means for women to organize or communicate independently of the state, any more than there were for anybody else.

Consequently, Cuba is one of the few modern societies in which there has been no public discourse about the extent of sexual assault and harassment of females, in part because the regime, specifically the FMC, has perceived it as being a divisive issue.[13]

While the Cuban leadership is formally committed to equalizing material relations between males and females, it is much more wary about erasing gender differentiation. Although some concern may be expressed about the "machismo" of young boys, for example, parents are nevertheless reminded of the necessity to nurture "the customs, inclinations and forms of behavior appropriate to females and males ... [since] both are different from the biological point of view as well as in many other respects."[14] Fidel Castro himself has emphasized that women should be protected because they are physically weaker than men and "have to be mothers [who are] the natural workshop where life is forged."[15]

There is scant evidence that the Cuban leaders have given much thought to the feminist critique of contemporary gender values, particularly those of males, except for their negative judgments about capitalism's exploitative values. Cuban society still seemingly condones an introduction to a 1986 text on the *Formation of the New Man in Cuba,* which blithely declares that "the principal characteristic of the new man is his great optimism and confidence in his creative possibilities, without fear of what is entailed. As Fidel Castro once said: a *man's man*" (emphasis added).[16] This glorification of conventionally masculine values suggests that Cuba's leadership has remained impervious to the way in which machismo has been challenged by the women's movement in modern countries since Che Guevara first popularized the notion of the "new man" in the mid-1960s.

This ideological reproduction of *machista* values that Cubans have inherited from the past—and its counterpart, the celebration of traditional female *hembrista* traits—remains the main problem. In the economy, however, there has been a remarkable transformation in the situation of women. During the 1970s the proportion of married women who entered the labor force rose from 16.3 percent to 36.7 percent and to 45 percent in Havana.[17] By 1984 women composed 38.9 percent of the total labor force.[18] Significantly, women's participation is rising most rapidly in non-traditional professional and technical occupations, which is consistent with the fact that a majority of university students are women, including those in fields such as geology, mining, and metallurgy. According to Isabel Larguía and John Dumoulin, who have carried out some of the most interesting research on women in Cuba, it is now not at all unusual to see women supervising men in construction crews, shipyards, and machine shops. These new roles are forcing men to confront their prejudices and acknowledge their dependence upon the professional and technical competence of women. Accordingly, age-old notions about the intellectual inferiority of women and of their inability to do work that is not directly related to domestic activities "have been profoundly undermined in recent years."[19]

Though Cuban women may still be regarded as "natural workshops where life is formed," in practice they have been progressively freed from biological destiny. Thanks to improved access to contraceptives, abortions, sexual knowledge, and medical care, birth rates as well as infant mortality have fallen to levels that match (and in some cases fall below) those of developed industrialized countries. Furthermore, Cuba has an extensive system of day-care centers—although far from sufficient—and boarding schools that have increasingly freed mothers from their homes. Divorce, too, has become much more accessible to Cuban women than to those elsewhere in Latin America. (The Cuban rate of divorce is approximately three times that of Costa Rica and twelve times that of Mexico.)[20] The ratio of divorces to new marriages fell from 1 to 19.1 in 1953 to 1 to 2.3 in 1988.[21] The trend is as discernible in rural provinces such as Sancti Spíritus as it is in Havana, where the ratio of divorces to new marriages has almost reached 1 to 2. Men's economic domination of women and women's forced confinement to maternal and domestic roles are rapidly coming to an end.

On the other hand, although divorce on terms of formal equality for women has been facilitated by changes to Cuba's civil laws, the government is constitutionally obligated to "protect the family, motherhood, and marriage." Families are expected to play a fundamental role "in everything related to the up-bringing of the new generation."[22] In return, children are formally locked into dependent traditional relationships with their parents and other adults. The Youth Code stipulates that in addition to maintaining "correct social behavior," they have a "fundamental obligation . . . to love their parents, and respect their teachers, professors and all adults in general."[23]

The revolutionary government might have been more radical and innovative in its approach to transforming the role of the family, particularly with respect to the reproduction of time-honored gender values. Many Cubans have been raised by single mothers, stepparents, and extended families. Today fewer than three out of five couples are formally married. "Unformalized marriages have become more flexible; multiple forms of relations between couples have been brought about" as a result of the broader social changes since 1959.[24] Such trends have not, however, been accompanied by an ideological questioning of the conventional nuclear family model. As with much else that relates to sexuality and gender, the Cuban state discourages or prevents the public exploration of alternative relational models.

Nevertheless, the improvement of education, together with its augmentation by an enriched formal culture and its extension to more and more Cubans, have broadened their horizons and stimulated their curiosity and creativity, be it with respect to music, dance, art, design, or fashion. Cubans, especially youth, are being increasingly exposed to cultural values that indirectly affirm the importance of self-expression and diversity of personal life. This tendency has been reinforced by Cuba's growing exposure to global youth culture, particularly pop music and fashion. Much as the leaders might have liked to retain a cordon sanitaire around the country, there has been little that they could do to prevent these trends from influencing young Cubans. The 1971 Congress on Education and Culture was adamant in its opposition to the penetration of mass culture emanating from the developed capitalist countries. According to those who were to implement its edicts, Cuba had "traditionally frowned upon the tendency for some to dress outlandishly, in poor taste . . . ultra tight pants and so forth."[25] This position sprang from *machista* beliefs about appropriate male behavior—Cuban women, excepting those from the upper classes, have always been expected to dress flamboyantly by Cuban men—as much as from an anticolonial or anticapitalist stance. Yet two decades later Cuba's leaders have seemingly accepted that they can neither control nor impose cultural tastes on Cuba's youth. Rock groups with appropriately bizarre names such as Naranja Mecánica (Mechanical Orange), Alta Tensión (High Tension), and Agonizer are increasingly popular. To curb such trends would risk completely alienating youth from the revolution. One young UJC leader put it very succinctly when he was questioned about his own fashionable clothes. Should the day come when UJC leaders turned their backs on fashion, while the majority of the young tried to keep abreast of it, the UJC would really be in trouble, he said. In fact, Roberto Robaina, the former UJC head who catapulted into the Party Politburo in the early 1990s, became one of the country's most popular and influential leaders largely by insisting that the contemporary values of Cuba's youth had to be respected in the formulation of public policies.

The tastes and preoccupations of most of Cuba's youth are diametrically opposed to the more conservative values of the generation that initially made the revolution. Willy-nilly, young Cubans respond not to exhortations to emulate Che Guevara but to the powerful mass global culture that has molded their personal tastes. Few may own a Walkman, ghetto blaster, or VCR, but nearly everybody knows what they do—offer escape to another world, just as they do everywhere. Not everyone, to say the least, can wear "designer" clothes, but an impressive number of young Cubans will do anything to wear brand-name foreign clothes. They are at least as sensitive about their public images as young people in any other Western country. This extends to gender identity.

In Cuba today there is less certainty and compulsion about how males are expected to behave, less need to interpret ambiguity of gender in a homophobic manner. Trendy young males *(pepillos)* are becoming less preoccupied with defensive *machista* postures, and there are more *civilizados* (gay-positive people). The new cultural climate creates more space for gay males, both more space to blend in and more space to create separate turfs. It is hard to tell who is gay and who is not on the beaches of the Playas del Este outside Havana. On the beach's half-mile Cayito section, however, one can assume that the majority are gay or lesbian.

A perusal of Cuba's youth magazines, *Somos Jóvenes* and *Muchachas,* reveals the extent to which the regime has had to come to terms with this fact. These periodicals obviously lack slick consumerist packaging, but the style of their sexually androgynous models and the subjects of their features would be familiar to North American readers.[26] From the perspective of traditional Cuban machismo, nothing could be more extravagant and decadent than Michael Jackson and Prince. Yet uncritical features on both these pop idols have appeared in *Somos Jóvenes.* So have articles on Juan Gabriel, Mexico's flamboyant balladeer, who could hardly be said to epitomize *machista* values. Michael Jackson was the subject of a one-hour TV special in January 1992. But for his persona, there is nothing remarkable about this fact, given that international rock stars are regularly featured on Cuba television.

The arts are also becoming much more open minded about sexual matters. Nude love scenes once considered too controversial to show on television now scarcely raise an eyebrow. Accordingly, few Havana residents are offended anymore by the sight of nude bodies when one of the city's excellent modern dance groups, such as Danza Contemporánea de Cuba or Danza Abierta, appears on stage or television. Defending, indeed asserting the obligation to present such scenes on television, TV director Ómar González Jiménez declared: "Art—and we are not only referring to film or television—must be ever more authentic. . . . Why then cover up nakedness with a veil of prejudice? If the act of love is a daily occurrence and our art is full of everyday scenes, why prevent us from showing that part of life?"[27] Who would have imagined, even a decade ago, that by the mid-1990s masturbation would have been openly discussed on Cuban television (El Doctor Responde)?

Lesbianism and male homosexuality are also beginning to creep into the arts, after long having been invisible.[28] A more liberal approach to the production and distribution of films and video is clearly discernible. In 1983 there was controversy over showing *Word Is Out* (an American documentary about the lives of older gays and lesbians) at the annual film festival in Havana, but by 1987 several films shown at the festival included lesbian or gay themes. Cubans have also begun to include homosexual characters in their own films. In most cases, such as in *La bella de Alhambra,* a film directed by Enrique Pineda Barnet, homosexuality is still presented as a problem, the stereotypical treatment it also usually received in Hollywood films until the 1970s. However, recently Francisco Gattorno, who played the role of the hot scuba instructor in *The Summer of Mrs. Forbes,* directed by the gay Mexican film director Humberto Hermosillo, became the first Cuban actor to portray a sympathetic homosexual personality in a contemporary film. To be sure, the Spanish production, which was shown in the Havana Film Festival, was not widely distrib-

uted in the rest of the country. Nevertheless, the fact that the
script was written by Gabriel García Márquez, a close friend of
Fidel Castro who is as widely admired within Cuba as he is in
the rest of Latin America, ensured that the film would attract
interest. It was followed by *Adorables mentiras* (Adorable lies),
which satirized homophobia among other aspects of contemporary Cuban society. These films paved the way for Tomás Gutiérrez Alea and Juan Carlos Tabío to make a film adaptation of the
prize-winning short story written by Senel Paz, "El lobo, el
bosque y el hombre nuevo" (The wolf, the woods, and the new
man). *Fresa y chocolate* (Strawberry and chocolate) based upon the
story was presented at the 1993 Havana Film Festival to wide critical and public acclaim. It subsequently played to packed houses
from noon to midnight in Havana's major cinema, the Yara, for
over three months. Although the film could be criticized for its
restricted portrayal of contemporary homosexuals, it undeniably
constitutes an enormous advance in terms of its treatment of gay
oppression.

The establishment of the International Film and Video School
outside Havana, with the active participation of Gabriel García
Márquez and other Latin American intellectuals and film personalities, has also contributed to the emergence of a cultural climate more favorable to the defiance of ideological censorship of
homosexual issues. Equally significant is the emergence of groups
like the Hermanos Saíz organization, an independent collective
of young "mediamakers" with an appropriately ambiguous relationship to established institutions such as ICAIC, the Cuban
Film Institute. Its members' work is both experimental and politically provocative in their determination to break fresh ground.
One example is the group's attempt to organize the first exhibi-
tion of gay film and video in Cuba.[29]

Similar changes are evident in the literary world. A decade ago
many gay writers, some such as Reinaldo Arenas with international reputations, were blacklisted and expressly prohibited

from representing Cuba abroad. Today, authors who are known to be gay occupy prominent cultural positions and are free to come and go as they will. *Paradiso,* the only novel with homosexual content published in Cuba since 1959, remained out of print for twenty-five years despite its universal acclaim as a literary masterpiece, but its author, José Lezama Lima, and playwright Virgilio Piñera, also blacklisted in the past, have been restored to their rightful place in Cuban literature and publicly honored. The homosexual identity of these writers has been rediscovered and acknowledged, at least in cultural circles.[30] If at one time homosexual professors were being purged from the universities, today they are beginning to supervise theses on homosexuality, for example, in the work of exiled Cuban novelist Severo Sarduy.

In time the publication of Senel Paz's short story "El lobo, el bosque y el hombre nuevo,"[31] which won France's prestigious Juan Rulfo prize in 1990, may come to be seen as a watershed in the regime's treatment of works with homosexual themes. The tale treated gays as participants in revolutionary Cuba, a reality that one of the story's protagonists, a straight UJC militant, was forced to acknowledge and indeed value. It also portrayed gays' alienation from a revolution within which they had suffered persecution in the past.

Onstage works with gay themes or subtexts are also becoming more common. There have been at least three different theatrical productions of Paz's story since its publication. Carlos Díaz's productions of works by Tennessee Williams and Federico García Lorca have been enthusiastically received by critics and audiences alike. His production of García Lorca's *El público* could hardly be outdone in terms of its radical sophistication and homoerotic panache. Artistic challenges to traditional norms have also increasingly occurred within such disparate places as the Yara cultural center on La Rampa in the heart of Vedado and the National Theater facing the hallowed monument to José Martí in the Plaza de la Revolución. Their creative administrators—including Fidel Pérez, who presented the first show of homoerotic art in Cuba in the Yara, and Nisia Agüero, who facilitated the production of an audacious musical (*Ocania: Pasión infinita*, replete with transvestites and effigies of erotic angels) in the Teatro Nacional—are at the forefront of the push for more artistic license. More marginal cultural spaces, such as the Sótano Theater, have presented plays (not necessarily good productions) containing homosexual content ranging from cruising to sex and frontal nudity (for example, *Encuentros nocturnos peligrosos*).

On television, too, homosexuality is becoming an ever more common focus of programs as the medium opens itself to a more frank and honest treatment of sexuality in general. Although the personal needs of Cuban homosexuals are still not addressed, homosexuality is present in lectures, documentaries, and films. In a period of two weeks at the end of November 1994, for example, Cuban viewers were able to hear Manuel Calviño, a psychologist at the University of Havana, offer a gay-positive presentation of homosexuality in his weekly program, "Vale la Pena"; they were able to see Randy Schilts's *And the Band Played On,* and Jonathan Demme's *Philadelphia.*

Musical artists, too, seem to have greater security than they once had to incorporate ambiguity about sexuality into their work. There is an increasing visibility of artists who have large gay followings and are regarded as gay-positive or even lesbian or gay, regardless of their formal marital status. Concerts by artists such as Annia Linares and Mirta Medina (now in exile) were notorious for the behavior of their gay and lesbian fans, who outdid themselves in the struggle to assert the preeminence of their favorite diva. Some other artists, such as Amaury Pérez and Xiomara Laugart, express gay and lesbian sensibility even more explicitly. Other popular musicians such as Pedro Luis Ferrer have been so outspoken about conditions in Cuba and the aspirations of its youth that they have on occasion been prohibited from making public appearances. Ferrer, who has been allowed to perform in public again, is known for the homemade cassette recordings of his performances in private fiestas, which include supportive songs about gays and jineteras. ( *Jineteras* are women who solicit male tourists, sometimes merely implicitly, in hope of gaining access to material and social opportunities that would otherwise not be available to most Cubans.) And Pablo Milanés, perhaps Cuba's most beloved musician, has done much to validate the rights of men who love other men.

Milanés, thrice happily married—his first wife has been immortalized in his most famous song, "Yolanda"—but who has never hidden his relations with other men, was himself a victim of state repression at the time of the UMAP. He has gone on to play an exemplary role in the development of Cuban culture. His foundation (now defunct) supported the work of innumerable playwrights, painters, and musicians. In May 1994, he became the first Cuban artist, and one of the first of such stature in the whole Western Hemisphere, to dedicate a song to the liberation of homosexuals—"El pecado original" ("The original sin"), on his 1994 album, *Orígenes*.[32]

The strength of these new artistic currents must not be exaggerated. As in other countries, Cuba's radical intellectuals find plenty of obstacles in their paths. They need all their wits to survive the opposition of bureaucrats, censors, funding agencies, and the like.[33] The usual material and political constraints are currently aggravated by the fact that the revolution is battling just to survive. Some obstacles may be greater in Cuba, but some may actually be less formidable than the deterrents to originality elsewhere. Cuban intellectuals and artists have to face the bureaucratic mentality fostered by an authoritarian state and party apparatus, but they also have the opportunity to satisfy the hunger for fresh ideas and experiences of the new postrevolutionary generation, whose burgeoning culture is unlike anything previously seen in Cuba. Such cultural developments are insufficient to eradicate homophobia, but they contribute to the erosion of *machista* beliefs about what constitutes appropriate masculinity. The Cuban state tolerates and in some cases supports such initiatives. It could not be interpreted otherwise given the insistence of the Communist Party that it alone has the right to establish the ideological parameters of culture and the mass media. But clearly the state will not go further than tolerance in most cases. It will not support any direct confrontation with machismo (let alone homophobia) on the grounds that such a position would be divisive. An additional unstated reason is that in the process the leadership's own machismo might eventually be questioned. This would particularly apply to Fidel Castro, who—whatever his affirmations to the contrary—exalts in his unquestioned role as the *caudillo,* the Comandante en Jefe, in short the epitome of machismo.

# SEVEN

## Gay Life in
## Havana Today

*IT WAS EVIDENT* by the mid-1980s that Cuban gays had begun to feel much less intimidated by the state in relation to the way they publicly expressed the sexual dimension of their lives. They have become once again a visible part of street life in downtown Havana and to a lesser extent in some of the larger provincial cities. They are for the most part discreet in their public behavior, but no more so than homosexuals in most Latin American cities. Gays cruising on their own, as well as couples and larger groups socializing together, have become part of the street scene in Old Havana and Vedado. If their dress and behavior are largely indistinguishable from that of straight males, how do they recognize each other? "By the way they walk, by the way they look at you. When they gaze at you, they undress you," explained an old hand.

More and more, young gays are developing a sense of gay identity and consciousness. They are beginning to break out of their individual as well as national isolation. They are becoming aware of the growing rights of gay males in other countries and of their own role in what has become an international social movement.[1] Although *entendido* may still be the most common self-description, *gay* is increasingly used by younger homosexuals. Nevertheless, very few homosexuals are "out of the closet" (as the term is understood in North America), even within their family circles.[2] And almost nobody has "come out" in public, just as in most other parts of Latin America.

Furthermore, even though some gays in Cuba have adopted terms such as "coming out of the closet," it is not clear that these terms have the same meaning and political significance they do in North America. "Coming out" in North America designates a process of assertive self-identification as a gay person that is undertaken in the context of a homophobic, individualistic, and fragmented capitalist society. To be sure, for many of us it is a moving and memorable part of our personal development as gay people. However, many gay activists go beyond this in asserting that it should be the central plank in the struggle for gay liberation. This is more open to debate, since the latter can only be secured by means of a broader struggle to transform a society and state that are oppressive overall. In Cuba (as is true of much of the rest of Latin America), many gays would see coming out as an unnecessary and divisive action threatening an individual's multifarious ties to his family and community as a whole. Other issues related to everyday life press down on most of them and their families—finding work and scrounging around for the money (increasingly dollars) that will permit them and their families to resolve food shortages, deal with house maintenance, and provide for transportation, clothes, entertainment, and everything else that is in short supply. A minority of homosexuals might go further and view coming out as a self-preoccupied distraction from the fundamental struggles to secure national sovereignty and overcome underdevelopment.

Americanized as Cuban mass culture may be, Cubans remain

Latin American in their attachment to familial and communal relations. The identity of most homosexual males is linked integrally to that of their family and barrio. They are used to sharing their resources. Most of them genuinely seem to need and enjoy the company of their families and neighborhood friends. Accordingly, in comparison to North American gay males, much less of their identity is derived from their sexual orientation. Provoking a possible rupture with their immediate and extended family by coming out is therefore not a step that most Cuban homosexuals are ready to contemplate unless their lives have been made intolerable, which is rarely the case.

Males, particularly young males, have considerable license to pursue sex as they see fit, particularly if it is not publicized. Families respect the privacy of their personal life outside the home, just as they in turn respect the primacy of their family ties within the home environment. Familial solidarity rather than individualistic one-to-one intimacy tends to characterize relations within the home. Men are not expected to reveal details of their personal lives or the feelings associated with them. A young gay journalist explained: "In Cuba, you should never tell it as it is. Everything is understood. That comes from the Spanish influence. Everything is inferred. Everything is known. But nobody says it." He added that even though he himself had never tried to hide his homosexuality, he could not see any point in coming out, as such. "The moment you put it in words, you are in a sense admitting guilt, as if you were repenting."

Coming out in North America is primarily concerned with the affirmation of a "deviant" sexual orientation in a homophobic puritan culture within which sexual practice is central to the definition of gender. This is not the case in Cuba and in most of Latin America. In Cuba, sexual orientation is inferred from gender identity rather than vice versa, as tends to be the case in North America. If you behave "normally," other Cubans will assume that you are basically heterosexual even if you have been known to have had sex with another man. In North America those who are perceived as failing to live up to expectations about what constitutes appropriate masculinity, particularly teenagers, are also frequently the target of ridicule that is implicitly or overtly homophobic. But the real litmus test that establishes your sexual identity is based on sex. You will be homophobically labeled gay or queer if you have been known to deviate to the slightest degree from the narrow path of conventional heterosexuality. The Cuban equivalent to coming out as a gay person in North America is to refuse to conform to traditional male mannerisms in public, knowing that such behavior will be perceived as "effeminate," as unbecoming to a "real man." This could apply, for example, to crossing a leg over one's knee, effusive hand gestures, or in the past to wearing sandals.

The relationship between Giovanni, a European who spent a couple of months teaching in the University of Havana, and Juan, his young Cuban boyfriend, throws some light on the way Cubans interpret and respond to same-sex interactions. Giovanni was older and conventionally masculine in his public behavior. He was relative open about his gay identity but only made a point of revealing it in relevant circumstances. Juan acted very macho in public and also sporadically dated women, even though he associated with the gay crowd in Havana. He frequently stayed overnight with Giovanni, who rented a room from a Cuban couple. Macho though he liked to consider himself, Juan never hid his sexual relationship from either his mother or from the woman in the house where Giovanni was living. In fact, Juan seemed to go out of his way to confirm the fact that he had slept overnight, secure in the knowledge that his machismo was not in question. His public *machista* persona did not prevent him from being quite tender in private. Although he normally played the *activo* role, he also eventually wanted to be fucked.

He introduced Giovanni to his brothers and to his best friend and was demonstratively affectionate with him in front of them.

It was not clear whether his goal was to show off his friendship with a foreigner, to manipulate Giovanni into buying rum for all of them to have a party together, or just to express his feelings. He introduced his girlfriends to Giovanni but also made it clear that his relationship to Giovanni was a priority for him. He was unusual because he had a very close relationship to his mother, who was younger than Giovanni, and had told her all about his relationship. She insisted on meeting Giovanni, who eventually visited her modest home in one of the poorer districts of Havana. To his astonishment he was presented to every member of the extended family, all the while wondering whether they, like Juan's mother and possibly his brothers, also knew the nature of his relationship to Juan. There was no way of knowing for he was greeted with extraordinary warmth as befitted a friend of Juan. In this interaction, the sexual aspects of their relationship were completely incidental. To cap it all, on his return to Italy Giovanni was surprised to receive a letter from Juan's mother thanking him for the influence he had had on her son!

Although young Cuban males who have sexual relations with other men may not "come out" as the term is understood in North America, they do not necessarily hide the fact either, as was the case with Juan. In addition, more and more of them are organizing their leisure time in a way that affirms the primacy of their relations in their social life with gay men—for example, by frequenting semipublic gay fiestas. There is also an increasing popular awareness and acceptance among society as a whole of the fact that gays are an inevitable fact of modern life. Although the majority of Cubans may not approve of gays, they are slowly beginning to regard them as just another manifestation of the radical transformation of young people's sexuality in general. As one young gay exile noted after returning from a visit to Cuba in the late 1980s, "People are more relaxed with each other. Young guys are less macho and more *civilizado* than they were when I left Cuba." A black member of Cuba's junior boxing team agreed that there had been a big change. "In the past, I got angry when a *maricón* came on to me. Now it is different. Wherever you go you see *pájaros*. People talk and hang out with them. It's no big deal." In some departments of the University of Havana, such as modern languages and fine arts, gays have become a visible and accepted component of student life. Gay students in some *becas* (residences), such as those in Bahía on the outskirts of Havana, are accepted by others in a way that is hard to imagine in most public universities in North America.

Many homosexuals frequent public places that have acquired somewhat of a gay reputation, suggesting that they must feel more secure about their rights than they presumably once did. They must also be more willing to accept the risk of being individually identified as gay by being there. There seems to be a growing recognition that the police who patrol the streets and squares of downtown Havana have more pressing priorities than to single out gay males for harassment. Certainly, the police are a much less intimidating presence than they once were in places like the Coppelia and the Parque de la Fraternidad. Identity checks remain common occurrences and even the occasional *redada* persists (just as they do in Mexico and Costa Rica), but the police are clearly more concerned with upholding public order in general than with persecuting gays in particular, as they did in the 1960s and 1970s. To be sure, the police also patrol beaches, but as individuals they are no more aggressively homophobic than the police are in most Latin American countries or Canada for that matter.[3]

In fact, the homophobic character of Cuban society has been exaggerated by Cuban officials ranging from Fidel Castro to Monika Krause, as a plausible explanation for why the government has done so little to combat the discriminatory treatment of gays and lesbians. Krause repeatedly emphasized in interviews that the attitude of Cuban parents to the possibility that their sons might be gay was "better dead than that." Though variants of the refrain "prefiero mi hijo muerto que maricón o ladrón" (better my son dead than queer or a thief) are not uncommon, they do not necessarily indicate how gay sons are treated by their Cuban parents. Some parents do react very negatively, just as in the past some families encouraged sons to emigrate to the United States after their homosexuality was discovered. Still, as a rule, relatives and particularly mothers will not reject any member of the family: "Pase lo que pase es la familia" (Regardless of what happens we are family). But they do not want to have to deal with the issue face to face as is true of many other personal issues that are never directly aired within the family. One young gay, who rued the day that he had come out to his family, explained, "They already knew but would have preferred me not to have told them. It is one thing to know and another thing to be told."

The same applies to the barrio, for in a sense the barrio is an extension of the family. "In Cuba, everyone knows all about their next-door neighbors, and their ups and downs—and even about those who live three or four houses away. When you have lived there for a year or more, they are almost like your family," explained a young Cuban writer. "They may be shocked when they first realize that you are homosexual, but they soon get over it, and it just becomes one of those things." Although there is less acceptance away from the barrio, rejection of homosexuals is expressed in a less violent way than it often is in North America.

"Queer baiting," which severely constrains the public behavior of many North American gays, is virtually absent in Cuba. A mass of bored gay males and their *civilizado* friends often congregate in places like the front of the Yara Cinema, at one of the most prominent intersections in Havana, typically without harassment of any kind. I have never seen or heard of antigay incidents happening there although its gay *ambiente* is becoming increasingly obvious. Passers-by may yell out *locas* or *pájaros,* but these are typically more like labels that stereotype rather than expressions of overt hostility. Occasionally, a group of marginalized black youths, for example, may make more antagonistic remarks, but their antagonism may be a product of the significance historically attached to homosexuality within a culturally and racially oppressed group (as opposed to being a reflection of a generalized license to taunt gays, as is so often the case in North America). From their perspective, the only thing worse than being poor, uneducated, and black would be to be perceived as homosexual—effeminate—as well. The *machista* assertion of their privileged "normal" status is also usually fleeting compared to the queer-baiting practice of marginalized working-class youths in North America. In short, the social phenomenon of queer baiting (let alone queer bashing) essentially does not exist in Cuba; nor do the homophobic graffiti that abound on the walls of toilets, schoolyards, and other public places in North America. Cuban gays find it hard to believe the extent of homophobic rage and violence that exists in most large U.S. cities. No doubt, some of their immunity to violent hostility is due to self-censorship and political invisibility. The situation may change if and when gays become more assertive, but for the moment at least they do not have to be constantly on guard against being assaulted in public.

Which are some of the places that have been frequented at one time or another by homosexuals? There are popular streets like La Rampa and Avenida 23 in Vedado, which are not only frequented by gays and *pepillos* but also by money changers, hustlers, and pimps offering a variety of goods and services ranging from sex to cut-rate rum, Havana cigars, and even medicines such as PPG (a new Cuban drug that aids blood circulation). There are specific spots on the Malecón, the seafront boulevard, as well as the Parque Maceo, the Prado, and the pedestrian Bulevar in Old Havana. Hundreds of gays have been known to congregate on the Malecón, near the foot of La Rampa, on many a weekend summer night. For a while in the early 1990s, they also became a distinct section at the informal public dances that were sponsored by the UJC in the Parque Maceo. There are plazas like the Parque Central and Parque de la Fraternidad where homosexuals cruise into the early hours of the morning, as well as in the general vicinity of the Coppelia, the famous ice-cream parlor opposite the Habana Libre Hotel and the Yara Cinema. *Pájaras locas* (outrageous queens) are notorious for frequenting places like the park in front of the central train station, the arcade in front of La Sortija store in Old Havana, and the Prado—so much so that many "decent" gays concerned about their public image will not go near such places for fear of being associated with them.

Gays also gather at events such as the Christmas Eve mass, which seems to be a gay "happening" in the cathedral and adjoining square as much as a formal religious service. As the hour approaches, all are talking about how they are going to get there since there are so few buses and taxis are virtually unavailable for Cubans. Still, one way or another, gays arrive in droves. They do not take much notice of the actual service but wander in and out of the cathedral onto the square to see who else is there. Few are practicing Catholics, but still they are there, partly because—unlike the North American Church—the Cuban Church, and particularly the archbishop of Havana, Cardinal Jaime Ortega, are seen as sympathetic to homosexuals. This impression has been made through the Church's defense of human rights in Cuba. Most gays have little knowledge of the homophobic edicts issued by Pope John Paul II.

Havana is similar to other large cities in that it contains a wide diversity of sexual desire, practice, and identity. Certain areas attract one type of homosexual more than another. In downtown Vedado you are much less likely to encounter the sort of flamboyant queens that you might see around the Prado in Old Havana. On the streets of Old Havana you would be more likely to find poor black and working-class homosexuals whom more educated, "respectable" gays would label as dangerous *chusma* (rabble), for middle-class gays tend to be as uptight in Cuba as they are everywhere else. Most are loath to admit that they might envisage a visit to cinemas like the Payret and the Astral in Old

Havana, which are known for the cruising and furtive sex that take place in the washrooms, not to mention other parts of the theaters. Nor would they readily admit to checking out notorious toilets such as that of the central bus terminal or to having furtive sex—"one last try before going home"—in the dark, leafy arbors of the Madriguera and the Loma del Príncipe adjoining the University of Havana. There, as anywhere else, lack of social opportunities may have channeled the desire of "decent" gays toward anonymous sex with partners from every social extraction. For some it becomes an erotic proclivity.

Until major hotels became de facto reserves for foreign visitors, more closeted homosexuals patronized bars such as those in the Inglaterra, Caprí, and Habana Libre hotels.[4] In contrast *tout le monde* tries to attend the performances of Cuba's famed national ballet company in the García Lorca Theater in front of the Parque Central—some "screaming" from the upper galleries while down in the orchestra, the more fastidious and decorous show off their elegance and culture. Upstairs or downstairs, the García Lorca is where you will find the *loca* that dwells in the heart of many a Cuban homosexual. At the other end of the spectrum are the new macho hunks who spend much of their spare time in gyms and strut their gorgeous bodies on the beach.

Various public beaches attract gays ranging from the uncomfortable coral and therefore more marginal Triton and Playita de 16 in Miramar to the Cayito Beach outside Havana, which is just as inviting as any other section of the famous Playas del Este. All have acquired a gay reputation, even though in reality they are mixed beaches of gays and *civilizados* who are attracted by the scene's nonconformity. Until the late eighties Varadero, today virtually reserved for foreigners, was a favorite holiday resort for gays, as it was for anyone else who could dream of going there. There too were well-known gay hang-outs and cruising places such as the Plaza de las Ocho Mil Taquillas and even discos known to turn a blind eye to men dancing together.

The negative cultural effects of foreign tourism reminiscent of those in other Caribbean islands are unfortunately increasing by the day. Style and image conscious as many young Cuban gays tend to be, they are not only likely to imitate the behavior of foreign tourists but also to invest more energy in gaining access to dollar discos and leisure outlets associated with foreigners. Since the government has to accommodate tourist demands, dollar discos like the Comodoro, the Marina, and Galeón are more tolerant of Cuban gays who accompany their foreign patrons. The Deauville attracts so many gays that it has acquired a gay reputation despite the fact that Cuban gays have to resort to the usual heterosexist subterfuges to gain admittance. Although such Cubans are far from representative of young homosexuals in general, these venues nevertheless excite the imagination of those who have no access to them and who until recently have had no alternative spaces to frequent. A by-product is that many young gay men are induced into *jineterismo* or the Grupo de Apoyo al Turismo Internacional (Support Group for International Tourism), the ironic name that a *jinetero* friend applied to his activities with tourists. This "support" is the only way they can acquire access to public places where gay men can dance together and to other benefits that only dollars can buy.

*Jineterismo* is a Cuban term for a practice that has spread in Cuba but is by no means restricted to that country. It is now associated with hustling foreigners who have dollars, but it has its roots in age-old relations between Cuban *entendidos* and would-be straight young men who could be induced or seduced into having sex as part of a night out. It was, and remains, much more reciprocal in its benefits than might be supposed by some of its moralistic critics. Since money is not fetishized in the way it tends to be in North America, this practice does not carry the same puritan emotional baggage as the exchange of sex and money does in North America. As the rich widow of a certain age confides to her gay confidant, of even more uncertain age, in the wonderful

Cuban *telenovela* (soap-opera) "El Año Que Viene," "There are three stages in one's life. In the first, others pay to be with you. In the second, you pay to be with them. In the third, you pay to get whomever you *really* want!" Using gifts to seduce someone is not seen as immoral by the vast majority of homosexuals, any more than it has been perceived as such by most Cuban heterosexuals. The person with more money is not only expected to grab the bill but regards it as a privilege to do so. Supposedly straight young men, for example military recruits, have their own reasons for accepting material favors. Many use the financial incentive as an excuse to satisfy their own need for sex. They can then claim that they just did it for money or because they were drunk. The resemblance of *jineterismo* to North American–style hustling is only superficial, for very few *jineteros* would dream of discussing a price for their company let alone for specific sexual favors. As one of them said, "eso sería muy feo" (that would be horrible). Moreover, unlike prostitutes, and even those who hustle part-time in North America, *jineteros* are not labeled with an identity that separates them from the rest of the community. Other Cubans appreciate that most *jineteros* relate to foreigners as a means of acquiring little luxuries—even necessities, for that matter. Male *jineteros* who target gays are vastly outnumbered by female *jineteras,* who are increasingly becoming prostitutes per se.[5] *Jineterismo* is really a way of intermittently relating to tourists rather than a full-time occupation. The minority who have become akin to full-time male prostitutes do not typically form part of the gay *ambiente.*

Semipublic gay parties where admission is by cover charge have emerged as a big feature of week-end life. They offer new social spaces to gays who had previously relied on *jineteando* for access to places where they could dance and be themselves. Havana has always been a party town, especially among gays and lesbians. Hosts of private parties have never had difficulty in finding fifty, sixty, or a hundred people who would cram into their often small quarters until the wee hours of the morning, even in the worst of times, such as the revolution's early phases, when they might be busted by a *redada*. What is different now is that the *fiestas de diez pesos* (ten-peso parties), as they have become known, are one of the entrepreneurial activities springing up all over Cuba. Although the organizers typically include gay people, they usually require the active cooperation of many who are not, since they are often run in multihome buildings and overflow in every direction. In some respects the fiestas are institutionalized in the sense that they are regular occurrences at the same address, so that their patrons are aware of the relative merits of competing fiestas. Some attract huge numbers of gays—not to mention lots of *civilizados* of both sexes—and only close at dawn. Some are associated with transvestites and feature drag shows. For a while there was even one on the outskirts of Havana that opened in the morning and took place around the swimming pool. In spite of the fact that the parties must be illegal since they charge admission and sell black-market liquor, the state seemingly tolerates their existence, much as it does the *paladares* (private homes that sell meals, snacks, and beverages for dollars). Neither the police nor the CDRs can be unaware of the fiestas' existence, given the number of patrons they attract, the noise level, and the fact that many take place on consecutive week-end nights.

The most popular summer fiestas happen on the *azoteas* (terrace roofs) of *solares* (tenements) in Central Havana. They provide a spectacular if hazardous setting. In fact, one of the most popular ones had to cease operations for a while in late 1994 after two young gays were severely injured when they fell off the roof. To reach them you must navigate narrow, unprotected stairs, often in semidarkness. Then you must remember not to get too near to the side of the *azotea,* since only a low, unprotected ledge would save you from plummeting to the ground three or four floors below. The sound system, when it works, is to say the least inadequate, so that only a few can actually dance to the music. Those who do not drink are fortunate because there may only be one or two toilets to meet the needs of several hundred people. In any event, drinks are beyond the reach of most because they have to be bought with dollars. This set-up may not sound appealing, but in fact the animated atmosphere and starlit setting more than compensate for the physical inconveniences. Though a lot of these party goers would undoubtedly do anything to see the gay scene in Miami and New York, many a visiting gay Cuban who actually lives in the United States laments what he has left behind in Havana.

What will he remember about these parties on his return to the United States? Certainly not the decor or the music, nor the drugs or rather lack of them. Nor the sex, for there is surprisingly little sexual activity going on, at least until the parties are about to end. (Which is not to say that Cuban gays are not as sexually aware of one another as are most gays everywhere.) As with so much else about Havana, the parties are made memorable by the animation and warmth of the people there and by the opportunity to connect, unmediated by fetishistic, market-driven preoccupations with looks and fashion. Fiestas are first and foremost opportunities to intermingle within a large and festive crowd, to pass from old friends to new friends, and to flirt with, rather than cruise, new acquaintances. In comparison with the North American bar and party scenes, particularly those of Toronto, you accordingly see few lost souls at a Havana fiesta. This is how one Cuban émigré on a return visit to Havana described the difference:

> In North America you arrive in a gay bar and find everybody wrapped up in themselves, talking only to their friends, or being distant and alone. They are impenetrable. They look at a new arrival, but nobody is welcoming. They only try to connect if they want sex. They are all separated as if they were islands. In Cuba it is not at all like that. As soon as you arrive everybody is mixing, everybody is talking with each other. People introduce themselves wanting to make friends. It's sad

but true that the majority of North Americans really don't
want to make new friends.

Most of the social spaces that I have mentioned are in Havana.
Yet it would be wrong to conclude that they are restricted to the
capital. Santiago homosexuals know exactly where to meet during the annual carnival, just as everybody knows that you go to
the Parque Maceo and in front of the Riviera Hotel during the
Havana carnival (currently in abeyance because of the economic
crisis). Cover-charge gay fiestas, though smaller and more discreet than those of Havana, are also beginning to be a feature of
gay life in Santiago. In more sophisticated cities such as Santa
Clara, the *fiestas de cinco pesos* (five-peso parties) are almost as
open as they are in Havana. There are country fairs like the *cha-
ranga de Bejucal* and the *parrandas de Remedios,* which were very
popular with out-of-town gays before the shortage of transportation associated with the current economic crisis. Even in sleepy
provincial cities like Cienfuegos it is not hard to find the places
where local homosexuals congregate on the Prado and Malecón.
In Santa Clara, a social and cultural center called the Mejunje becomes transformed into a delightful gay club at week-end. The
club is located in the heart of the city, and while its character is evident to all, it has the full support of the local government and
Party. De facto gay-positive social spaces are increasingly being
accepted in other cities, such as Sancti Spíritus, Camagüey, and
Holguín. In general, however, the social life of homosexuals who
live in the interior continues to be much more conservative than
it is in the capital.

Clearly not all gay males frequent these social spaces for in
Cuba, as elsewhere, many homosexuals (particularly older ones)
prefer to socialize privately in small groups and do not necessarily choose to construct their leisure lives around their sexual orientation. Furthermore, since the bulk of men who engage in
same-sex sex may not admit to being homosexual or even bisexual, it is understandable that some rarely if ever visit places fre-

quented by gays. Many do not want to risk being *quemado* by associating with them.[6] They tend to be more preoccupied with their masculine images and to project effeminacy onto the gay males who congregate in public. Their sexual contacts are as often as not made in the course of their everyday lives, at bus stops, on buses, on the streets, in cinemas.

The *fiestas de diez pesos* and street life are just two of the most obvious indicators of the growing collective gay consciousness in Havana. Still, their widespread occurrence shows a change in general attitudes to homosexuality. It may be countered that there is no real shift since homosexuals have been a part of public life in Cuba since long before the revolution. Regardless, the important fact is that there has been a major change in the number and personal style of gays who are more open about their sexual orientation. This represents an important step in combating the restrictive equation of homosexuality with effeminate *maricones*. They may not always be recognized as such, but today there are far more "masculine" gays out in public whereas once only flamboyant *locas* were visible to the public at large. Moreover, the new visibility of gays encourages a growing sense of collective awareness among gay males themselves. It publicizes homosexuality to latent or repressed homosexuals by showing the range of self-expression that is possible. The importance of this should not be underestimated because *machista* values are almost as deep-rooted within the *ambiente* as elsewhere, and most latent homosexuals are fearful of expressing their sexuality for social reasons as much as for fear of political repression.

In short, the behavior of younger gays in particular and the public spaces available to them reflect an important change since the sixties and early seventies, when homosexuals were systematically persecuted by the police. It could also be argued that except for the absence of explicitly gay bars, there is considerably more public space available to homosexuals than before the revolution. As one older *entendido* put it to me, "Before the revolution the *ambiente* was fabulous, but it was mostly restricted to the area around the barrio Colón. Today *entendidos* are all over the place."

My attention here to some of the positive changes affecting social attitudes toward homosexuality, and to the public spaces where Cuban gays can relate to each other, is not meant to suggest that homosexuals have been freed from oppression. Homophobia is still structured into the fabric of Cuban society and state institutions, as much as it is in the rest of Latin America and everywhere else. Homosexual oppression exists almost by definition so long as society is *machista* and the state accords privileges to certain forms of gender and sexual relations—physical expressions of affection among heterosexuals in public, conventional definitions of what constitutes a family, and heterosexual parenting and custody of children, to cite some of the most obvious examples—and reinforces their superior status through the educational system and especially in the mass media. Homosexual oppression is also a fact of life so long as gays and lesbians are subjected to prejudicial treatment, explicit or not, at work and in public life.

How gay males and men who have sex with other men but do not consider themselves gay will respond to this oppression will vary according to their social and cultural background. Many who have themselves internalized *machista* and heterosexist values will end up leading isolated lives and repressing much of their sexual desire. Let there be no doubt about it, many homosexuals in Cuba, as elsewhere, still have a great deal of difficulty in integrating their sexuality with other aspects of their lives. In Cuba, as elsewhere, the pain and loneliness of many homosexuals continues to be either ignored or attributed by society as a whole to self-destructive behavior.

As one would expect, age, education, race, and social class affect homosexuals' sense of themselves and the way they relate to each other and to society in general. Racial prejudice reinforces homophobic prejudice, most obviously in the stereotyping of black *maricones* as particularly effeminate for their failure to live up to the stereotype of black men as the incarnation of masculinity. In addition, racial prejudices affect relations among gays just as much as they do in any other sector of Cuban society. Racist comments abound in conversations among gays and not infrequently go beyond verbal prejudices to become hardened discriminatory attitudes. Most dark blacks (as opposed to *mulatos*, who comprise the majority of Afro-Cubans), particularly those with little education and consequently low social status, are indisputably marginalized from the gay mainstream, but Cubans contend that this has more to do with class-based cultural difference than skin color. Accordingly, expressions such as *negro negro* refer to a perceived lack of culture rather than the intensity of a man's black skin.

Within the gay community, as elsewhere, there is little or no space for blacks to articulate their feelings about racial prejudice let alone to respond to it in terms of self-organization. Nevertheless, despite these real obstacles of racism, most blacks and *mulatos* participate in the gay milieu to an extent that would be unimaginable in any American or even Canadian city. Dark-skinned blacks and fair-skinned whites rarely date, and when they appear together they are the object of prejudicial gossip, but black and *mulato* and *mulato* and white intermixing is common. Whites who explicitly ostracize people of color within the gay "community" are rare, but they and many light-skinned *mulatos* clearly consider themselves to be superior to blacks. One *mulato* law student responded with astonishment to my statement that he was a person of color; he said, "Yes, but I am very advanced" in reference to his light skin, pointing out as well that his hair was not really "bad" (crinkly).

Blacks are objectified as being particularly *caliente* (hot). In Cuba as elsewhere, the attribution of extraordinary genital size and sexual potency to blacks is an integral component of racist stereotyping, even though the conflation of eroticism and racism is very complex and is usually done unconsciously by most gays. This attitude is evident in the remarks of one older homosexual: "Sexually blacks are good, they have quality. There are many whites who prefer them. They are a shameless race, but they are good for that." But at the risk of overgeneralization, it seems to me that it is *mulatos* who are most envied by gays and Cubans generally for their looks and sensuality.

As with race, class distinctions are much more fluid within the Cuban gay community than they are in North America, Mexico, or Costa Rica. Class demarcations are less evident among Cuban homosexuals because the old class stratification (which was never particularly rigid) was shattered by the revolution and the new social classes have yet to gel. Inheritance is an insignificant factor, and the depreciation of the Cuban peso in relation to the American dollar has deprived higher salaries of much worth because almost all nonrationed goods are paid in dollar equivalents. Economic privilege therefore depends on access to dollars, and the means to obtain them include remittances from relatives abroad and the underground activities of *jineteros* and nonsexual hustlers engaged in *el bisne* (the black market). The private taxi driver could be a moonlighting doctor, an unemployed Slavic linguist, or anyone else searching for dollars. Advanced education, which had previously been very influential in determining access to given careers and therefore served as a determinant of income differentials as well (although it was never as great a factor as in capitalist countries), no longer ensures access to an enviable standard of living. To be sure, there are some educated gays who are elitist in their identification with subcultures such as the artistic intelligentsia or the sophisticated theater community, which has a cosmopolitan perspective. Yet, in the final analysis, even they are subject to the same leveling influences that affect the material circumstances of most Cubans. In short, although education and culture may be contributing factors with respect to the viability of long-term gay relationships, class does not differentiate the lives and relationships of most Cuban gays to the extent it does in North America.

The only classes or social strata that are clearly identifiable either by privilege or conversely by deprivation are, on one hand, elites affiliated with the government, military, and organizations such as joint ventures associated with foreign enterprises; and on the other hand, those who have only minimal educations and probably a marginalized culture that tends to set them apart from the middle sectors, broadly defined. One rarely finds representatives of either group in gatherings of mainstream homosexuals. It follows that these groups' experiences of homosexuality are not similar to that of most Cuban homosexuals.

If the gays that I have come to know over the years—who include teachers, writers, doctors, librarians, engineers, cabaret dancers, athletes, manual laborers, and sons of *campesinos*—are at all representative of Cuban homosexuals as a whole, then it can be said that there is little that typifies most Cuban homosexuals other than strong family ties and alienation from the government (not to be equated with opposition to the revolution itself). Other than a few shared attitudes, such as suspicion and distrust of the state (and obviously sexual attraction to other men), self-identified gays in Cuba have no more in common with each other than they do in most other countries. Still, I will venture this generalization about gay life in Cuba: the older the person, the more likely he is to have withdrawn into a private life and to have adopted traditional role-playing mannerisms and sexual practices. It is also harder for him to shake off the traumatic effects of the early phases of the revolution. The younger and more educated he is, particularly if he lives in Havana or in more cosmopolitan provincial cities such as Santa Clara, the more likely he is to have developed some gay consciousness and to reject sexual role playing. Lovers are developing relationships based more on mutual self-respect than was the case in the past. I doubt that as many of the new generation of homosexuals will get married to gain social acceptance as was once the case. In the interior of Cuba, traditional roles will no doubt change more slowly. The same applies to working-class males, especially those who are black and whose lives are tightly bound to historically marginalized subcultures. Those who are economically and socially disadvantaged are less able to assert new sexual forms of behavior.

Though it is hard to generalize about any group's sexual practices, there can be little doubt that although more and more young gays are *completo* (reciprocal in sex), most Cuban homosexuals have incorporated *machista* attitudes into their sexuality. These are evident in the persistence of sexual roles—that is, that a person must be identified as *activo* or *pasivo* and that privileged status belongs to the *activo,* who is much more likely to incorporate gender attributes that evoke conventional masculinity. In this respect, Cuba is not all that different from other Western patriarchal cultures that celebrate masculinity. As oppressed as gays may feel by straight men within this kind of culture, many still envy and indeed lust for the proverbial "real man." Cuban homosexuals are by no means unique in their phallocentric preoccupations, yet the size of penises acquires a significance among Cuban homosexuals that has few parallels. No rejection is quite as conclusive as this classic Cuban dismissal: "Era bonito, pero figúrate, la tenía muy chiquita" (He was gorgeous, but imagine, he had such a small cock). Nor is anyone celebrated quite as much as the man of mythical proportions.

Celebrating and fantasizing about attractive men is central to being gay. That does not mean that gay men do not socialize with or are unaware of women. On the contrary, in Cuba as elsewhere it is common to see homosexuals in the company of women. Some of these women are lesbians and some are gay-positive *civilizadas.* In fact, the presence of many women at gay functions, such as the *fiestas de diez pesos,* persuades many Cuban homosexuals that they are supportive of lesbian rights and women's liberation. They contrast their apparent ease in socializing with women with the tension that frequently characterizes relations between gays and lesbians in North America. In reality, however, most Cuban gays appreciate and welcome women only if they are prepared to abide by conventional feminine and *machista* norms. As a rule, lesbians who challenge and refuse to conform with such oppressive stereotypes are no more part of an integrated homosexual scene than they are anywhere else in Latin America.

There are few other generalizations that may be made about Cuban gays or about the extent of state intrusion into their personal lives. In general, there has been a significant reduction in state surveillance, for example by the block Committees to Defend the Revolution (CDRs), since oppression of homosexuals was at its peak in the 1960s and 1970s. Even in the past sanctions against homosexuals were mainly directed at men who, by Cuban standards, would have been perceived as "flaunting" their homosexuality—that is, behaving in an "unmasculine" way. For example, the resolutions of the 1971 Congress on Education and Culture were directed at *"reconocidos homosexuales,"* which is best translated as "notorious homosexuals." This limitation does not in any way excuse such oppression, but it does make it more comprehensible in terms of traditional Cuban and Latin American attitudes toward "effeminate, ostentatious" homosexuals. Since the vast majority of Cuban males who engage in same-sex sex are either closeted homosexuals or do not admit to being homosexual at all, they would not have been directly affected by state repression of "notorious" homosexuals. Even the latter had access to much more sex than might be supposed from the regime's persecution of homosexuals. In fact, Reinaldo Arenas argued that repression had actually incited homosexuality as an act of defiance against the regime's celebration of machismo and the "new man." "There was never more fucking going on than in those years, the decade of the sixties, which was precisely when all the new laws against homosexuals came into being."[7] To illustrate his point Arenas claimed to have had sex with no fewer than five thousand men in the 1960s, an impressive number given that he was still in his twenties!

It has always been evident that "known" (as opposed to "notorious") homosexuals abound in the educational, cultural, and health fields. An impressive number of prominent writers, artists, actors, and musicians are widely known for having sexual relations with other men. Some of them have occupied prominent official positions in organizations such as UNEAC. They do little to camouflage their homosexuality, other than having marriages of convenience and making sure not to question the state's homophobic policies. Although they may have stunted their creativity by repressing its gay component, they have hardly suffered in other respects. They are courted by foreign visitors and have easy access to foreign travel. In distancing themselves from *maricones,* whom they criticize for being too ostentatious and immoral, they become accomplices of the system. They remain silent in the face of the oppression of the majority, reinforcing the belief that there is a pathological difference between decent and "antisocial" homosexuals. Though they may present themselves as gay to foreigners, most Cuban gays perceive them as being *oficialista*—in short, not to be trusted with respect to gay issues. Reinaldo Arenas is not the only Cuban intellectual who, having paid the price for his inability or refusal to repress the way in which he manifested his homosexuality, had bitter feelings about those who had accommodated themselves to the system.[8]

The sexual orientation of less privileged and necessarily more discreet homosexual professionals is probably inferred by their colleagues from their social and leisure activities as well as from their marital status. Still, if the rituals of masculinity and deference to heterosexist conventions are observed—for example, by occasional attendance at public social functions with a wife or ostensible *novia*—the privacy of their personal life will be respected. The majority of "known" gays are not hassled at work or in public. That would not accord with customary Cuban politeness and respect for people's privacy (but it would not preclude malicious gossip, of course). Needless to say, they would have to play their part by refraining from explicit allusions to the taboo part of their private lives. Nevertheless, hiring and particularly promotion in most fields are detrimentally affected to the person who has not succeeded in masking all traces of his homosexuality. Here again Cuba is no different from most of Latin America and indeed much of North America. In all these countries, a person's lot will be determined more by the extent of homophobia in the people who have immediate power over him than by institutionalized discrimination. In almost every case, this discrimination is justified on grounds other than sexual orientation.

Much the same is true of the CDRs' impact on the domestic lives of homosexuals. Because their original purpose was tied to civil defense, they were entrusted with surveillance of the civil population. Over time the need for such surveillance has declined. The CDRs are now much more concerned with the collection and dissemination of general information. They usually deal with issues such as health and education and also with mundane but pressing matters like water, power, and garbage. These committees usually do not make it their jobs to spy on what people do in bed. To be sure, some Cubans remain sensitive to the possibility of being overheard by zealous CDR members, but this trepidation does not seem to stop them from engaging in black-market and other activities that are nominally illegal. In short, it would be wrong to conclude that most CDRs are preventing gay males from "tricking" in their own homes, from living together as lovers, or from having gay parties. After all, the CDRs are mostly composed of ordinary Cubans who may well have frequent contact with their neighbors over other matters. To be sure, some CDRs may be dominated by officious individuals who try to cramp other people's lives, but there are far more whose basic policy is to live and let live. The case of one *solar* or tenement that I am familiar with in Centro Habana may illustrate the point. Over one hundred people are crammed into the building, of whom more than a dozen are reputedly homosexual. The incredibly crowded circumstances in which they live determine that "peaceful coexistence" will be the rule, one that in this particular case is extended to a gay couple whose tempestuous live-in relationship is overheard by all and sundry. The head of the CDR happens to be a closeted *entendido* himself. But even if he were not, it is quite apparent that he would be wise not to report the myriad "antisocial" activities that abound within the building, ranging from money-changing to prostitution of one sort or another. In other cases, admittedly not common, CDRs have been headed by openly gay people. When I asked one gay man whether he had problems with the CDR on account of running *fiestas de diez pesos* in his home, he replied, "Hardly. I am its president."

Where intrusion occurs it is likely to be by meddlesome people who would make bad neighbors under any circumstances, CDR or no CDR. How the CDRs impinge on the private lives of gay males is also affected by how much the gay person is esteemed or not for other reasons and also by how much power homosexuals project onto their neighbors because of their own internalized homophobia. All this does not change the fact that for many gays the CDRs have been symbols of the Cuban state's power to police the most private aspects of people's behavior. The fact that this power is not commonly exercised, and that the CDRs' effectiveness has steadily diminished in recent years, in no way lessens their oppressiveness for those who oppose the regime on other grounds.

The remaining sociopolitical restrictions on sex and gender in Cuba may seem onerous compared to the freedom that many gay inhabitants of North America's cosmopolitan downtown cores presently *seem* to enjoy. Still, from a historical and comparative perspective, Cuba is not all that different from other Latin American countries. Furthermore, fears, myths, and in some cases official restrictions do not prevent gay Cubans from cruising, "tricking," and living together.

Lack of privacy is actually the biggest constraint on the sexual and relational aspects of the lives of most homosexuals (as is true much of Latin America). There is a serious housing shortage in Havana and most other cities. The majority of gays live in incredibly cramped homes with their parents and other relatives. There are no legal restrictions upon single males having (including buying) their own homes, but at present this is an option that most gays can only dream about. And in reality, an impressive number are ambivalent about leaving their family homes. Family ties and affection are so great that even when a homosexual man has acquired an apartment or house, he will typically offer to share it with other members of his family, relatives, or friends. Strange as it may sound to many North American gays, who place a premium on having their own space, many and perhaps most Cubans (like other Latin Americans) are appalled by the idea of living alone—although they would love to share space with an ideal *pareja* (lover). Because so few of them have come out to their families, they consequently have to resort to all sorts of subterfuges if they are to have sex in their own homes. And many would consider it a *falta de respeto* (disrespectful) to do so, in any event.

So where can single Cubans have sex or spend a night together? For heterosexuals it is somewhat easier since they can either rent a hotel room (if they can afford it and have the right connections) or line up to rent a room by the hour in a *posada* (a trysting establishment), a somewhat embarrassing experience. Neither option is open to gay males, at least not in their hometown hotels. Two men would not be allowed to rent a hotel room unless they had an official reason. To do so they would have to find a pretext to spend a night in a nearby town. Cabins in the *campismo popular* resorts that have been created in the last few years are also becoming very popular for those involved in longer affairs. Such campgrounds tend to be less restrictive than hotels for two men who want to spend time together. (Even so, many homosexuals mask their sexual orientation by sharing adjacent cabins with lesbians.) There is also a good deal of mutual support among friends by, for instance, allowing their homes to be used when parents are not around. Less fortunate ones have to resort to renting private rooms from people who exploit the housing shortage by charging exploitative prices. Until resort areas virtually became the exclusive preserve of foreigners, it was also quite common for groups of better-off gays and lesbians to rent private homes by the beach for weekends.

Casual sex is obviously a complex matter usually requiring much imagination and experience. There are large parks like the Lenin and shady nooks off the Quinta Avenida in Miramar. There are hidden rugged beaches such as the Playa del Chivo beneath the Castillo del Morro close to Old Havana, the more appealing sand dunes on the Playas del Este outside Havana, as well as toilets,[9] cinemas, stairwells, rooftops, shells of ruined buildings, and empty lots—all involving considerable risk of detection and discomfort. Then there is the problem that the circumstances of such sex tend to separate the physical pleasure from other forms of emotional intimacy and connection.

It is very difficult for gays to go out for a night on the town. Most of the better clubs and cabarets restrict the entrance of men not accompanied by women. Until recently there were no public spaces (with the possible exception of "dollar" discos in Havana and Varadero) where gay males could dance together even with women partners as covers. Many gays resort to double-dating with lesbians if they want a night out together. If they are prepared to grease the palm of the doorman, a gay couple may sometimes be allowed to sit in some hidden corner of a cabaret. There are also places like the *casas del té* (tearooms) that are well known for their gay patronage. However, even though no straight people may be present, gays usually "no se sienten en su casa" (do not feel at home). The management may not kick them out, but they are not secure in feeling welcome either.

In short, until the advent of the *fiestas de diez pesos,* there were no social spaces where homosexuals could socialize together out-side private parties and feel free to be spontaneous and intimate with each other. On the other hand, the struggle to find and cre-ate space within which such closeness can occur may have indi-rect compensations. Since a sustained effort is required to develop and retain a relationship, couples tend to attach value to nonsex-ual forms of contact. Like other Latin Americans, Cubans are in some ways more sentimental than many contemporary North American gays, and they may find it easier to accept such limita-tions so long as they can be in contact with their *compromisos* (boyfriends) and *parejas* in other ways. Furthermore, although Cubans are much more *sato* (promiscuous) than their criticism of alleged North American promiscuity would suggest, in Cuba there may be less emphasis on sex and more value placed upon connecting to people in other ways than there is in Canada. One gay exile, who admittedly felt much freer in his everyday life in Toronto, put it this way:

> It is much more difficult to have a relationship here. Everyone wants to be free; nobody wants to get involved or commit themselves. I think that it is because of the permissiveness and promiscuity. It is not that I don't like pornography and videos, or don't cruise around myself. But the fact is that you can have an overdose of that sort of thing so that sex loses significance and becomes mechanical and boring.

Now that the police and the law are less immediately repressive, the need most commonly expressed by younger gays, in particular, is for access to cafés, discos, and bars where they can relax and have fun. They are not unique in this respect, since virtually all of Cuba's youth say the same thing. This should not necessarily be equated with a demand for something equivalent to a gay ghetto bar in North America. Cuban homosexuals may be intrigued when foreign visitors show them advertisements for such places or tell them about them, just as many Cubans want to get hold of

pornographic magazines. But I suspect that this desire is for ex-
otica as much as it is for erotica. There is no particular reason
why Cuban homosexuals, any more than other Latin Americans,
would choose to build their social lives around commercial spaces
that cater exclusively to gay males. On the contrary, most would
ideally prefer to socialize in integrated mixed spaces. That said, it
does not mean that some would not prefer to patronize such gay
bars exclusively nor that the rest would not like to visit them occasionally, perhaps even accompanied by *civilizado* friends.

Cuban gays have been deprived of many of the benefits that accrue from the social centers, support services, media, and public
events that are associated with gay liberation in the United States
and Canada and that are beginning to emerge in Mexico and Costa
Rica. On the other hand, they may have benefited from the fact
that their identities have not been as narrowly defined as those predominantly produced within North America's highly regulated
and commodified society. One Cuban gay intellectual—necessarily unfamiliar with the complexities of contemporary gay and
"queer" cultures—argued "that gays in North America and other
capitalist countries cannot develop a more radical and progressive
political consciousness precisely because the bars, the gay neighborhoods, and their vaunted sexual freedom distract them from
the social and political problems of their countries."

Most Cuban gay exiles in North America revel in the newfound freedom of their everyday lives, but many also maintain
that they felt much less sexually constrained in Cuba. Some gay
exiles even insist that they "were never excluded from predominantly heterosexual bars, discos, and sporting events, where we
always had a chance of picking up a *pepillo.*" Reinaldo Arenas,
too, recalled Cuba as a place where "gays were not confined to a
specific area of a club or beach. Everybody mingled and there was
no division that would place the homosexual on the defensive.
This has been lost in more advanced societies, where the homosexual has had to become a sort of sexual recluse and separate

himself from the supposedly non-homosexual society, which undoubtedly also excludes him."[10]

An impressive number of Cuban homosexuals are emphatic that they want greater integration and acceptance in society as a whole rather than separation and lives built around a gay ghetto. Their undoubted desire to "lead a freer and more open homosexual lifestyle, without the social pressure and repression to which we have been subject" does not mean that they necessarily want "gay" institutions as such. As the gay intellectual quoted above added:

> I don't think that it is a question of whether or not this or that exists. That is a superficial, phenomenological question, that doesn't deal with the essence of the problem. The issue is that gays should not be limited in any way. They should be free to go to any bar, without the present restrictions. Opening a bar or hotel specifically for gays would not signify much in itself. In fact, from one point of view it could be seen as a form of discrimination rather than liberation. Everyone who went there would immediately be labeled as gay. It might even represent a more effective way of controlling all gays.

It is a reflection of the powerlessness of Cuban gays to assert and defend the legitimacy of their personal everyday life that they have not been able to envisage the way a more open society might be created, one that would allow them to develop their full potentialities without being boxed into the role of being "a gay." It is not merely a question of juxtaposing this commodified separate gay identity with a vision of a liberated but socially integrated homosexual person. At its best being gay means not merely "coming out" but being part of gay interactions, social activities, and organizations that expand and challenge the meaning of gay identity. This process and struggle contribute not only to affirmation of a gay presence but also inevitably contribute to questioning the meaning and worth of being "a straight," or *cheo,* as Cubans would put it.

# £IGHT

## The Impact
## of AIDS

*BECAUSE OF* good fortune, circumstances, and certainly not least its commitment to preserving the health of its population, Cuba has so far been spared the worst effects of the global AIDS epidemic. As of December 31, 1994, Cuba had reported a total of only 342 people who had contracted AIDS, 218 of whom had died from the disease. An additional 1,099 individuals were reported as having tested HIV seropositive. Of these 783 were male and 316 female. Heterosexual males and females represented a clear majority of people who had AIDS or were HIV positive.[1] However, over time homosexual or bisexual males have constituted an increasing proportion of seropositive males, rising from 41 percent in October 1990 to nearly 62.8 percent in December, 1994.

Transmission of the infection has almost invariably occurred through sexual intercourse. Intravenous drug use is extremely rare in Cuba and apparently nobody has been exposed to the infection this way. No more than a handful of people have been infected by exposure to contaminated blood, reflecting the fact that

Cuban blood donors have been effectively checked for HIV antibodies. Initially, a majority were infected by sexual contact with non-Cubans, either at home or abroad, with some Cubans no doubt infected during their residence in Angola or other African countries during the 1980s.[2] By 1991, the proportion of those infected by non-Cubans had dropped to less than a quarter. Currently, the vast majority of those who are seropositive have been infected by sexual contacts within Cuba.

Because Cuba's AIDS-prevention program has been highly controversial, it is important to examine it unemotionally. A good starting point is to recognize that the incidence of reported AIDS cases is very low in Cuba relative to that in Mexico, Costa Rica, and most of the neighboring Caribbean countries.[3] American critics of Cuba's AIDS program would do well to remember that Cuba's rate of HIV infection is also much lower than that of Latinos living in the United States, specifically including Puerto Ricans, who are more affected than any other ethnic group. The rate of infection in Puerto Rico itself is almost eight times higher than that in Cuba.[4] The low incidence of HIV infection must be due in part to the quality of Cuba's public health system. It allowed the Cuban government to organize a systematic response to the impending threat of an AIDS epidemic as early as 1983. Most Latin American countries are still unable to do so given the paucity of their public health resources. And unlike in the United States, where almost a third of those who acquire AIDS have no health insurance, all infected Cubans have had the opportunity to receive excellent health care free.

In some respects the low incidence of AIDS in Cuba offers an almost textbook illustration of "one of the oldest and most fundamental truths of medical science: public health measures are always more effective in controlling disease than are all the medicines in the world." Robert Root-Bernstein, the prominent AIDS specialist, continues that "if we want to control AIDS, it is not vaccines, antiretroviral drugs, or other medical miracles that we need. We need to solve the social, economic, health education, and medical care problems that create the conditions that permit AIDS to develop in the first place."[5]

The figures say that Cuba has been able to contain the spread of HIV. Cuba has not had anything remotely resembling an exponential increase in AIDS, in contrast to the experience of many other Third World countries. Although there has been a slight increase in the incidence of HIV seropositives, the rate of that increase has rapidly declined. Cuba has also been able to offer better medical treatment to those who are seropositive or who actually have AIDS. For example, in Cuba the average life expectancy of people with AIDS is nineteen months, almost twice that of Mexico.[6]

Opponents of the regime, such as Néstor Almendros, the late director of *Improper Conduct,* have argued that AIDS is much more widespread than official figures suggest.[7] Some gay physicians in Cuba agree that "all the facts about AIDS are not revealed in Cuba." This may be true, but Cuba would not be alone in this regard since almost every country has underreported the real number of people who have AIDS or who have tested seropositive. (In part, this is inevitable because of the difficulty of tracking the spread of the disease, which is invisible in its initial stages.) Critics have not been able to demonstrate why Cuba's AIDS statistics would not have the same integrity as its other highly reliable epidemiological statistics.[8] There may be some dispute about the relevance of Cuba's health statistics to an overall evaluation of the revolution's success, but no serious student of the revolution questions their basic accuracy.

Cuba's initial policy of quarantining—that is, seemingly imprisoning—for life all people who had tested positive to HIV antibodies was radical, indeed draconian. It evoked an emotional response abroad where it was seen as an illiberal contravention of basic human rights. Even some of the more uncritical supporters of the regime have been forced to acknowledge that the "harshness of the quarantine" effectively ensured that the "hospital-like facilities . . . resembled a prison more than a sanatorium."[9] The original prison-like external appearance of the Havana sanatorium, popularly known as Los Cocos, was indicative of its primary function. The grounds of the sanatorium, which was administered until 1989 by MINFAR, the Ministry of Defense, were surrounded by a high concrete wall. Inside the grounds, was a *calabazo* (cell) where recalcitrant internees could be locked up. People in perfect health, except for the fact that they were infected with HIV, were confined against their will, and those who escaped ended up in the Combinado del Este prison, which is a jail in every sense of the word.

Some gay critics abroad interpreted the quarantine program as further evidence of Cuba's repressive discrimination against homosexuals. Yet in Cuba it was not perceived as either unusual or discriminatory. The program seems to have been supported from the outset by the majority of the Cuban population, including a majority of homosexuals, whose experience of Cuba's health system has led them to place enormous trust in the country's medical policies. In fact, the quarantine measures were quite consistent with Cuba's radical response to other epidemics such as dengue and African swine fever. They were also consistent with the authoritarian philosophy that characterizes the relationship of Cuba's health authorities to the population as a whole.[10] In exchange for having their health taken care of, Cubans submit to the dictates of medical officers who "know what is best for them."

Although the quarantine program was not motivated by a homophobic agenda, homophobia was clearly an underlying factor in some of the initial responses to the epidemic. While homosexuals were a minority among those first infected, AIDS was prejudicially viewed as a gay disease by the government as much as by the population as a whole, as it was almost everywhere else. The government's preoccupation was to protect the "normal" majority from the disease and only secondarily to respect the human rights of those who were infected with HIV. Gay internees, for instance, were subject to discriminatory policies within the Havana sanatorium. They initially lived in segregated quarters and were subject to greater restrictions than other residents with respect to the external passes that allowed them to make brief visits outside the sanatorium. They had to wait longer for such passes and were subject to greater supervision by the nursing staff, who chaperoned them to ensure that they had no opportunity to infect others.

As Marvin Leiner has argued in *Sexual Politics in Cuba: Machismo, Homosexuality and AIDS,* the quarantine program reflected *machista* assumptions in other ways, especially the belief that male sexuality is uncontrollable and unchangeable.[11] Accordingly, no one who was infected could be trusted to act responsibly; a corollary was the belief that people—especially homosexuals—who were not infected would not change their own sexual behavior in response to sexual education—that is, take responsibility for their own health by refraining from unsafe sex.

Although the machismo of Cuba's leaders affected the way they initially responded to the AIDS epidemic, there is no evidence that the government publicly exploited homosexuals as scapegoats for the epidemic. Although the AIDS prevention program's public presentations have consistently incorporated heterosexist language and assumptions, the Ministry of Public Health has always emphasized that "the illness can be contracted by normal relations between men and women" and has underlined the fact that "AIDS is not something exclusive to homosexuals."[12] The emphasis has always been on the number of sexual partners and the type of sex performed rather than on the sexual orientation of those involved.

Yet some gay Cuban doctors insist that the "AIDS information that is released is prejudicial rather than factual" in its association of the disease with homosexuality. Cited as an example is the fact that the first person reported by the press to have died of AIDS was identified as a theater designer who became infected on a New York visit, an account that plays into the stereotypes of theater people in Cuba. There may be a grain of truth in such contentions, difficult though they are to substantiate in terms of intent. Yet here again complaints must be set in the context of the homophobic exploitation of AIDS in most other countries. Compared to the initial homophobic statements made by public health officials in Costa Rica and Mexico, the comments made by Cuban officials were not particularly homophobic. To be sure, their initial response did nothing to undermine the popular equation of homosexuality with AIDS, but its homophobic implications (such as they were) surely fell far short of those contained in government reactions elsewhere in Latin America. In Costa Rica, for example, posters and pamphlets were distributed to doctors and to the public warning that sex with homosexuals, prostitutes, and drug addicts represented the major risk of AIDS infection. The social democratic government of Oscar Arias also carried out a series of highly publicized raids against gay bars in the name of AIDS prevention.

In Cuba, homosexuality has been linked to AIDS mostly as part of a critique of the decadence of U.S. capitalism rather than as a criticism of the "pathological" or "antisocial" behavior of homosexuals per se, as might once have been the case.[13] Official surveys of the epidemic's etiology, largely based on American data and experience, are equally devoid of homophobic allusions. On the other hand, the studied avoidance of any acknowledgment that gays and bisexuals are among those who have been most affected by the epidemic can also be interpreted as a form of inverse discrimination.

If the assumption is made that those who engage in same-sex sex may be on the way to becoming the largest category of Cubans infected with HIV, then the Ministry of Public Health should be faulted for failing to undertake AIDS-prevention education that specifically addresses gays and bisexuals, or at the very least explicitly includes them among its target groups. The paucity of such safe-sex education is regrettable, given that anal intercourse is the preferred sexual practice among Cuban males who have sex with other males and that condoms are used by only a minuscule percentage of the population.[14] Once again, however, it is important to place the defects in Cuba's AIDS-prevention program in context. Safe-sex education directed to gays and bisexuals is insufficient, but general AIDS-prevention education is also in short supply. On the other hand, the extensive public health network, recently supplemented by the family physician program, ensures that a much higher percentage of the population will be systematically exposed to health education (including information about AIDS prevention) than would be the case in Mexico and most other Latin American countries, where much of the rural and urban poor population is deprived of ready access to health clinics and doctors. Still, the measure is clearly not enough, as evidenced by the fact that even gays known to have AIDS admit to having been pressured to have unsafe sex. Such attitudes reflect the dare-devil machismo that infects homosexuals as much as other Cuban males. Then there is the fact that condoms are not always accessible.

The official explanations for the low profile of Cuba's AIDS information program are that there is no need to create a panic within the population because the incidence of AIDS is low and that Cubans are traditionally uncomfortable about discussing sexual hygiene in public. Officials also contend that they want to avoid encouraging the belief that gays are responsible for AIDS. That, supposedly, is why avoidance of certain high-risk practices associated with homosexuality was not stressed in AIDS-prevention education prior to the mid-1990s.[15] Many Cuban gays respond that the real reason the government does not address the needs of homosexuals is that to do so would imply public recognition and therefore legitimation of homosexuality in

Cuba. This may be so. In any event, the pressure of circumstances has not yet forced Cuban health authorities, unlike those of countries such as the United States and Canada, to confront openly the means by which many gay men have been infected. The total number of Cubans infected by HIV has not been sufficient to outweigh Cubans' (including homosexuals') *pudor* with respect to public discussion of intimate sexual practices such as anal intercourse.

Furthermore, it would be very difficult to carry out effective safe-sex education among those who engage in same-sex sex without arousing their fear of being labeled as homosexuals. This difficulty has been aggravated by the absence prior to the mid-1990s of official or unofficial gay social spaces where safe-sex information could be distributed. Despite the relatively low number of homosexuals infected so far, the further spread of the HIV infection among those who practice same-sex sex could be best contained if AIDS-prevention measures were preceded or accompanied by efforts to end the marginalization of homosexuals in society as a whole.[16] Since the Cuban government does not concede that gays are oppressed and marginalized, its refusal to acknowledge the need to reach out to them is not surprising. Nongovernmental AIDS education initiatives, particularly those identified with gays, are not encouraged. Attempts even to discuss safe-sex education from a gay perspective were thwarted in the November 1994 Congress on Sexual Education.

The most controversial aspect of Cuba's AIDS-prevention program was the initial decision to place all those people who were HIV-positive as well as those who actually had AIDS in special AIDS sanatoriums that were physically isolated from the rest of society.[17] Initially it appeared that innocent people were being confined for life—incarcerated to all intents and purposes—not for what they had done but for what they might do in hypothetical circumstances, with hypothetical consequences.[18] However, in all fairness it should be noted that Cubans assumed that quarantining would be only a temporary measure since they, like many others, expected that an effective AIDS vaccine would soon be found.

In implementing this quarantine policy, Cuba acquired the distinction of being the only country that rejected the World Health Organization guidelines regarding the use of quarantine. Not only did the policy appear to disregard completely the human rights of people with AIDS but it may also have been a deterrent to the cooperation in AIDS prevention of people who engage in "high-risk practices." As Valentin Pokrovski, the one-time director of the Soviet Institute of Epidemiology, argued in rejecting such a policy for the Soviet Union, "people will try to avoid medical examination so as not to risk being essentially incarcerated for the rest of their life, and the disease will spread out of control."[19] Ironically, the quarantine policy also seemed to contradict the belief of the Cuban Ministry of Public Health, which itself admitted that in the "final analysis it is individual behavior that will determine what will happen in each case, given that there are basic aspects of [AIDS] prevention that cannot be regulated by the health system and that require each person to adopt specific preventative measures."[20]

The announcement of the initial quarantine policy was accompanied by other measures, such as the compulsory disclosure of sexual contacts by those who were seropositive,[21] that disturbed people who highly value a liberal conception of human rights—for example, the need to uphold individual privacy and freedom as much as possible vis-à-vis the state. The government also announced that everyone would undergo HIV antibody tests. Although these tests were not compulsory,[22] Cubans were subject to social and political pressure to submit to them voluntarily. In addition, people in high-risk groups—including Cubans who had been abroad and those with a history of sexually transmitted diseases—were to be barred from donating blood (a reasonable restriction) and would have this fact entered on their identity cards. This unnecessary labeling might have few adverse consequences for women or for most Cuban men who had served overseas, but it would effectively identify as homosexual the vast majority of the remaining single men with the identity card notation. The identity card policy was soon discarded, but widespread testing of the population continued for some time, although not to the extent once envisaged. By 1993 over 13 million tests had been carried out. In time, tests were restricted to members of what were considered high-risk groups, such as workers in the tourist and entertainment industries, sailors, and anyone returning from extended periods abroad. Homosexuals qua homosexuals have *not* been defined as a high-risk group. Eventually all tests became truly voluntary except for blood donors, and doctors were obliged to obtain consent before doing an HIV test. It is expected that by 1995 facilities will be available for completely anonymous testing.[23]

The government insists that its twin policies of mass testing and quarantine measures were initially responsible for preventing the spread of HIV and AIDS within the country. No responsible critic denies that the epidemic has been contained in Cuba, but this fact is not necessarily solely attributable to the present Cuban AIDS-prevention program. It may be that similar results could have been achieved with methods more respectful of individual human rights. For example, Cuba may have benefited from the fact that it is an island subject to an embargo that prevented travel to and from the United States, whose major cities initially harbored the largest number of people infected with HIV in the Western Hemisphere. Furthermore, Cuba's tourist industry was relatively undeveloped prior to the onset of the epidemic and was still very much geared to "family style" vacations. The effectiveness of the public health system, evident in early testing of blood supply, coupled with the relatively low level of venereal diseases among the Cuban population, may also have helped to deter the spread of the epidemic, in contrast to underdeveloped countries where opposite conditions prevail. Last but not least, the opportunity for Cuban homosexuals to have full intercourse has been restricted by the lack of private places for lovemaking, and this limitation may also have slowed the disease's spread.

The question is therefore whether similar results could have been attained through widespread safe-sex education and voluntary and anonymous testing of the population. Cuba would have been uniquely equipped to carry out such a program because of the size and scope of its mass organizations, which have demonstrated their effectiveness in inoculation campaigns and mobilizations in response to hurricanes. Unfortunately, as if to prove that this was not a viable alternative, Cuba never conducted safe-sex education programs widely enough or often enough to alter traditional sexual practices. To be sure, there have been periodic informational radio and television programs, some of them very well executed, but there have been no massive safe-sex campaigns as such.[24] The low incidence of HIV, coupled with ingrained sexual habits that would have required immense funds to change and the paucity of financial resources during the "special period," were no doubt additional factors that affected the extent of safe-sex education.

Another limitation of the mass-testing and quarantine programs is that they may serve to deemphasize the crucial need for individuals to assume responsibility for preventing transmission of the virus by avoiding unprotected intercourse. This characteristic of Cuba's AIDS-prevention program is consistent with the overall character of the Cuban health program, which fails to empower the individual to assume responsibility for personal health care and continues to mystify the power of professional, centralized medical expertise in a way that in this case is detrimental to the eradication of disease.[25] The system may foster a false belief that sexual partners outside the sanatoriums are free from the disease. Cubans as a group still have little knowledge about AIDS. The continued, albeit moderate spread of HIV, particularly among young people, reveals that mass testing and epi-

demiological contact tracing do not guarantee that people will not
be infected by their sexual partners.[26] This is not surprising, considering the scarcity of condoms and the reluctance of Cuban
males to use them.

Mass testing and contact tracing might only be truly effective
if they were done universally, simultaneously, and recurrently,
which would be beyond the resources even of Cuba's public
health system.[27] Furthermore, the enormous expansion of the
tourist industry currently underway makes the strategy even
more problematic. Cuba received over six hundred thousand
tourists in 1994 and hopes to attract two million visitors annually
by the end of the decade. No doubt a considerable number of
them will have sex with Cubans. Contrary to government propaganda, an impressive number of Cubans go to bed with foreigners not merely because Cubans are *calientes* and foreigners from
capitalist countries are "decadent." Cubans do it partly out of
boredom, given the limited leisure outlets in the country, and increasingly for material reasons. Commercially organized prostitution may have been dramatically reduced since 1959, but the
number of part-time prostitutes and *jineteros* of both sexes increases every year. Pimps can now be encountered in Havana
hawking the services of girls in their early teens. Clandestine
brothels and call-girl services are reemerging. Short of completely
altering the relatively open character of the tourist industry and
thereby compromising its attractiveness to Westerners, it will be
impossible to ensure that there are no HIV carriers among these
foreign tourists or to prevent them from having sexual contact
with Cubans.

Paradoxically, the effectiveness of Cuba's current quarantine
program increasingly depends upon safe-sex practices to which
the Cuban health authorities have given relatively little attention
in their AIDS-prevention initiatives. The implementation of
quarantine has become much more liberal and humanistic (at
least in the Los Cocos sanatorium in Santiago de las Vegas) than

it was at first. According to a worldly seventeen-year-old who has been actively gay since he was eleven and who has spent the last couple of years in the sanatorium, "there is less repression of gays in Los Cocos than anywhere else in Havana."[28] Havana residents who are HIV positive are housed in very comfortable, and in some cases even luxurious, conditions by Cuban standards in the original and principal sanatorium.[29] The grim concrete wall has been torn down and replaced by a less intimidating wrought-iron fence. Most residents live in attractive houses surrounded by spacious grounds, truly an oasis of physical tranquility. Residents who are in established relationships (including homosexuals) have their own separate accommodations. Most are free to leave the grounds at will provided they clock in and out. Evening visits to Havana are facilitated by a sanatorium bus that leaves at 4 PM and returns at midnight, quite a privilege given the transportation crisis that bedevils the lives of most residents of the capital. Internees may be visited by family members and friends throughout the week. Furthermore, as one former internee recalls, prior to the "economic crisis of the special period we ate better food in the sanatorium than any tourist was able to do outside it." In addition, they had free access to all drugs and the best medical treatment that Cuba could provide. It is clear that no expense was spared before the economic crisis that followed the collapse of trade with the former Communist camp.

During the first stage of their isolation, internees may not leave the sanatorium unless they are chaperoned by a staff member. However, once they have satisfied the sanatorium staff that they will respect the need to abide by safe-sex guidelines, and their families have indicated their willingness to guarantee such behavior—a formality—they are free to return home every weekend. Furthermore, they receive full salaries from their previous jobs during their stay in the sanatorium, a practice that allows them to keep contributing to their families and homes and to provide for personal expenses.

While Cuba officially remains committed to quarantining some of those who are infected by HIV, in practice the administration of the sanatorium—now responsible to the Ministry of Health—is increasingly concerned with medical and therapeutic support, behavior modification, and public education. In fact, its goal is directed toward "the integration of patients in society to the fullest extent possible" coupled with holistic health support that is unsurpassed by any Third World country and probably by few developed countries.[30]

Since 1994, furthermore, a new system of outpatient treatment has allowed patients who are deemed *confiable* (trustworthy)— about three quarters of all seropositives—to live at home with their families. Over one hundred have thus far chosen to do so in Havana. This step will also create space in the sanatorium for HIV-positive people who could not previously be accommodated. Still, the economic crisis has begun to affect the diet and even the health care available for outpatients, much as the crisis has afflicted the rest of the population.

In principle, outpatients receive special allocations of protein-rich food; in practice, the food supplement is inadequate and erratic in its distribution. It is much inferior to what they would have received if they had remained in the sanatorium, mainly on account of the problems that plague all food distribution in Havana. Moreover, those who have opted to return home face the same problems of meal preparation that plague all Cubans, compounded by the dilemma of enjoying enriched diets when other family members may be in almost equal need for different reasons. Accordingly, many internees have opted to remain in the sanatoriums. Much as they may have preferred to live at home, living conditions there could rarely match those of the sanatoriums. Yet whatever the difficulties associated with life outside, no former internee has opted to return to the sanatorium. As one of them said, "the freedom to do what you want with your life on a daily basis has no price."

The mind-set of Cuban authorities does not seem to encompass the fact that human rights have a subjective dimension that is as important as the satisfaction of people's material needs. They seem bent on demonstrating that regardless of the criticism directed at the quarantine program, it is still better than any alternative. This determination may be the reason for the termination of the stipend received by former internees within three months of their choice to return home. From then on they are left to their own resources. In addition, like all other Cubans, they must pay out of their own funds for many of the minor drugs that they formerly received free of charge within the sanatorium. Given the unemployment situation in Cuba and the fact that most of the former internees no longer have marketable skills, such a policy seems bureaucratically insensitive. So does the imposition of petty restrictions upon the freedom of those who have decided to remain in the sanatorium. They have to abide completely with the terms that have been set for them by its administrators.[31] In short, although the material conditions and health care they receive are impressive, the fact remains that adults are still subject to the paternalistic edicts of those who are empowered to determine what is best for them.

Fortunately, such restrictions are being increasingly undermined by the continuing transformation of the overall AIDS-prevention program in the light of experience and new information. In Los Cocos, Cuba's main AIDS sanatorium, changes have also occurred in response to the struggles of internees, doctors, and other personnel to humanize and liberalize the nation's AIDS-prevention program. Much has been achieved. Long-term patients have been central to the work of the semiofficial Grupo de Prevención del SIDA (GPSIDA, the AIDS Prevention Group), which emerged from within the sanatorium with the support of Dr. Jorge Pérez Avila, its director, who is highly regarded by most internees in contrast to those who preceded him. Needless to say, members of Proyecto Vida (Project Life), the other AIDS-prevention group, which unlike GPSIDA is openly gay, are much more ambivalent about the administration of the sanatorium, which does not support their activities in part because it does not want AIDS to be equated with homosexuality.[32]

GPSIDA carries out safe-sex and AIDS-awareness education on television, in schools, and other social centers. Its members, who are HIV positive themselves, also undertake the very important work of being the first to interview those who have been newly infected, counseling them with respect to their options (whether they will be interned or not). More and more of those who are HIV positive only enter the sanatoriums when it is necessary because of their health or personal circumstances. In this respect, the deteriorating accommodations and nutrition of most Cubans brought by the economic crisis will surely affect their choices. Some of those who have been newly infected with HIV will still be obliged to enter and remain in the sanatoriums if they do not demonstrate a commitment to the guidelines of safe sex.

Overall, quarantine policies may have improved enormously over the last few years, but the same cannot be said of AIDS-prevention education in general. For a variety of reasons, probably including collective self-deception and the economic crisis, the program has been deficient. There has been little public promotion, condoms have been scarce, and sexual practices have barely changed. Some of the deficiencies are bureaucratic in origin. On the other hand, the scarcity of funding and material resources cannot be overemphasized. It is truly humbling to observe the conditions in which people of undoubted good-will must work in places like the Buró del SIDA (AIDS Center) administered by the National Center for Health Education. Posters and pamphlets are not available because of the scarcity of foreign exchange and the belief that money would be better spent on importing expensive drugs, like AZT, for those already infected or sick. In their place, more effort is being given to using the resources that Cuba has in abundant supply, such as family doctors, local government agencies, and mass organizations. CNES has established branches in every province to coordinate the AIDS support and prevention program.[33] Still, given the massive increase in tourism and the type of tourist increasingly attracted to Havana by its renewed reputation as a sexual mecca, it will be surprising if there is not a big increase in AIDS in the future.

Although internees find it hard to reconcile themselves to quarantine, temporary though it may be, and although most gays have little positive to say about the regime, Cuban gays seem supportive of the AIDS program in general. Most gays are as likely to view the quarantine measures as protections of their own interests as to criticize them as an unnecessary restriction upon individual rights. However repugnant quarantine measures may be to those who espouse liberal conceptions of human rights (not to mention those who until recently have been deprived of the right to assume responsibility for how they live with HIV), the majority of Cubans may have come to see human rights through a different prism. Many and perhaps most Cubans have come to agree that collective social rights may conflict with and even supersede those of the individual. Yet it is also true that they do not have any more opportunity to participate in an *informed* debate about appropriate responses to the AIDS epidemic than they have about the disposition of any other public issue.[34]

One problem in Cuba is that its leadership reacts defensively to any external criticism of its policies. As a result, its programs are often misunderstood abroad and, even worse, are often perpetuated at home when they are not working or not working as well as they might. As Medea Benjamin, an informed but critical supporter of the revolution, has so aptly put it, policy reforms are impeded by "machismo, or what I call the *cojones y más cojones* (balls and more balls) syndrome. Once committed to a certain course of action, there is no pulling back."[35] In the case of AIDS, Fidel Castro has declared in a typically vainglorious response to foreign criticism that Cuba's AIDS-prevention program not only ensures an "almost total guarantee" against its spread but is also "the most humane and the most scientific that can be done, and the most useful for both the infected as well as for the rest of the healthy population."[36] Perhaps so, but that does not change the fact that none of those who initially feared that they were incarcerated for life were consulted about how their lives were being handled.

AIDS is a very complex disease that has evoked more social panic and ideological response than any other modern sickness. Few if any countries should be satisfied with their response to the AIDS epidemic. This applies to the support given to those people who are HIV positive or have AIDS and to the extent and quality of AIDS-prevention education. Cuba should be criticized for its illiberal quarantine program and for its failure to offer sufficient safe-sex education. But in doing so we should also acknowledge the holistic health support that it has offered those who are seropositive or who have AIDS. Cuba has much to teach those countries who do not consider that health is a basic human right and deprive large numbers of their citizens of adequate medical care.

# NINE

## An Imperfect Revolution
## in an Imperfect World

Some people who look at us from afar see us as an immutable society, and make us accountable for what happened five, ten, fifteen years ago, and even for events that never happened. I don't mean to imply by this that the problem [homophobia] has been completely resolved in our country. If that had been the case we would have been the first to solve it in the whole world.

*—Senel Paz*

Let us agree that in recent times coercion against gay groups has considerably diminished and that we are already experiencing more acceptance by the heterosexual part of society. . . . It is a step forward for Cuban gays who, as a result of our hardships, begin to be conscious of our situation.

*—Manifesto of the Gay and Lesbian Association of Cuba,*
*July 28, 1994*

*THE CURRENT* situation of Cuban gays is much more oppressive than the Cuban government is willing to acknowledge. Yet it is also much less restricted than it was a decade ago and much better than many émigré gays and lesbians are willing to concede in public. Gay males are subject to discrimination, but their hardship is more a product of the society's inherited *machista* prejudices and of the regime's generally authoritarian character than it is of any policy singling out homosexuals for persecution. Still, because the government does not permit issues to be raised outside its purview and because its leadership remains *machista* and homophobic (at least at the unconscious level),[1] such prejudices continue to be reproduced in the absence of any serious effort to combat or supplant them.

An overview of the changes in Cuban society since 1959 reveals the extent to which homosexual oppression has diminished. It also indicates what will have to be accomplished if Cuban gays are going to participate successfully in the movement for gay liberation that is such an important feature of the modern world.

The lot of Cuban gays continues to be tied to the overall revolutionary process with all its strengths, defects, and problems. The relative importance that is assigned to the strengths and the defects of the revolution (including the oppression of gays) by commentators in Cuba and elsewhere will depend on their whole social and political worldview. Cuban gays have good grounds to complain and battle against the discriminatory treatment they have endured, and they must be supported in this struggle. Nevertheless, no foreign criticism of the situation of Cuban homosexuals deserves respect if their oppression is treated as a unique fault of the revolutionary regime. It is vital that Cuban homophobia be viewed also in the context of Cuba's traditional machismo and in the comparative context of the contemporary oppression of homosexuals elsewhere in Latin America, where cultural and familial values are similar to Cuba's.

Furthermore, the continuing oppression of Cuban gays must be seen in the context of all the other forces that have helped to deform the revolution. The United States has done everything in its power short of outright military intervention to prevent the revolution from succeeding and thereby offering an alternative economic and social model to the rest of Latin America. Since the

collapse of the Communist bloc, the U.S. government has intensified its efforts to isolate and destroy the Cuban economy. It has
never been able to crush the revolution, but it has built enormous
economic and political barriers to Cuba's free development. In
the bipolar world that prevailed until recently, Cuba had little
choice but to align itself with the Soviet bloc, which was neither
democratic, pluralistic, nor economically dynamic. Soviet influence reinforced the undemocratic tendencies already present in
Cuba's traditional political culture. Cuba's uncritical support for
the USSR included acceptance of the racism, sexism, and not least
the homophobia that permeated the Soviet society and institutions. By applying the Soviet political model to Cuba, Fidel
Castro's regime ensured that these social problems would not be
adequately confronted in Cuba either but rather concealed by its
professed democratic centralism.[2]

Though the creation of a new society has doubtless been limited by external factors, the Castro regime has aggravated Cuba's
problems—be they social, economic, or national in scope—by
preventing many Cubans from lending their energy and creativity to solving them. While most blacks, women, and poor
people have been empowered by the revolution in some areas of
their lives, many others have been alienated by the regime's
authoritarian character. Its triumphal claims regarding the democratic participation of the Cuban people in the resolution of
the country's problems continue, despite the fact that more and
more Cubans are withdrawing their commitment to the revolution and are seeking individual solutions to their problems. Collectivist rhetoric increasingly substitutes for democratic practice
and respect for the opinion of ordinary Cubans. As Carollee Bengelsdorf has noted, this was particularly evident during the 1991
Fourth Party Congress. "The themes of the Congress echoed the
traditional themes of the Cuban Revolution—unity, sacrifice, and
struggle—at a time when, in the face of a very different world
and a radically transformed internal situation, such themes by

themselves rang hollow, and even unbearably archaic, for large sectors of the population, across all ages or political dispositions."[3]

Cuba is not a pluralist or liberal state where personal realization is valued as an end in itself. The government's attitude toward personal, everyday life is that individual fulfillment is a by-product of social solutions to material problems. There is no recognition that personal, everyday needs are as significant for many people as national problems. Nor is there any acknowledgment that individuals discover their diverse needs and potentialities at a personal as well as a collective level in the struggle to liberate and develop their country. The contributions of feminism and other kinds of sexual politics to the reevaluation of the hierarchical practices that have characterized most socialist parties up to now hardly fit the Cuban paradigm of socialist democracy.

The Cuban state is still indisputably homophobic in the broadest sense of the term. It sees nothing positive in homosexuality and tries to contain and marginalize it. At best it views gay males as individuals who can make a contribution to the revolution and the construction of a new society *in spite of* their sexuality. Nevertheless, indirectly and unwittingly, the Cuban revolution has contributed to the eventual liberation of Cuban homosexuals. Cuba's revolutionary regime has been repressive in many ways, but it has also planted the seeds of liberation for gays and others. Its restrictions, diminishing though they may be, continue to be experienced by so many as oppressive precisely because the revolution also unleashed the expectation of personal development, an ambition absent from the lives of those trapped in the miserable material and social conditions that prevail throughout much of Latin America.

Just as liberal capitalism has facilitated the economic development of industrialized countries, expanding material consumption for much of their population, so did state socialism advance the social welfare of much of the population in Communist countries. Where capitalism cultivates possessive individualism, in principle socialism addresses a wider range of human needs. Greater access to health, education, and culture, together with more security and equality, should help to develop human potentialities in all their diversity. This socialist principle remains rational. It should not be invalidated by the fact that in practice Communist regimes have impeded people's full development.

Whether the humanist potential of the Cuban revolution can still be realized will depend upon the government's ability to regenerate an economy that collapsed along with the Communist bloc. Development in this direction will also depend on the willingness of the regime to democratize itself, that is to say, reject the Communist model and replace it with something completely new. There is no clear indication that it has the resources to accomplish the former or the will to do the latter. Cuba's future will also hinge on whether the United States adopts a policy toward Cuba that is consistent with its liberal democratic pretensions and that recognizes the Cuban people's right to determine their future on their own terms. The United States must end the economic blockade and all other initiatives aimed at overthrowing the revolution. Its present policies will not facilitate a peaceful transition to a more democratic society in Cuba. They only contribute to the exacerbation of the hardships of its people.

The effort to separate good from bad in the revolution is very difficult because it has always had a contradictory character. Its strengths and achievements have in many ways been symbiotically tied to its defects and failures. Centralized power, enforced political unity, and mass mobilization played a major role in consolidating the revolution initially, and in defending the country from the continuous efforts to overthrow or undermine it, primarily instigated by the United States. But this defensive effort has also entrenched an authoritarian, bureaucratic political regime that has alienated more and more Cubans.

Initially, the revolution raised the standard of living of most Cubans through its redistributive and egalitarian policies. Cuba's ability to do this was in no small measure strengthened by its links to the industrialized Communist countries, particularly the Soviet Union. But the costs of its command economy have also become increasingly evident. There has been an enormous waste of resources in the pursuit of ill conceived and dogmatically pursued goals. Despite support from the Soviet Union, Cuba had experienced only modest economic growth by the mid-1980s. Especially noticeable was its failure to make much progress in lessening the dependent character of its economy, which was still dominated by the export of raw sugar.

External geopolitical factors, such as the embargo on trade with the United States (which dominated Cuba's economy before 1959) and the distance from its Communist partners, have been major obstacles to Cuba's economic development. So has the enormous cost of military defense necessitated by the ever-present threat of invasion from the United States. Still, even considered together, these obstacles do not account for all Cuba's economic problems. Long-time supporter of the revolution Medea Benjamin has noted: "Cuba's economic problems did not begin with the upheavals in the socialist world. Huge swings in economic policy over the years have caused massive disruptions. . . . In addition to inefficient central planning and coordination, corruption, bureaucracy and low worker productivity have hampered Cuba's development."[4]

Despite these problems, by the mid-1980s Cuba had "developed more than any other Third World country," according to Pablo González Casanova, Mexico's most distinguished social scientist.[5] Janette Habel, author of *Cuba: The Revolution in Peril,* concurs: "It is precisely the spectacular reduction in social inequalities, with the poorest groups benefitting from increases in the lowest wages, full employment and free social services (education, health and housing) which has turned Cuba into the country with the most extraordinary and egalitarian social gains in Latin America."[6] No responsible Latin American specialist questions the enormous progress that Cuba had made by the mid-1980s in all three respects, even though they may differently evaluate the political methods used to achieve such progress.

Conversely, there was and continues to be a steady deterioration in living standards for the majority in the population of the rest of Latin America. Even such an unlikely figure as William Rogers, former U.S. Assistant Secretary of State for Inter-American Affairs, has admitted: "Everywhere [in Latin America]—except among the privileged, whose invulnerability to economic disasters stands in starker contrast every day to the lot of the common people—life has been getting worse year by year."[7]

Until the economic crisis precipitated by the collapse of the Communist camp, the poor and working classes in Cuba were spared the worst consequences of the economic debacle that entrapped the rest of Latin America in the 1980s. To be sure, personal consumption had scarcely risen, but social services were not dismembered as they were elsewhere. In fact, in some sectors such as public health, services were expanded, as in the cases of the family doctor program and the material care extended to people living with AIDS.

Despite Cuba's impressive social development in the 1980s, there was considerable and increasing discontent among sectors of the population who resented the restrictions on their personal lives. This unrest increased when the collapse of communism in the Soviet Union and Eastern Europe led to a sharp drop in living standards. Yet until 1994 the Cuban government refused to recognize let alone respond to this discontent. Demonstrations in Havana and the ensuing flight of tens of thousands of people on makeshift rafts in August 1994 finally prompted the government to initiate reforms, such as the reintroduction of private farmers' markets, which offered hope that the everyday needs of the population might be met in the future.

This vertical style of socialism is the political and economic context for any social change in Cuba. The regime's approach to emancipating women and blacks, prejudice against whom is intermittently acknowledged, suggests the difficulty faced by minorities such as homosexuals who are not even officially recognized as a separate and oppressed group. According to Fidel Castro, "women's oppression" and "racial oppression" have been eliminated by the revolution. As far as he is concerned, since it is indisputable that Cuba already enjoys "complete equality of all citizens,"[8] there is no further need to debate the issue. This attitude is consistent with the way his emphasis upon national unity has always minimized the significance of issues that are not defined as a priority. Castro is determined "to rule out not just the slightest debate, but even the mention of different or contradictory positions."[9]

There is no disputing the fact that more progress has been made in combating institutional discrimination against blacks and women in Cuba than elsewhere in the region. The initial redistribution of wealth and equalization of incomes improved the condition of Afro-Cubans in particular since they accounted for a disproportionate number of the unemployed and poor. The regime has also recognized how much traditional prejudices have impeded the full participation of women in public life, but the acknowledgment of discrimination against blacks has been much less vigorous.[10]

Whether these advances have been rapid enough or whether they meet the various needs of those affected by racial and sexual discrimination is another matter. Since Cuba does not allow truly independent organizations or media to operate, it is difficult to publicize ideas and opinions not sanctioned by the government.[11] The official government position on racist prejudice until very recently was that no such thing existed in Cuba.[12] Any suggestion that Afro-Cubans might experience the contrary was indignantly rejected by Cuban officials. If pressed they would respond with favorable comparisons to racial discrimination in the United

States. Yet anyone familiar with Cuban culture and society can confirm that racial prejudice is widespread and that most people of color are aware of it. Informal discrimination, at the very least, naturally follows.

That this occurs is not surprising. It would be extraordinary if discrimination had been extirpated so easily from Cuban culture after centuries of black slavery and oppression. Failure to acknowledge the extent of racism does not necessarily mean that Cuban leaders do not want to eliminate it. Their denial is a product of their paternalistic belief that all social problems have been (or soon will be) solved by the Communist Party, which has the insight to define these problems even better than the people experiencing them can do.

The same brand of stifling paternalism is applied to women, who, as a group, may have benefited more from the revolution than blacks. Women in the highest echelons of the Party, such as Vilma Espín, leader of the Federation of Cuban Women (FMC), have symbolically represented women in the Politburo.[13] Blacks, in contrast, have never had a representative in that position because there is no equivalent to the FMC for blacks. Yet the FMC is in no sense an autonomous feminist organization that raises issues independently of the Party. As Vilma Espín once emphasized to a foreign interviewer, the FMC is a "feminine, not feminist" organization.[14] A wide range of issues raised by feminists elsewhere are still invisible within Cuban public discourse including rape, assault, incest, and lesbian sexuality.[15] It is as astonishing to be told that these are not concerns of Cuban women as to hear the often-made claims that neither racial discrimination nor homosexual oppression exist in Cuba.

Unwilling to be challenged or to admit any fundamental errors, Fidel Castro continually makes bombastic claims about Cuba's progress that are not only specious but also have the effect of intimidating anyone who might be rash enough to disagree. Thus Cubans and foreign journalists are told that Cuba has the best health system in the world, the best education system, the best social services, the most democratic institutions, least repression, and so forth, while at the same time any alternative viewpoint or dissent is silenced or at least rendered invisible. Prior to 1991, this also extended to any debate about the nature of the Communist camp as a whole.[16] The Cuban version of the history of communism is devoid of reference to internal debates, struggles, and errors. When glasnost emerged in the Soviet Union, Cubans were told that the new politics of openness was not relevant to Cuba since its equivalent had always existed in their country. Nothing could be further from the truth.

Unlike Soviet leader Mikhail Gorbachev, who acknowledged in his 1989 speech to the Cuban National Assembly that "socialism had underestimated the importance of people's immediate interests and had often failed to meet their everyday needs,"[17] the Castro regime initially responded to the crisis that confronted the communist camp by becoming more dogmatic. Instead of facing up to the root causes of Cubans' discontent, the regime urged them in billboards plastered throughout the country to "Defend and Develop the Ideology Created by the Revolution." The regime took this position at its own peril because exhortations from above would not in themselves exorcise the "moral corrosion, apathy and selfishness" to which Castro attributed the collapse of communism elsewhere.[18] As Gorbachev, following Marx, well knew, "it is not the consciousness of people that determines their existence, but, on the contrary, their social existence that determines their consciousness." Castro's pronouncements at the time seemed to contradict this fundamental tenet of Marxism. "Socialism still has many defects and shortcomings, but these deficiencies are not in the system, they're in the people," he said in an interview with a Mexican journalist.[19]

Fidel Castro's paternalistic *caudillismo* and Cuba's lack of a democratic tradition are political problems as serious as the centralized bureaucratic system installed by the Communist Party.

In theory, policies are democratically debated within the Communist Party, the Organs of Popular Power, and within the mass organizations. In practice, this has not really happened because information is denied to the public and opinion cannot be organized around differing visions of the public good. Instead public opinion is orchestrated and manipulated by the leadership. Adolfo Gilly, the prominent Mexican Marxist, has pointed out that the Cuban leaders treat Cubans like children: "the Party and the state will listen like a father does with his children, but they will decide on their behalf what is good for them."[20]

Until recently, almost no information that reflected poorly on the revolution's achievements was made available to the Cuban public in the mass media. Even now that the country is supposedly undergoing "rectification" of its errors and problems, no coherent critical opinion is permitted in the press, radio, or television. Cubans are exposed only to isolated, fragmented criticism of details but never of substance. Only Fidel Castro and those who echo him are allowed to address fundamental policies in public. His seeming candor about Cuba's problems is self-serving since his own authority is never in question. After thirty-three years of "socialist" democracy, power remains as centralized around his person as always. How could it be otherwise in a state where the most common revolutionary slogan, "Comandante en Jefe, Ordene!" (Commander-in-Chief, Command!") is still as operative as ever.[21] His power is unassailable because he is first secretary of the Central Committee of the Communist Party, the president of the Council of State, the president of the Council of Ministers, and the commander-in-chief of the armed forces.

Since the nation's executive power is so highly concentrated, is it any wonder that Cuban leaders respond in a defensive and authoritarian manner to any criticism of their homophobic policies or of most anything else? Typically, the Cuban government has dismissed out of hand "the incredible charge [that] it represses homosexuals. . . . The charges cannot be answered because the lies are so grotesque that decorum prevents us from accepting that they be debated."[22] The questionable political motivation of some who have raised the issue of homosexual oppression in Cuba[23] is no justification for a blanket refusal to allow debate of the issue, particularly in a state that claims to combat all forms of oppression in the name of humanistic socialism. It should be possible to address the issue openly, with all its historically rooted complexity, without making the regime responsible for every manifestation of homophobia in the country. Still, the Cuban government refuses to allow the discussion for much the same reason that it represses free debate about sexism and racism, despite its formal commitment to the advancement of women and blacks. It fears that it would foster division and as a result weaken the cohesion of the revolutionary process—not to mention its own control of the Cuban people.

Despite the fact that Cuban laws are more homophobic than those of Mexico and Costa Rica, the private lives of most Cuban homosexuals, qua homosexuals, are currently organized in ways that are not substantially different from those in the other two countries. Social restrictions are essentially the same. Gays are tolerated so long as they know their place, are discreet about their sexual orientation, and do not contravene gender norms in their public behavior. As in the other two countries, a privileged minority of homosexuals are allowed to excel in their respective fields but the majority remain oppressed.

Cuban gays are particularly affected by lack of privacy because of overcrowded housing and their restricted access to the cheap hotels that elsewhere in Latin America cater to extramarital sex. Yet this problem of Cuban homosexuals is not uniquely theirs. Mexican homosexuals who are either poor or very poor are scarcely better off in this respect. What distinguishes the lives of Cuban gays from those living in prerevolutionary Cuba or elsewhere in Latin America is their complete lack of access to commercial social spaces such as the bars, cantinas, discos, cafés, and bathhouses that serve the needs of gay males in Mexico City and San José.[24] Here again it should be said that only a minority of Mexican and Costa Rican homosexuals can easily afford them or may even want to patronize them. Furthermore, it should not be forgotten that in Latin America the majority of those who engage in same-sex sex (whether sporadic or habitual) do not necessarily identify themselves as homosexuals, let alone want to build their social lives around gay institutions. It is the members of the emerging gay community, composed of homosexuals who define their identities primarily in terms of their sexual orientation, who feel most oppressed in Cuba. They are the ones who are most sensitive to the most negative feature of Cuban public life—that is, the absence, indeed prohibition, of the means to publicize those needs and rights that the state otherwise simply ignores. Still, a sense of perspective is in order. The suppression of civil society in Cuba is an inexcusable wrong that is aggravated by the dictatorial nature of the Castro regime. Yet this defect is characteristic of the Latin American political tradition as a whole. Civil society is only just beginning to manifest itself in Mexico and for that matter is weak in Costa Rica, despite the government's formal liberal democratic character.[25] The kinds of gay institutions that have emerged in industrialized capitalist countries are still very recent phenomena in Mexico and Costa Rica.

Yet gay organizations have begun to emerge in these two countries, and gay or gay-positive viewpoints are increasingly presented in the media—two developments still unheard of in Cuba. On the other hand, Cuban homosexuals, unlike those in Costa Rica and Mexico, are not subject to continuous abuse by the tabloid press. Nor are they hounded by the Catholic Church, whose homophobic campaigns scarcely rise above those of the two nations' yellow press. Nor have they been subjected to the type of witch hunts, city-wide mass arrests, and assassinations that have been orchestrated by local politicians and the police in Mexico and even in Costa Rica.[26] Class limitations on the exercise of civil rights within capitalist societies also should not be overlooked. Working class, economically marginalized, and cross-dressing homosexuals are far from enjoying the "privileges" that are available to the middle- and upper-middle-class homosexuals in the two countries. In many respects upper-class gays benefit from the oppression of the majority of people (heterosexual and homosexual) in Mexico and to a somewhat lesser extent in Costa Rica.[27]

The above comparison does not detract from the fact that, in the past, the Cuban revolutionary state was particularly repressive toward homosexuals. Still, unwittingly, it was also contributing to their future liberation by meeting their basic social needs. The improvements in economic security, social equality, and access to culture that had occurred by the mid-1980s contributed to the growing self-esteem of younger gays. These changes also helped to create a more positive response among the whole population to the growing gay presence within its midst. This was especially true of the generation of young Cubans raised since 1959. The effect of all this was that young gays began to be more at ease with themselves and more open about their homosexuality.

In short, gays and lesbians were among the beneficiaries of the fact that, by the mid-1980s, Cuba had created the first truly modern society in Latin America, that is, one that *potentially* offered the vast majority of the population the opportunity to experience personal fulfilment that was not severely constrained by material deprivation.[28] The new Cuba found expression especially in the large educated population that enjoyed the increasingly rich and diverse cultural life of Havana.

The contradiction between the sociocultural development of Cuba and the outmoded bureaucratic authoritarianism of its regime also contributed to the beginnings of a new gay awareness. The expectations of many gays were heightened by their participation in the revolutionary process, even though the regime did not honor its professed humanism when it came to their own specific needs. As one gay intellectual put it:

> Here in Cuba there are a large number of gays who have ac-
> quired a radical political consciousness as a result of the revo-
> lution, but nevertheless they cannot develop themselves in the
> way they would like because of their situation as homosexuals.
> True, some of those who are exceptionally able and talented
> have done so, but they are a minority.

The easing of legal prohibitions over the years was no longer sufficient for the new generation of young gays and lesbians. For
them and for an increasing number of other young Cubans, tolerance was an inadequate substitute for the government's failure
to recognize and help meet their personal, everyday needs.

Cuba's failure to address the issues that have contributed to the
alienation of homosexuals is due to lack of will and not to the
absence of suitable conditions for doing so. It is simply not true
that the Cuban people—at least those in Havana and the larger
provincial cities—would not accept a gradual and systematic extension of rights to homosexuals if it were coupled with the initiation of a public discourse on gender and sexuality that affirmed
the legitimacy of homosexuality. There is no reason why the developments beginning to occur in Communist Eastern Europe
and in Mexico and Costa Rica could not also take place within
Cuba. It is paternalistic and authoritarian for the Cuban government to contend that the Cuban people are not ready.[29] The
enthusiastic public response to *Fresa y chocolate* and to Pablo Milanés's "El pecado original" demonstrates quite the contrary. The
regime's refusal to acknowledge the needs and rights of homosexuals is really motivated by fear that doing so would undermine
its claim to regulate personal behavior in general.

*MY ANALYSIS* of the gradual improvement in the conditions
facing Cuban homosexuals is essentially based on the circumstances that prevailed before the collapse of the Communist bloc,
which accentuated the social, political, and economic problems
that had begun to surface in Cuba in the mid-1980s. The current

crisis has affected every aspect of Cuban life (including the lives of homosexuals) and has called into question the survival of the regime. Although the Castro government still proclaims that it will not sacrifice any of the revolution's fundamental goals, all of them have been undermined in one way or another, intentionally or not.

The regime's political responses to the crisis have in some ways been contradictory. On the one hand it is still adamant that it will not tolerate any organized challenge to its existence. As has been amply documented by Amnesty International and others, there has been an increase in political repression and in the violation of civil rights since the start of the "special period."[30] On the other hand, the regime has shown signs of recognizing that its attempt to control every aspect of cultural, intellectual, and social activity is ineffectual and counterproductive. There is more latitude for youth and intellectuals to express themselves (but always within boundaries that the regime can ultimately control). Cubans now seem much less intimidated about voicing their needs and criticisms. It is quite possible that the regime may even be trying to allow some discontent to be released at the institutional level, such as within the National Assembly and within mass organizations such as the Union of Young Communists (UJC) and the Confederation of Cuban Workers (CTC). This tolerance is still no more than a safety valve because there is little evidence that these are becoming the kinds of institutions whose members express the diverse, even polarized needs and opinions of the Cuban people. Nor is there much evidence that the Cuban government feels obliged to respond to such testimony.

How have homosexuals fared in these new circumstances? In immediate and direct terms, life has become much harder for them. Like everybody else, they must expend most of their energy on simply getting by—trying to get enough food to eat, finding the means to get to and from work, and recouping the energy to face another day. An added hardship for homosexuals is that they typically depend more than heterosexuals upon access to extra-familial spaces where they can socialize. The drastic cutbacks in food, transportation, and electricity make it much more difficult for them to develop satisfying sexual and emotional relations with other gays. It has instead made them even more dependent upon their families as a means of survival.

From another point of view, however, their situation is more promising than previously. Until recently, the regime effectively prohibited more than a handful of people from congregating in public, and special permits were required for even private house parties. The state has seemingly lost the capacity (and hopefully the will) to control people in this fashion. As a result, there is more opportunity for gays collectively to share their discontent, needs, and aspiration. The foundations for future struggles for gay liberation are tentatively (albeit unconsciously) emerging.

The production and distribution of *Fresa y chocolate* was a landmark for Cuban gays. It unleashed a popular discourse about a culturally tabooed and politically repressed issue that went beyond the confines of the film itself. There have been many great and politically important Cuban films since 1959, but perhaps none has had such immediate social repercussions. Both homosexuals and homosexual oppression became visible in a totally new way. In a sense, the release of the film was also a concession by the regime that its homophobic policies have been counterproductive. The film could not have been made (and certainly not distributed) without the explicit approval of the top leadership.

The film was refreshingly innovative since it portrays the oppression of homosexuals in the context of everyday life in Cuba as it actually is, complete with black market, racial prejudice, *jineteras,* Santería, and urban decay. It is especially significant because the implied criticism of the regime's treatment of gay males in the film is conjoined with a wider critique of other repressive, obtrusive interventions of the Cuban state into everyday life. The oppression of Cuban gays does not stem from the prohibition of homosexuality as such but from the restrictions on everyday life suffered by all Cubans and by gays more acutely. The fact that the film's gay characters are unnecessarily stereotypical of *maricones* is at least counterbalanced by the fact that the only unsympathetic character in the film represents the ugly side of the UJC and of the Ministry of Interior. The film's enthusiastic reception by the Havana public, perhaps based on pity rather than respect because of the way the film framed the victimization of its homosexual characters, offers conclusive proof of the erosion of traditional homophobia within Cuban society but not necessarily within the state. For the Cuban Film Institute, ICAIC, was prepared to support the project of brilliant, apparently heterosexual directors Tomás Gutiérrez Alea and Juan Carlos Tabío, but it simultaneously blocked all attempts by its gay members, some of whom are almost as accomplished, to produce work with gay themes.[31]

*Fresa y chocolate* has not been made in a cultural vacuum. Although the expression of homosexual viewpoints may seem somewhat dated by middle-class gay standards in Mexico City and San José, these are at last beginning to be publicized in Havana. "Gay" literature, public lectures about homosexual novelists and poets, and theatrical productions containing homosexual characters are beginning to form part of the capital's cultural scene and mass culture.[32] The acclaim for recent theatrical productions dealing with homosexuality, such as Virgilio Piñera's *La niñita querida* and Federico García Lorca's *El público,* directed by Carlos Díaz, is surely indicative of a gay-positive sophistication in the Havana theater community comparable to that in Mexico City or San José. Gay intellectuals are making their sensibility felt in public as they have not done for a long time.

In a similar view transvestites are becoming visible in venues that may be more accessible to the majority of gays. Since the outset of the revolution, when "La China Musmet" was prohibited from appearing cross-dressed as a woman, *travestis* have been the homosexuals most subject to repression. They are still harassed by

the police if they appear on the street (just as they are the prime
targets of homosexual oppression in Mexico and Costa Rica), and
for much the same reason, their victimization arises from their association with prostitution, valid or not, as much as from their
renunciation of masculinity. Nevertheless, they have gradually
been allowed to appear on stage, first as individual female imper-
sonators in peso cabarets such as L'Arlequín and the Café de Paris
and in dollar ones such as the Comodoro. Then in 1994 complete
*travesti* shows burst onto the stage of the Alegría theater and in
cultural centers associated with cinemas such as the Fausto and
the Payret in Old Havana. The bureaucracy at the Ministry of
Culture was flummoxed by the new phenomenon, which was already attracting many gays. It decided to have the shows shut
down on the grounds that they were a cover for homosexual gatherings. After the *travestis* organized themselves into groups such
as Trasvisión, formerly "Muñecas Marginadas" (Marginalized
Dolls), and insisted that a commission be established to verify that
they were legitimate artists, the shows were duly reopened.

The authorities were even further taken aback by the dazzling
transvestite spectacle that took place in the Rita Montaner (formerly the América) Theater on February 28, 1995. It was named
Gunila 95 in honor of Guillermo Ginesta, known as Gunila, who
was the first transvestite to have died of AIDS. Nothing like it
had ever taken place in Havana. In addition to every one of the
seventeen hundred seats being occupied, hundreds more people
were jammed into the aisles. Many more were unable to buy seats
or gain entry to the event that had been advertised only through
word of mouth. It was a triumphant night for its participants and
the Proyecto Vida organizers and a memorable one for members
of the incipient gay community, who had come together as they
had done at no time before. The authorities responded by declaring that it was inappropriate for public theaters, such as the Rita
Montaner, to be used for such purposes, despite the fact that the
event had nominally been an AIDS fund-raiser. The response of

Proyecto Vida was to seek alternative venues within Havana and the rest of the country for similar events. And they may yet succeed in transforming Gunila into an annual celebration of transvestite, and implicitly gay, culture, since the attitude of more and more Cubans, gay and straight alike, is that they will do whatever they are not expressly forbidden from doing.

The newfound assertiveness of gays in Havana is as evident as their renewed visibility. It is noticeable in the way gay patrons of cover-charge fiestas react to the unexpected arrival of police. (A permit is required for parties that extend beyond 1 A.M.) There is no panic, as there would have been a few years ago, and much more likelihood of an arrangement that respects the interests of the party goers as much as those of the neighbors. In short, there is less fear of the state and greater awareness of the needs and rights of gay people. Cuban gays may now live in Third World material conditions, but their aspirations are based on a culture that increasingly mirrors the First World.

Still, their growing awareness may have few lasting consequences unless they find the means to organize themselves and consolidate the spaces that have begun to open up to them. Although there is good reason to believe that the vast majority of homosexuals feel oppressed by the regime's homophobia, until recently few gays could conceive of organized action to challenge its policies. Most homosexuals either waited for the moment when they could leave Cuba or resigned themselves to the status quo. Their failure to assert their presence was a reflection of the regime's success in extirpating any expression of civil society within Cuba.

On July 28, 1994, however, the first steps were taken to promote gay and lesbian rights in an organized manner. Despite a torrential downpour, more than a score of young gays and lesbians met in the Parque Almendares, some distance from the usual gay gathering places. No fewer than eighteen signed their names to the founding manifesto that protested the discrimination they had historically suffered.[33] They proclaimed that henceforth July 28 would be celebrated as Cuba's Gay Pride Day. Calling for an end to discrimination, the manifesto declared that:

> The state should not make moral judgments, only juridical and legal rules. Whether or not a couple is heterosexual or homosexual should not affect the standpoint of the state. . . . The question is personal and intimate, it relates strictly to private life. Organizations connected to the state have to accept that this is a social fact and should create policies that do not discriminate in principle against those who are already subject to considerable discrimination, be it with respect to sexual orientation or anything else. [The full text appears in Appendix C.]

The organizers emphasized that their concern was merely to assert gay and lesbian needs and rights and that their action was not to be construed as an expression of political opposition to the regime. Unfortunately, the establishment of the new organization, the Gay and Lesbian Association of Cuba (GLAC), was immediately overshadowed by the street demonstrations and "raft-refugee" crisis a week later. Nevertheless, for a few days word of the new organization spread like wildfire among the gays and lesbians who gathered along the Malecón and at the weekend fiestas. Because of the youth and inexperience of its founders, GLAC was notable more for the enthusiasm than the organizing skills of its members. This was the reason it foundered, a fate that has befallen many attempts to found gay organizations elsewhere in Latin America. Members of the GLAC were not subject to any specific repression, although they, like many other Cubans, lived tense moments that included more street *redadas* in the weeks that followed the refugee exodus in the late summer of 1994.[34] Its remaining members have reorganized themselves into the new Grupo de Acción por la Libertad de Expresión de la Elección Sexual (GALEES) and eventually hope to gain official recognition as the representatives of the gay and lesbian communities in Cuba.

Havana's cultural and intellectual *apertura,* and the gay community that is emerging as a result, are to be welcomed. But these developments will not have real political significance unless they are accompanied by the democratization of the whole country. Central to democratization would be the emergence of civil society, which would enable popular needs and interests to be expressed by independent organizations controlled by their rank-and-file members. Also essential is the dismemberment of the centralized bureaucracy that ultimately stifles all public life in Cuba. Unfortunately, as Janette Habel and Carollee Bengelsdorf (both long-term sympathizers with the revolution) have underlined, such developments still seem remote possibilities.[35]

The regime's fear that individualism and social pluralism might weaken Cubans' collective resolve to resist the United States has fostered a siege-like mentality among its leaders and reinforced its undemocratic, authoritarian character. Rather than risk democratizing the nation's public life, Cuba's leadership has tried to deflect increasing popular discontent by pointing to the defects of the United States, the chaos in the former Soviet Union, and the deepening crisis in the rest of Latin America.

The issue of human rights illustrates the point. That the United States has no more genuine interest in the human rights of Cubans than it has in those of Haitians or racial minorities within its own borders is self-evident. The fact that the professed U.S. concern for human rights in Cuba is demagogic and determined by its underlying goal of overthrowing the regime, however, does not alter the fact that the civil liberties and human rights of individuals should be as important concerns for Cuba as they are anywhere. Fidel Castro is just as demagogic as U.S. politicians are when he claims that "no country has done more for human rights than Cuba."[36] He is downright dishonest when he denies that "anyone has been arrested for criticizing" the Cuban regime or claims that there has been no "single case of a popular demonstration being disbanded by the police."[37] It is repugnant for Castro to argue that independent human-rights organizations are not needed because "in Cuba, it is the state that defends human rights."[38]

From the perspective of gays, not to mention all the other Cubans who feel that their personal opinions and needs are being ignored, the contrary is true. No government can uphold rights unless it is truly accountable to its citizens. A genuine democratization of the Cuban state and the development of civil society are essential to uphold people's rights to participate in public and political life. Democratization does not necessarily require a multiparty system—which has hardly brought liberation to the oppressed either in the United States or in Latin America—but it does entail "the institutionalization of effective decision-making power and control by the popular masses over economic and social choices"[39] and the establishment of nongovernmental organizations and an independent media to monitor the state and inform the public. It also necessitates the separation of party and state and the disappearance of all notions of vanguards and democratic centralism. These Leninist principles have nowhere reflected the interests of the majority of the people, nor have they subjected the state to the scrutiny that is required to avoid irrational and wasteful policies.

An open state and a vibrant civil society are particularly necessary for gays—and even more so for lesbians—since gays are less visible and their oppression is frequently less evident than that of other minorities. In Cuba as elsewhere there is a need for gay organizations to assert and defend their rights because there is no reason to believe that other organizations, let alone broadly based political parties, will have the same motivation to represent those interests.

The challenge confronting Cuba is enormous given the chaotic condition of its economy and the level of public discontent that is now apparent. Yet the crisis is so acute that it also offers Cuba an opportunity to make a "revolution within the revolution." There is little time left. Rapid democratization of Cuban public life is the only choice left to the revolutionary state if it wants to regain popular support and elicit the heroic effort from Cubans that will be required to overcome the forces pitted against the island nation.

Some exploratory steps are being taken in this direction. Since the Fourth Party Congress, more public recognition has been given to diverse opinions within the Party. A dialogue is beginning with Eloy Gutiérrez Menoyo and other leaders of the moderate Cuban opposition in exile. Conferences in Havana and Santiago have been organized to facilitate the exchange of opinion between exiles and Party leaders with regard to the democratization of Cuba.[40] Intellectuals and academics are being given more opportunity to prepare and voice critical appraisals of government policies. The impact of joint enterprises is becoming more evident by the day. So is the presence of the self-employed private sector, whose members can only mushroom with the expulsion of hundreds of thousands of redundant state employees in 1995. Catholicism and Afro-Cuban sects attract more and more adherents, and their leaders become more assertive in voicing their needs and demands. Civil society, an indispensable element of any meaningful modern democracy, is tentatively trying to establish roots within Cuba. But self-evidently, there is no guarantee that they will be allowed to grow in such a way that the Party's present monopoly of power will be imperiled.

Trying to preserve the revolution by repressive—or even worse, military—means could only be a short-term measure that would sacrifice the revolution's ideals and achievements and presage the collapse of the revolutionary state. In the best case, its successor would be a neoliberal regime that would dismantle the social achievements the Cuban people fought so hard for. At worst, the revolution's fall would result in a bloody counter-revolution imposed by the most reactionary elements in Miami and elsewhere in the United States who seek to restore the status quo before Castro.

The majority of homosexuals are highly unlikely to benefit by either turn of events. Only a small minority of Latin Americans, gay or straight, have benefited from the installation of neoliberal regimes, whereas the majority have been impoverished in every respect. Their situation has deteriorated so markedly that the *Latin American Weekly Report,* noted for the objectivity of the information that it passes on to its business and academic readers, has reported on the widespread concern among the region's elites that "the have nots, goaded beyond endurance by hunger, unemployment and the spectacle of others doing very nicely" will erupt in a social explosion throughout the region.[41]

The experience of Nicaragua, where the U.S.-engineered downfall of the Sandinista regime led to its replacement by a neoliberal government, indicates what might lie ahead for Cuban homosexuals if the revolutionary regime is overthrown because of external pressures. In Nicaragua, social advances put in place by the Sandinistas were reversed by the Violeta Chamorro government. Under pressure from the Catholic Church, the government also promptly introduced a new law that punishes with one to three years in prison anyone who "induces, promotes, or practices in scandalous form sexual relations between persons of the same sex."[42] The imposition of a counterrevolutionary regime directed by the Cuban American National Foundation in Miami would be even worse for most Cuban homosexuals, for racism, sexism, and homophobia—not to mention appalling economic inequality— are much more entrenched in the mainstream of the Cuban exile community in Miami than they are in Cuba itself.[43] As Reinaldo Arenas found out when he arrived in Florida, "typical Cuban machismo [had] attained alarming proportions in Miami. . . . [a] place which was like a caricature of Cuba, the worst of Cuba."[44] There is thus no reason to believe that homosexuals any more than women or blacks would in most respects benefit from the overthrow of the revolution, which with all its defects may yet be recognized as having done more for their ultimate liberation than any previous Cuban regime.

This viewpoint may seem somewhat equivocal, and it has to be acknowledged that not all gays in Cuba would agree with it. Still, the fact remains that there have been significant positive changes for Cuban gays. Even more important are signs that a new generation of gays conscious of their rights is currently emerging. Without them gay liberation in the future is not even conceivable.

# APPENDIX A

## Cuban Sexual Values and African Religious Beliefs

### by Tomás Fernández Robaina

It has been argued that there are no basic differences between Spanish and African attitudes toward sexuality, particularly with respect to the *machista* positions contained in the religious creeds or cults of African origin that are practiced in Cuba.

The practice of the Sociedad Secreta Abakuá, which is solely made up of men (known as *abakuás or ñañigos*), is particularly instructive on this matter. The slightest sign of effeminacy, or even the suspicion that a person is homosexual, is enough to deny him membership or prompt his expulsion.

This prohibition does not mean that an *abakuá* cannot have sexual contact with a homosexual, always provided that the *abakuá* acts as the "male" or active partner. It is said that there was a famous *abakuá,* much respected by his hierarchy, who died of old age without ever having been known to have had sex with women while the

Tomás Fernández Robaina is a specialist in Cuban bibliography and in Cuban racial studies. He has written *El negro en Cuba: 1900–1958* (Havana: Editorial de Ciencias Sociales, 1990) (the forthcoming English edition will extend its coverage to 1990); and *Hablen paleros y santeros* (Havana: Editorial de Ciencias Sociales, 1994).

contrary was true with respect to men. The *machista* values upheld by the *ñañigos* are undoubtedly an influence on many men raised in the barrios adjoining the docks of Havana, Matanzas, and Cárdenas in particular; these are the sites of most of the *tierras* or *plantes ñañigos*—that is, the spiritual centers of those who practice *ñañiguismo*. It should be stressed that the Sociedad Secreta Abakuá is not really considered to be a religion or creed as is the case with the Regla de Palo, the Regla de Ocha, and the Regla de Ifá.

The Regla de Palo (originating in the Bantu culture), in contrast to the Sociedad Secreta Abakuá, allows homosexuals some limited participation in its rituals, such as receiving counsel or doing some work for it, but it prohibits them from being initiated and consecrated as *paleros* or priests, whereas the office is open to women. Yet according to recent research, for quite a while there have been some homosexual *paleros,* who are much criticized by conservative and orthodox priests. In general, homosexuals do not feel that the rituals of the Regla de Palo discriminate against them completely. Instead they regard their exclusion from some activities as a practice passed on by custom, tradition, and religious dogma.

On the other hand, the Regla de Ocha or Santería seems to be the most open of all the Afro-Cuban creeds about gender and sexual orientation. That accounts for the visibility of large numbers of male and female homosexuals who have been initiated as *santeros* or who are simply believers. Still, some ritual ceremonies may not be carried out by *santera* women, such as becoming *oriatés* (akin to shamans) and slaughtering four-legged animals. This prohibition does not apply to homosexual *santeros* who play the "active" role. Likewise, effeminate males are not allowed to participate in the playing of Reglamento drums.

Quite recently, the role of women within the Regla de Ocha has begun to be debated in Cuba. In the main, the restrictions on women have been seen not as discrimination but as a show of respect for tradition, so as to preserve and pass on Yoruba beliefs. The same argument is put forward in response to the limited participation of women in the Regla de Ifá (a special cult within Santería) and its total prohibition against homosexuals becoming *babalaos* (or priests). In this respect, a female who has received Kofa, the hand of Orula for women, is only allowed to become an *apetabi,* the wife of the *babalao* who helps prepare the room in which the rituals will take place but who is excluded from the *babalao's* basic initiation ceremonies. Of course there cannot be a rule without an exception. Despite the fact that the Regla de Ifá is so insistent upon prohibiting homosexuals from becoming *babalaos,* homosexuals can receive the hand of Orula and as such they may consult and receive the attention of a good *babalao.* Furthermore, some *babalaos* are known to be homosexual. How can this be? Quite simply they were initiated when they were too young to have acquired a sexual orientation, so that as they grew up and became homosexual they were able to retain their role of *babalao*, regardless of criticism and rejection by conservatives who probably exclude homosexual *babalaos* from their fiestas and initiation ceremonies. It is possible that similar cases can be found within the Sociedad Secreta Abakuá.

The involvement of women and homosexuals requires socioeconomic, sociocultural, and psychological studies that can reveal more about common, highly visible events, such as the possession of believers by *orisha* spirits. Such research might explain why women and homosexuals tend to be possessed by male and female *orishas,* whereas men are rarely possessed by female *orishas,* at least in current times.

Women and homosexuals generally do not recognize that the restrictions on their roles in African creeds constitute discrimination against them. Instead they tend to accept that the role they play is a result of long-standing customs, traditions, and standards of the Regla de Ocha.

According to current research, a conservative orthodox tendency to return to the oldest African rituals has become manifest in the practice of the Regla de Ocha and the Regla de Ifá; some *babalaos* and *santeros* have become very critical of the increase in homosexuality among their adherents. Although attitudes toward homosexuality are contradictory, it is evident that black Cubans are not more homophobic than whites, a fact that is even more true of those blacks who adhere to cultures with African origins. There remains a pressing need for more intensive research that could provide greater understanding of the behavior of women and homosexuals not only in Afro-Cuban religions but also in other religions that have developed in Cuba.

# ₳₱₱Ɇ₦ĐłӾ ฿

## El Pecado Original

### by Pablo Milanés

Dos almas
dos cuerpos
dos hombres que se aman
van a ser expulsados del paraíso
que les tocó vivir.
Ninguno de los dos es un guerrero
que premió sus victorias con mancebos.
Ninguno de los dos tiene riquezas
para calmar la ira de sus jueces.
Ninguno de los dos es presidente.
Ninguno de los dos es un ministro.
Ninguno de los dos es un censor de sus
propios anhelos mutilados . . .
y sienten que pueden en cada mañana
ver su arbol,
su parque,
su sol,

---

Text taken from the program of the inaugural concert of *Orígenes* presented in the Teatro Karl Marx, March 19 and 20, 1994. The translation is by Ian Lumsden.

como tú y como yo . . .
que pueden desgarrarse sus entrañas
en la más dulce intimidad con el amor
así como por siempre hundo mi carne
desesperademente en tu vientre
con amor también
no somos Dios.
No nos equivoquemos otra vez.

## The Original Sin

Two souls
two bodies
two men who love each other
are going to be expelled from the paradise
in which they were destined to live.
Neither of them is a warrior
who celebrated his victories with young men.*
Neither of them has riches
with which to placate the fury of his judges.
Neither of them is president.
Neither of them is a minister.
Neither of them is a censor of his own mutilated desires . . .
and each morning they can feel that they can
see their tree,
their park,
their sun,
like you and I . . .
that they can surrender their hearts
in the most sweet intimacy of love
just as I always sink my flesh
desperately within your womb
also with love
We are not God.
Let us not repeat the mistake.

---

* Mancebos has no exact equivalent in English. It is a literary term on occasion associated with the ephebi of ancient Greece.

# ∏PP∈ND∏X (

## Manifesto of the Gay and
## Lesbian Association of Cuba

Hello,

Today on Thursday, July 28, 1994, slightly after 5.00 P.M., we are meeting here. It is certainly the Cuban gay community's most important day.

Will the Parque Almendares, at present a space for a formal and disguised meeting, become a place that is remembered? Time will tell. It will be responsible for giving us the answer.

The gay and lesbian population is the part of society that throughout *machista* and homophobic history has been most victimized by discrimination and marginalization; our culture has been denounced from generation to generation. Perhaps five years ago there were far more gays and lesbians who hid their real sexual identity as the only way to find a space among heterosexuals, the majority of society who were considered "normal" and who condemned and obscured the existence of any sexual orientation that was different—condemning with their accusatory finger thousands of human beings who only sought to have their rightful place in society.

Obscurity was the degrading condition to which we were sentenced:

lack of space

lack of meeting places

lack of freedom

lack of means of expression.

Remember for example the homosexual victims of the UMAP who were despotically sent to work camps on the grounds that they were antisocial, the constant raids on gays in public spaces for "disturbing the public peace" when they were only trying to have fun. Remember the gays and lesbians who have had to live part of their lives in jail, accused of transgressions they never committed; the numerous university students expelled from their faculties for having long hair, for not dressing "according to socialist morality," for using earrings, for dressing in an effeminate way, or simply for sexually desiring someone of the same sex, even though it could never be proven. Let us also remember the outrages and discrimination committed against homosexuals in other parts of the world. These facts can serve to make us reflect upon the extent to which we have been humiliated, the extremes to which our natural rights to exist in liberty have been denied by the homophobic and *machista* society in which we live. But today darkness begins to give way to light—light that is necessary to show the way; and light that we alone have the responsibility of ensuring will never again be extinguished.

Today we have not met here in order to say who is responsible for all that has happened to us over time. Today is the moment to define the issues necessary to achieve social recognition; it is the moment to unite ourselves behind one national voice that demands our rights with strength and dignity.

Let us agree that in recent times coercion against gay groups has considerably diminished and that we are already experiencing more acceptance by the heterosexual part of society. The gay and lesbian world already has a small space, "a brief reference" in the means of communication, in cultural institutions (film, theater, literature), in the streets in which we share our love, in Saturday night fiestas. And this is important; it is a step forward for Cuban gays who, as a result of our hardships, begin to be conscious of our situation. That is why we are here, to defy censorship, to defy any distorted information that condemns us.

Our prospects depend upon ourselves and on our own capacity to demand our rights. Society may marginalize us; but we have to offer an image that we are people who have virtues and defects, just as anybody else, that the choice of being gay, lesbian, or heterosexual does not imply anything else; this is and will be our battlefield to believe in ourselves and for society to believe in us.

For how long must we endure being treated as if we are sick or pathological?

Why should we allow them to accuse us of being antisocial?

For how long must we be an object of discrimination, of prejudices, of abuses, of blackmail, of repression, of phobias?

Let us show them that we are not sick, that we are not antisocial, and let us struggle against discrimination, abuses, and blackmail.

For the first time we have consciously gathered here in unity. Being afraid can only help the ideas of our detractors.

Being afraid is absurd if we want to defend our rights.

It is necessary to act proudly, to make a daring gesture; it is necessary to act with courage. We will struggle without rest and will conceive our struggle as one of cultural and personal liberation.

Politics are inevitable in any struggle, but it is not what unites us here; let us leave that to the faithful.

It is more important to search for the freedom of which we have dreamt. Ending homophobia is fundamental; it is essential to destroy *sidafobia* [the fear of AIDS], to stop this disease, whatever it may cost, and let us show loving solidarity with those who are seropositive, so that they will feel that we are on their side, so that they will know that our struggle is their struggle and on their behalf.

It is necessary to obtain antidiscriminatory measures that will guarantee people who live together the same rights that any couple is entitled to.

The state should not make moral judgments, only juridical and legal rules. Whether or not a couple is heterosexual or homosexual should not affect the standpoint of the state . . . that is our belief.

If society can help the lives of individuals, why should it make them more difficult?

The question is personal and intimate, it relates strictly to private life. Organizations connected to the state have to accept that this is a social fact and should create policies that do not discriminate in principle against those who are already subject to considerable discrimination, be it with respect to sexual orientation or anything else.

Every individual's sexual freedom should be respected. The means to enjoy such freedom should be established.

It must be understood that the sexuality of our species has no natural limits.

There is much to say but much more to do. Action is power.

Let us defend the right to sexual freedom.

Let us unite with strength.

This will be our first triumph and the day that we will celebrate.

Let us name the 28th of July "Gay Pride Day of Cuba" and let us celebrate it every year.

On behalf of gay and lesbian rights,
                        Liberation.

                    The Organizers.

# NOTES

## Introduction

1. *Homosexuality, Society and the State in Mexico/Homosexualidad, sociedad y estado en México* (Toronto/Mexico City: Canadian Gay Archives/Solediciones, 1991).

2. *Manchester Guardian Weekly,* December 19, 1993.

3. Armando Valladares, *The Prison Memoirs of Armando Valladares* (New York: Alfred Knopf, 1986), p. 358.

4. Duncan Green, *Faces of Latin America* (London: Latin American Bureau, 1991), p. 144.

5. See Jeffrey Weeks, *Coming Out: Homosexual Politics in Britain from the Nineteenth Century to the Present* (London: Quartet Books, 1977), p. 235; and Barry Adam, *The Rise of a Gay and Lesbian Movement* (Boston: Twayne, 1987), p. 173.

6. Allen Young, *Gays under the Cuban Revolution* (San Francisco: Grey Fox Press, 1981).

7. The film's script is contained in Néstor Almendros and Orlando Jiménez-Leal, eds., *Conducta impropia* (Madrid: Editorial Playor, 1984).

8. Aart Hendriks, Rob Tielman, and Evert van der Veen, *The Third Pink Book: A Global View of Lesbian and Gay Liberation and Oppression* (Buffalo: Prometheus Books, 1993), p. 272.

9. Israel Vazquez, "Our Man in Havana," *Lexicon* (Toronto), May 1993.

10. See Chris Bull and Jorge Morales, "AIDS Crisis in Cuba," *The Advocate,* January 24, 1995. Carlos Otero, the seventeen-year-old gay resident in the AIDS sanatorium who was allegedly interviewed by the authors, denied everything that had been attributed to him in the article when I interviewed him in the privacy of his home in Old Havana in April 1995. So did his mother.

11. Sheldon Liss, *Fidel! Castro's Political and Social Thought* (Boulder, Colo.: Westview Press, 1994), p. 16.

12. See Carlos A. Heredia and Mary E. Purcell, *The Polarization of Mexican Society: A Grass Roots View of World Bank Economic Adjustment Policies* (Washington, D.C.: Development Gap, 1994), p. 10

13. Lourdes Casal, "Race Relations in Contemporary Cuba," in Philip Brenner, William M. LeoGrande, Donna Rich and Daniel Siegel, eds., *The Cuban Reader: The Making of a Revolutionary Society* (New York: Grove Press, 1989), p. 484.

## Chapter One

1. See Chapter Two for a discussion of the distinctive character of Cuban religious beliefs and practices, which permit Cubans to make vows simultaneously to both Santería deities and Catholic saints.

2. Philip Elliot Slater, *The Pursuit of Loneliness: American Culture at the Breaking Point* (Boston: Beacon Press, 1970).

3. For example, there is no possible excuse for the fact that in such a fertile country there should still be a serious shortage of fresh fruits and vegetables. Its persistence, indeed aggravation over time, is the result of Fidel Castro's dogmatic refusal to countenance meaningful incentives for private farmers and markets to sell their produce directly to consumers. When the policy was at long last reversed in the fall of 1994, as part of a series of market reforms, Fidel Castro was notably silent, in contrast to his direct intervention in the Fourth Communist Party Congress in 1991 to prevent a similar position from being adopted.

4. See Andrew Zimbalist, "Teetering on the Brink: Cuba's Current Economic and Political Crisis," *Journal of Latin American Studies* 24, no. 2 (May 1992).

5. See Sandra Levinson, "Gallup Poll in Cuba: First Independent Poll in More than Thirty Years," *Cuba Update* 16, no. 1 (1995), p. 9.

6. See Saul Landau, "After Castro," *Mother Jones* 14, no. 6 (July/August 1989), p. 23.

7. The increase in sexually transmitted diseases (STDs) that has occurred in Cuba since the mid-1960s suggests a change in sexual mores. Gonorrhea and syphilis have reportedly increased from 8.9 and 29.7 cases per 100,000 population in 1965 to 381.9 and 82.2 in 1989. See Sarah Santana, Lily Faas, and Karen Wald, "Human Immunodeficiency Virus in Cuba: The Public Health Response of a Third World Country," *International Journal of Health Services* 21, no. 3 (1991), p. 515.

8. See Natividad Guerrero, *La educación sexual en la joven generación* (Sex education in the young generation) (Havana: Editora Política, 1985), p. 30.

9. See Monika Krause, *Algunos temas fundamentales sobre educación sexual* (Some fundamental themes concerning sex education) (Havana: Editorial Científico-Técnica, 1985), p. 11.

10. Ibid., p. 26. Birth rates have since begun to fall from 128 per thousand teenagers in 1980 to less than 80 per thousand in 1988. Interview with Monika Krause, February 2, 1989. See also Alina Perera Robio, "Madres con caras de niñas" (Mothers with the faces of children), *Sexo Sentido* (Edición especial, Séptimo Congreso Latinoamericano de Sexología y Educación Sexual), November 14 to 18, 1994.

11. "Machismo" is a term that has only recently become popularized in Cuba. Even though it is in some respects synonymous with sexism, it really means celebration of conventional masculinity, of the values associated with being a male *(macho)*. Cubans do not necessarily associate the term "macho" with oppression of women, nor is the term necessarily used in a pejorative sense. The female counterpart of *macho* is *hembra:* the celebration of womanly attributes is known as *hembrismo.*

12. See the survey of sexual attitudes among university students carried out by the Centro de Estudios de la Juventud. Eighty-one percent favored premarital sex. *Juventud Rebelde,* July 14, 1985.

13. No pun intended, notwithstanding the fact that *mariposa* (butterfly), *pájaro* (bird), and *pato* (duck) are among the countless pejorative terms for homosexuals in Cuba.

## Chapter Two

1. *Maricón* is a derogatory term used by straight people. *Entendido* tends to be the self-description of most homosexuals (as to a lesser extent "gay" is among the younger educated crowd in Havana). Nevertheless, *entendidos* also use the term. It often reflects internalized homophobia, but sometimes it is used in a more defiant sense. A more common and less pejorative term used by homosexuals to refer to *maricones* is *loca,* a term that is also problematic given that it literally means a crazy woman.

2. Even today, it is commonplace for ostensibly heterosexual men, such as rural military recruits, to have sex with *maricones.* Although material compensation may be an important consideration, as often as not it is also a question of *faute de mieux* since such recruits tend to be looked down upon by Havana women on account of their rural appearance and manners.

3. The term *bugarrón* is applied to males who play the role of inserter in anal intercourse but who do not consider themselves to be homosexual. This can be a bit confusing since the term sounds as if it may derive from *buga,* which in Mexico is reserved for those who are strictly straight. In Cuba, homosexuals use *normal* to refer to heterosexuals, or pejoratively, *cheo.*

4. Reinaldo Arenas, *Before Night Falls,* trans. Dolores M. Koch (New York: Viking Press, 1993), p. 108.

5. The notion of *pudor* seems peculiarly Spanish. It conveys shame mingled with modesty as well as the censure of open reference to anything deemed indecent.

6. Until 1979, Cuba's penal code (Article 573 of the prerevolutionary Social Defense Code) actually prohibited males from being in public in their undershirts, a practice equated with immoral behavior. This prohibition continues in contemporary Cuba, inasmuch as the quasi-official *Manual de educación formal* (Guide to proper manners) also insists that it is incorrect to appear bare chested even on the doorstep of one's own house (3d edition [Havana: Ministerio de Educación, 1983], pp. 87–88. *Pudor* in relation to nudity is also reflected in the reluctance of many homosexual males to reveal themselves completely undressed before or after sex. Underpants are kept on until the last possible moment and replaced as soon as possible.

7. Mirta Mulhare de la Torre, "Sexual Ideology in Pre-Castro Cuba: A Cultural Analysis" (Ph.D. diss., University of Pittsburgh, 1969), p. 141.

8. Ibid., p. 142.

9. Ibid.

10. According to Roger Lancaster, "It is not that homophobia is more intense in a culture of machismo but that it is of a different sort altogether. . . . An altogether different word is necessary to identify the praxis implicit in machismo, whereby men may simultaneously desire to use, fear being used by and stigmatize other men" ("Subject Honor and Object Shame: The Construction of Male Homosexuality in Nicaragua," *Ethnology* 27, no. 2 [April, 1988], p. 121).

11. Arenas, *Before Night Falls,* p. 19. Reinaldo Arenas's lyrical depiction of the rampant libido of Oriente campesinos, including that of young boys directed toward farmyard birds and animals, has been supported in interviews that I have conducted with young gays who grew up in the Holguín countryside.

12. Ibid., p. 48.

13. Virgilio Piñera, "La vida tal cual" (That's life), *Unión* 3, no. 10 (April–June 1990), p. 27. The English translation of the original Spanish text is my own as are all subsequent translations unless the translator's name is given.

14. See Tomás Fernández Robaina, *Recuerdos secretos de dos mujeres públicas* (Secret recollections of two public women) (Havana: Editorial Letras Cubanas, 1983), p. 62.

15. See Benjamín de Céspedes, *La prostitución en la ciudad de la Habana* (Havana: Establecimiento Tipográfico O'Reilly, 1888), pp. 190–91; Pedro Giralt, *El amor y la prostitución* (Havana: n.p., 1889), pp. 84–85; and *La cebolla* (Havana), September 9, 1888.

16. Piñera, "La vida tal cual," p. 23.

17. See Ana María Simo and Reinaldo García Ramos, "Hablemos claro," (Let's speak clearly), *Mariel* 2, no. 5 (Spring 1984). See also Guillermo Cabrera Infante, "Mordidas del caimán barbudo," *Mea Cuba* (Mexico City: Vuelta, 1993).

18. Lourdes Arguelles and B. Ruby Rich, "Homosexuality, Homophobia and Revolution: Notes towards an Understanding of the Cuban Lesbian and Gay Male Experience," Part 1, *Signs* 9, no. 4 (Summer 1984), p. 687.

19. Isabel Larguía and John Dumoulin, "La mujer en el desarrollo: Estrategía y experiencia de la revolución cubana" (Women in development: Strategy and experience of the Cuban revolution), *Casa de las Américas* 25, no. 149 (March/April 1985), p. 39.

20. Wyatt MacGaffey and Clifford R. Barnett, *Cuba: Its People, Its Society, Its Culture* (New Haven: HRAF Press, 1962), p. 54.

21. Mariana Ravenet Ramírez, Niurka Pérez Rojas, and Marta Toledo Fraga, *La mujer rural y urbana: Estudios de casos* (Rural and urban women: Case Studies) (Havana: Editorial de Ciencias Sociales, 1989), p. 63–64.

22. *Piropos* are compliments, typically accompanied by insistent staring and on occasion physical molestation of women out in public. Although ideally witty, they are invariably sexist and sometimes vulgar. Males will frequently persist with their *piropos* until they have evoked a response from the female, even if it is merely a gesture of discomfort. However, *piropos* may not be seen by many Cuban women in quite the same way as they are by some North American feminists. Some foreign female residents insist that it is more honest—a game of innocent flirting—as opposed to what they experience as leering by males in cultures where *piropos* are unacceptable.

23. See Marifeli Pérez-Stable, "Cuban Women and the Struggle for 'Conciencia,' " *Cuban Studies,* no. 17 (1987) pp. 53–54.

24. Mulhare de la Torre, "Sexual Ideology in Pre-Castro Cuba," p. 143.

25. See Elsa Gutiérrez Baró, *Mensajes a los padres* (Messages for the parents) (Havana: Editorial Científico-Técnica, 1985), p. 71.

26. *Manual de educación formal,* pp. 64–65.

27. The extent of Spanish influence can be gauged by the fact that in the first three decades of the twentieth century 750,000 immigrants arrived from Spain. Though not all remained, they must have had a considerable impact upon the island given that the total population of Cuba was less than four million in 1931. Raúl Hernández Castellón, *La revolución demográfica en Cuba* (Havana: Editorial de Ciencias Sociales, 1988), p. 194.

28. Miguel Barnet, *Biografía de un cimarrón* (The biography of a runaway slave) (Havana: Bolsilibros Unión, 1967), p. 140.

29. Vertena Martínez-Alier, *Marriage, Class and Color in Nineteenth Century Cuba: A Study of Racial Attitudes and Sexual Values in a Slave Society* (London: Cambridge University Press, 1974), p. 2.

30. Lourdes Casal, "Race Relations in Contemporary Cuba," in Philip Brenner, William M. LeoGrande, Donna Rich, and Daniel Siegel, eds., *The Cuban Reader: The Making of a Revolutionary Society* (New York: Grove Press, 1989), p. 476.

31. Juan René Betancourt drew attention to this surprising fact in "Fidel Castro and National Integration," *Bohemia,* February 15, 1959. As if in reply, Castro addressed the issue of racism for the first time on March 22, 1959 (*Hoy,* March 24, 1959). See the forthcoming expanded English edition of Tomás Fernández Robaina, *El negro en Cuba: Apuntes para la lucha contra la discriminación racial en Cuba, 1900–1958.* (Blacks in Cuba: Notes for the struggle against racial discrimination in Cuba, 1990–1958) (Havana: Editorial de Ciencias Sociales, 1990), which will extend coverage to 1990. This curious omission should not be construed to suggest that he is any way a racist, for Castro was actively involved in antiracist struggles at university.

32. *Marianismo* refers to the cult of the asexual, self-abnegating qualities associated with the Virgin Mary and by extension with the Virgin of Guadalupe. *Hembrismo* is derived from *hembra,* a term used colloquially for women that properly refers to the female of any species of animal. *Hembrismo* is the counterpart of machismo in its celebration of female attributes. It has no association with feminism as understood in

North America. A popular *hembrista* saying is "soy tan hembra como tú macho" (I am as much a woman as you are a man).

33. Cited by Fernando Ortiz, *Historia de una pelea cubana contra los demonios* (History of a Cuban battle with the demons) (Santa Clara: Universidad Central de Las Villas, 1959), p. 510.

34. See Frei Betto, *Fidel y la religión: Conversaciones con Frei Betto* (Havana: Oficina de Publicaciones de Estado, 1985), an interview that is typical of the means by which Fidel Castro periodically orchestrates his public image at home and abroad.

35. Likewise, in the last few years the regime has begun to acknowledge the significance of *santero* traditions. Perhaps it has had no alternative, given that they have become ever more popular among the Cuban people.

36. See Rafael Carrasco, *Inquisición y represión sexual en Valencia: Historia de los Sodomitas (1565–1785)* (Barcelona: Laertes, 1985), pp. 30–50.

37. Cited by Francisco Guerra, *The Pre-Columbian Mind: A Study into the Aberrant Nature of Sexual Drives, Drugs Affecting behaviour, and the Attitude towards Life and Death, with a Survey of Psychotherapy, in Pre-Columbian America* (London: Seminar Press, 1971), p. 53.

38. See Diana Iznaga, introduction to Fernando Ortiz, *Los negros curros* (The black dandies) (Havana: Editorial de Ciencias Sociales, 1986), pp. xviii–xix.

39. Ortiz, *Historia de una pelea,* p. 374.

40. Monika Krause, interview, April 28, 1989.

41. Victoriano Domingo Loren, *Los homosexuales frente a la ley; Los juristas opinan* (Homosexuals before the law: The jurists opine) (Barcelona: Plaza y Janes, 1977), p. 11.

42. Marc Daniel, "Arab Civilization and Male Love," *Gay Sunshine* (San Francisco) no. 32 (Spring 1977), p. 3.

43. Ibid., p. 10. See also Maarten Schild, "Islam," in Arno Schmitt and Jehoeda Sofer, eds., *Sexuality and Eroticism among Males in Moslem Societies* (New York: Haworth Press, 1992), pp. 182–83.

44. Vern L. Bullough, *Sexual Variance in Society and History* (Chicago: University of Chicago Press, 1979), p. 238.

45. See the extensive commentary by Tomás Fernández Robaina in Appendix A.

46. Enrique Sosa, *El carabalí* (Havana: Editorial Letras Cubanas, 1984), pp. 50–51. "Complying with a rigid *machista* ethos, *[abakuá]* members are not allowed to sleep with their backs toward their wives, nor ever allowed to have intercourse without the man being on top of

the woman and being the only one who is allowed to be active": Manuel
Martínez Casanova and Nery Gómez Abréu, *La sociedad secreta abakuá*
(Santa Clara: Universidad Central de Las Villas, n.d.), pp. 16–17.

47. Fernando Ortiz, *Entre cubanos: Psicología tropical* (Among
Cubans: Tropical psychology) (Havana: Editorial de Ciencias Sociales,
1987), pp. 88–89.

48. See Betto, *Fidel y la religión,* pp. 103–4.

49. Quite consistently, the Spaniards also used the fact that homosexuality was attributed (among a host of other defects and vices) to the indentured Chinese laborers who were brought in during the mid-nineteenth century to justify their appalling treatment. See Hugh Thomas,
*Cuba: The Pursuit of Freedom* (New York: Harper and Row, 1971), p. 188.

50. José Agustín Caballero y Rodríguez de la Barrera, "Exposición
relativa al matrimonio entre esclavos y otros asuntos relacionados con la
población de la isla, así como algunos aspectos de la vida sexual de los esclavos" (Treatise relating to marriage between slaves and other matters
concerning the population of the island, as well as some aspects of the
sex life of the slaves). C. M. Morales no. 9, Biblioteca Nacional José
Martí, Havana.

51. Fernando Ortiz, *Los negros esclavos* (the black slaves) (Havana:
Editorial de Ciencias Sociales, 1987), pp. 28, 70. Although many of Ortiz's early views were undoubtedly racist, such as these remarks that
were originally published in 1916, they changed over the years.

52. See Manuel Moreno Fraginals, *El ingenio: Complejo económico social cubano del azúcar,* vol. 2 (The mill: The economic and social complex
of sugar in Cuba) (Havana: Editorial de Ciencias Sociales, 1978), pp. 38–57.

53. Julio Le Riverend, "El esclavismo en Cuba: Perspectivas del
tema," in Colectivo de autores, *Temas acerca de la esclavitud* (Havana:
Editorial de Ciencias Sociales, 1988), p. 20.

54. The fusion of homophobic with racist prejudices was not only directed against blacks. For example, Benjamín de Céspedes described his
revulsion at the sight of "drugged pederasts" belonging to the "miserable
. . . degenerate race" of Chinese in his account of prostitution in Havana
(*La prostitución en la ciudad de la Habana,* pp. 198–202). Fernando Ortiz
added that "homosexual vices and other refined corruptions" were characteristic of the "yellow race" (*Los Negros Esclavos,* p. 28).

55. Barnet, *Biografiá de un cimarrón,* p. 41.

56. Martínez-Alier, *Marriage, Class and Color,* p. 118.

57. Benjamín de Céspedes makes a point of noting that the "grotesquely effeminate pederasts" who abounded in old Havana in the late

nineteenth century were as likely to be black or *mulato* as white (*La prostitución en la ciudad de La Habana,* p. 190).

58. Senel Paz, "El lobo, el bosque y el hombre nuevo" (The wolf, the woods, and the new man) (Mexico City: Ediciones Era, 1991), p. 36.

59. Larguía and Dumoulin, "La mujer en el desarrollo," p. 38.

60. Ibid., p. 39.

61. Lowry Nelson, *Rural Cuba* (Minneapolis: University of Minnesota Press, 1950), p. 195.

62. Thomas, *Cuba,* p. 188.

63. See Hernández Castellón, *La revolución demográfica,* pp. 114–16.

64. *El Mundo,* April 15, 1965.

## Chapter Three

1. Exceptions to this generalization would include the poorest black people. They were most affected by the legacy of slavery, which had broken up families and encouraged changing sexual partners. See Manuel Moreno Fraginals, *El ingenio,* p. 45.

2. Mulhare de la Torre, "Sexual Ideology in Pre-Castro Cuba," p. 126.

3. However, the term *antisocial* only became current after the revolutionary regime had begun to use it as a way of labeling homosexuals as undesirable people.

4. See Fernández Robaina, *Recuerdos secretos,* pp. 16, 61.

5. See Carlos Franqui, *Family Portrait with Fidel* (New York: Random House, 1984), pp. 138–41, and Guillermo Cabrera Infante, in Almendros and Jiménez-Leal, *Conducta impropia,* pp. 134–35.

6. Franqui, *Family Portrait,* p. 139.

7. Ibid., p. 141.

8. See Guillermo Cabrera Infante, *Mea Cuba,* p. 109.

9. See Juan Goytisolo, *En los reinos de Taifa* (In the kingdom of Taifa) (Barcelona: Editorial Seix Barral, 1986), p. 175.

10. Cited by Carlos Franqui in Almendros and Jiménez-Leal, *Conducta impropia,* p. 85.

11. *Revolución,* December 2, 1961.

12. Cited by Janette Habel, *Cuba: The Revolution in Peril* (London: Verso, 1991), p. 93.

13. The role of the former militants of the PSP in the formulation of the new homophobic policies has yet to be clarified. It is possible that

the initial mystification of the Soviet Union, rather than the specific influence of the PSP members, was the determining factor, for in reality the PSP included many of the most sophisticated people in prerevolutionary Cuba. Carlos Franqui notes that two of its most prominent members, Carlos Rafael Rodríguez and Blas Roca (among many others), were disturbed by the adoption of these policies (*Family Portrait,* p. 140).

14. See Ben de Jong, "An Intolerable Kind of Moral Degeneration: Homosexuality in the Soviet Union," in *IGA Pink Book, 1985: A Global View of Lesbian and Gay Oppression and Liberation* (Amsterdam: COC, 1985), p. 79.

15. See John Lauritsen and David Thorstad, *The Early Homosexual Rights Movement (1864–1935)* (New York: Times Change Press, 1974), pp. 62–70, for an account of the regulation of homosexuality during the early years of the Soviet revolution.

16. See, for example, José Agustín Martínez, *El homosexualismo y su tratamiento* (Mexico City: Ediciones Botas, 1947). See also Luis Salas, *Social Control and Deviance in Cuba* (New York: Praeger, 1979), chapter 4.

17. *El Mundo,* April 15, 1965.

18. José Yglesias, *In the Fist of the Revolution: Life in a Cuban Country Town* (New York: Pantheon Books, 1968), p. 275.

19. Interview with Armando Suárez del Villar, one of the few prominent Cubans (who include Jaime Ortega and Pablo Milanés) who have remained in the country even though they spent time in the UMAP camps. April 15, 1995.

20. Samuel Feijoo, cited by Henk van de Boogaard and Kathelijne van Kammen, "Cuba: We Cannot Jump over Our Own Shadow," *IGA Pink Book, 1985,* p. 34.

21. Cited by Juan Goytisolo in Almendros and Jiménez-Leal, *Conducta impropia, p. 85.*

22. Ernesto Cardenal, *En Cuba* (Buenos Aires: Ediciones Lohlé, 1972), pp. 262–63.

23. One of Ernesto Cardenal's interviewees, in fact, suggested that Jehovah's Witnesses were the worst-treated inmates in the UMAP camps (*En Cuba,* p. 263).

24. Interview with Armando Suárez del Villa, April 15, 1995.

25. Young, *Gays under the Cuban Revolution,* p. 26.

26. See Jorge Domínguez, *Cuba: Order and Revolution* (Cambridge: Harvard University Press, 1978), p. 357.

27. This account is based on interviews with Raquel Revuelta and Armando Suárez, April 15, 1995.

28. Cabrera Moreno's lyrical depiction of peasant militias and Raúl Martínez's celebrated pop-art portrayal of Che Guevara now occupy a prominent place in the Museo Nacional de Bellas Artes in Havana.

29. Almendros and Jiménez-Leal, *Conducta impropia,* p. 88.

30. Ministerio de Educación, *Memorias del primer congreso nacional de educación y cultura* (Havana: Instituto Cubano del Libro, 1971), p. 200.

31. Information provided by one of Arenas's closest friends in Cuba.

32. *Bohemia,* April 11, 1969.

33. Ministerio de Educación, *Memorias,* p. 203.

34. According to one delegate who wished to remain anonymous, people like Celia Sánchez, Haydée Santamaría, and Alfredo Guevara struggled valiantly to resist homophobes like José Llanusa and José Ramón Fernández, who dominated the field of education during that period. Since Fidel Castro was apparently more absorbed by other matters at the time, hard-line party ideologues like Tony Pérez and Belarmino Castilla also had undue influence.

35. Ian Daniels, "Interview with Ana María Simo," *Torch* (New York), issue dated December 15, 1984/January 14, 1985.

36. His experience and that of countless others was vividly captured in the portrayal of Diego, the gay protagonist in Senel Paz's short story "El lobo, el bosque y el hombre nuevo," and in its screen adaptation, *Fresa y Chocolate.*

37. See van de Boogaard and van Kammen, "Cuba: We Cannot Jump over Our Own Shadow," p. 32.

38. *Granma,* April 10, 1980.

39. *Granma,* May 2, 1980.

40. *Granma,* April 7, 1980.

41. Cited by Young, *Gays under the Cuban Revolution,* p. 105.

42. There have been intermittent and very rare criticisms of homosexuals in the United States contained in broader denunciations of American society, as was the case in a *Granma* editorial on AIDS in New York (April 3, 1983).

43. Sexuality, including homosexuality, is regulated in every society in the sense that rules, either codified or enforced by custom, limit the way it can be expressed and practiced—for example, age of consent, sexual violation, definitions of what constitutes "indecent" public sex, and so forth.

## Chapter Four

1. The scope of the Law of Social Dangerousness, which has been applied against Cuban homosexuals, may have been amplified under the current Cuban regime, but its original breadth is no invention of the revolutionary government. Juan Goytisolo, the Spanish novelist who has been a harsh critic of the Cuban government in other respects, has pointed out that the Spanish Ley de Peligrosidad Social "indiscriminately persecute[d] vagabonds, gypsies, homosexuals, drug-addicts and other abnormal species." See "Remedios de la concupiscencia según Fray Tierno" (Remedies for concupiscence according to Friar Tender), *La Cultura en México (suplemento de Siempre)* (Mexico City), August 9, 1978, pp. 7–8. The law was only removed from the Spanish penal code in 1978.

2. See Victoriano Domingo Loren, *Los homosexuales frente a la ley,* pp. 43–50.

3. See Article 378 (15) of Costa Rica's Penal Code.

4. *Indicaciones para la imposición de multas por contravenciones* (Regulations for the imposition of misdemeanor fines), Decreto 141 (1p) (Havana: Ministerio del Interior, 1988) p. 34.

5. *Second ILGA Pink Book: A Global View of Lesbian and Gay Liberation and Oppression,* Utrecht Series on Gay and Lesbian Studies no. 12 (Utrecht: Interdisciplinary Gay and Lesbian Studies Department, Utrecht University, 1988), p. 202.

6. The use of the *present* tense and of generalizations is unfortunate because they give a very misleading impression of the current treatment of homosexuals. There are no public records of how many homosexuals were sentenced to four years in prison for such offenses in the late 1980s, but I suspect that there were few if any. Nevertheless, the Penal Code remains a continuing menace to the human rights of homosexuals since it permits preventive detention in a psychiatric hospital or work center for up to four years. The *Second ILGA Pink Book* also makes a serious error in its statement that homosexuals could be sentenced to up to twenty years in prison under Article 359 of the Penal Code. Formerly nine months, the maximum sentence was raised to twelve months in 1988. Overall, the book gives a somewhat misleading impression of the extent of homosexual oppression even as far back as the late eighties, which unfortunately feeds into other anti-Cuban campaigns. The article on Cuba in the first *Pink Book* gives a much more balanced picture

of the situation of homosexuals in Cuba (see van de Boogaard and van Kammen).

7. See Article 98 (6) of Costa Rica's Penal Code.

8. Cuba's legal discrimination against homosexuals must once again be placed in comparative context. Twenty-four U.S. states still prohibit "sodomy" between males, and a variety of federal, state, and city laws discriminate against homosexuals in other ways. In 1986, the U.S. Supreme Court in *Bowers v. Hardwick* upheld Georgia's criminalization of private consensual "sodomy." In Britain, Section 28 of the new Local Government Act makes it illegal to "promote homosexuality or its acceptability . . . as a pretended family relationship" using local government funding.

9. A singularly un-Marxist concept!

10. Although the maximum sentence has been reduced from eight to five years, the minimum sentence has been raised from one to two years as compared to the 1979 code.

11. For example, sexual assault against adult males is penalized more severely (seven to fifteen years in jail) than that carried out against women (four to ten years). See Articles 298 and 299.

12. See speeches by General José Abrantes, Minister of the Interior, *Bohemia,* January 8, 1988, and *Granma,* July 21, 1988.

13. Ramón de la Cruz Ochoa (Cuba's Attorney-General), *Granma,* April 29, 1988.

14. Arguelles and Rich, "Homosexuality, Homophobia and Revolution," p. 694.

15. Debra Evenson, *Revolution in the Balance: Law and Society in Contemporary Cuba* (Boulder, Colo.: Westview Press, 1994), p. 159.

16. *Redadas* still occur on a minor scale, in the sense that two or three patrol cars may appear from time to time in places like the Yara/Coppelia corner, where gays and gay-positive *civilizados* congregate at night. However, it is clear that their main objective is to intimidate in order to deter too many people from congregating there. Some people are carted off to the police station, but unless they are suspected of having committed specific crimes they are soon released. If anybody has been charged recently with scandalous behavior, it certainly has not deterred many a flamboyant queen from acting up. At times, the intersection offers a truly gay scene that can typically be found only within the gay ghetto in North America.

17. Salas, *Social Control and Deviance,* p. 154.

18. See, for example, the exchange between Aryeh Neier and Debra Evenson in the *New York Review of Books,* September 29 and October 13, 1988.

19. Valladares, *Prison Memoirs,* p. 358, and Arenas, *Before Night Falls,* pp. 177–201.

20. Gianni Miná, *Un encuentro con Fidel* (Havana: Oficina de Publicaciones del Consejo de Estado, 1987), p. 36 and chapter 2 passim. He repeats the claim in Tomás Borge, *Fidel Castro, Un grano de maíz: Conversación con Tomás Borge* (Havana: Oficina de Publicaciones del Consejo de Estado, 1992) p. 227. The point is not that conditions in Cuban prisons are necessarily bad—it is quite possible that they are better than in most countries, particularly compared to the treatment of minorities in U.S. prisons—but rather that Castro's triumphal claims contribute to the foreclosure of any debate within Cuba with respect to what actually takes place in Cuban prisons.

21. Lee Lockwood, *Castro's Cuba, Cuba's Fidel* (New York: Macmillan, 1967), p. 123.

22. Those who applaud the achievements of the revolution in other respects all too often are left grasping at straws when it comes to finding concrete evidence that the regime has reversed its discriminatory policies toward gays. For example, Debra Evenson, who correctly foresaw that the Communist Party would reverse its official policy of excluding religious believers from membership, concluded on the basis of "private conversations" that the new policy would be extended to "all forms of discrimination, including against gays and lesbians." But this was an irrelevant point since gays as such, unlike religious believers, have never been formally excluded from the Party. They are de facto excluded because the Cuban Government refuses to support their rights by combating homophobic prejudices in the population as a whole. Debra Evenson, "Channeling Dissent," *NACLA: Report on the Americas,* 24, no. 2 (August 1990), p. 28. See also Liss, *Fidel!* p. 159. Significantly, in his 1992 interview with Tomás Borge, Fidel Castro avoided saying whether gays could become members of the Party. Borge, *Fidel Castro,* p. 238.

23. The Ochoa affair focused attention upon supposed laxity and corruption within the Ministry of Interior. It also coincided with increased public anxiety about the extent of theft and violence in Havana. Nevertheless, despite the fact that the Party tightened political surveillance in response to the crisis, the progressive policies that were initiated by Abrantes were not reversed by his successors. "Street" homosexuals were among the most obvious beneficiaries.

24. *Bohemia,* January 8, 1988.

25. Ministerio del Interior, *Indicaciones para la imposición de multas,* p. 34.

26. Lockwood, Castro's Cuba, p. 124.

27. Some people have interpreted the election of Alfredo Guevara (the head of ICAIC, the Cuban film institute, who is widely known to be homosexual) to the Central Committee of the Communist Party in October 1991 as a harbinger of greater acceptance of homosexuals within the Party. However, Guevara has never been known to identify himself publicly with the rights of homosexuals.

28. However, the important issue once again is whether the homosexual is perceived to be ostentatious in his public behavior. The experience of one of my friends may indicate the boundaries. His homosexuality could easily be inferred since he shares a small apartment with his lover, makes and sells clothes in his free hours, and makes no attempt to disguise the fact that his visitors are almost exclusively male. On the other hand, he is no screaming queen and has very good relations with his neighbors. His homosexuality has not been a barrier to his selection as educational secretary for the zone-level CDR.

29. See *Juventud Rebelde,* June 24, 1990.

30. Articles 23, 24, and 26 of the Youth Code expressly stipulate that admission to universities is contingent on the "political attitude," "social conduct," and "integral attitudes" of the applicants. But once again, although these formal stipulations give the state discretionary power, it is obvious that they are not currently strictly enforced judging from the number of gays who are enrolled in such faculties as law and medicine. They may not be "out" at college, but many of them must surely be known to be or suspected of being homosexual.

31. Although the National Center for Sexual Education has sponsored workshops and publications for teachers aimed at developing more enlightened views about homosexuality, it is unclear to what extent these are being incorporated into the classroom. I have yet to meet secondary-school or university students who have been exposed to gay-positive material in their course work.

## *Chapter Five*

1. Borge, *Fidel Castro,* pp. 236–38.

2. This is the only occasion in which the Cuban people have been directly exposed to Fidel Castro's opinions about homosexuality. The

interview was also subsequently printed in weekly installments in *Bohemia*, which currently has a very small circulation.

3. Interview with Monika Krause, February 21, 1989.

4. Marvin Leiner, *Sexual Politics in Cuba: Machismo, Homosexuality and AIDS* (Boulder, Colo.: Westview Press, 1994), p. 93.

5. See "Educación Sexual: una Grieta entre el Estado y la Iglesia," (Sex education: A split beetween the State and the Church); Efraín Valerio, "El Estado no Debió Doblegarse ante la Iglesia," (The State should not have given in to the Church); and Monseñor Antonio Troyo Calderón, "El Control de la Natalidad es una Imposición Colonialista," (Birth control is a colonial imposition), *Esta Semana* (San José), August 18–24, 1992.

6. East Germany led West Germany with respect to legalizing homosexuality. Although homosexuality was not fully legalized until 1968, the government had officially announced as early as 1957 that homosexual acts would not be prosecuted unless they involved coercion or under-age partners. See Hans Vonk, "Homosexuality in the GDR," in International Lesbian and Gay Association, ed., *IGA Pink Book, 1985: A Global View of Lesbian and Gay Oppression and Liberation* (Amsterdam: COC, 1985).

7. See John Parsons, "East Germany Faces Its Past: A New Start for Socialist Politics," *Outlook* 5 (Summer 1989), pp. 43–52.

8. Despite Cuba's overwhelming economic dependence upon the Soviet Union, its cultural policies (along with others) soon ceased to be conditioned by the Soviet model. For this reason, Article 121 of the Soviet penal code (repealed in 1993), which made male homosexual relations punishable by up to eight years imprisonment, fortunately had no bearing on the formulation of Cuba's new policies.

9. Cited by Leiner, *Sexual Politics in Cuba,* p. 101.

10. Natividad Guerrero, *La educación sexual en la joven generación.* See also Raquel Fernández Pacheco, Natividad Guerrero Borreco, and Elena Socarrás de la Fuente, *La sexualidad en la adolescencia* (Adolescent sexuality) (Havana: Editorial Científico-Técnica, 1981).

11. Aloyma Ravelo García, *Del amor, hablemos francamente* (Havana: Editorial Gente Nueva, 1989). Significantly, the editorial advisers included Monika Krause, Celestino Alvarez Lajonchére, and Elsa Gutiérrez Baró, the most prominent sexologists in Cuba.

12. See Siegfried Schnabl, *El hombre y la mujer en la intimidad* (Havana: Editorial Científico-Técnica, 1979), p. 328.

13. Guerrero, *La educación sexual,* pp. 34, 64.

14. Whereas the footnote implies that any male under the age of six-

teen is a child—hardly the case in Cuba—there is no similar explication in the reference to Article 353, which deals with sexual violence against females under twelve years of age even though the article refers to them as women!

15. Kurt Bach's "Homosexuality, Society and Sexual Education" and Siegfried Schnabl's "The Counselling That Is Offered within the Sexual and Marital Counselling Centers with regard to Homosexuality [in East Germany]" (informal translation by GNTES) are much more progressive and gay positive than anything that has yet been made available to the Cuban public in general.

16. Stephen J. Risch and Randolph E. Wills, "From Cuba and GDR: Positive Views of Gays," *Gay Insurgent* 6 (Summer 1980), p. 6.

17. Heinrich Brückner, *¿Piensas ya en el amor?* (Havana: Editorial Gente Nueva, 1981), p. 210.

18. See Heinrich Brückner, *Denkst du Schon an Liebe* (Berlin: Der Kinderbuchverlag, 1980), pp. 201–3, and Brückner, *¿Piensas ya en el amor?* pp. 209–10.

19. William H. Masters, Virginia E. Johnson, and Robert C. Kolodny, *La sexualidad humana* (Havana: Editorial Scientífico-Técnica, 1987).

20. Siegfried Schnabl, *El hombre y la mujer en la intimidad*, 2d Cuban edition (Havana: Editorial Científico-Técnica, 1989), pp. 301–12.

21. Monika Krause Peters, *Algunos temas fundamentales*, p. 28.

22. Interview February 21, 1989.

23. Ibid.

24. See A. X. van Naerssen, ed., *Gay Life in Dutch Society* (New York: Harrington Park Press, 1987).

25. Krause, *Algunos temas fundamentales*, p. 3. See also *Granma*, June 14, 1982.

26. In January 1989, an incident occurred on Cuban television that gives a flavor of the treatment of homosexuality by the mass media. In response to a question about his views about love, viewers were astounded to hear Mario Benedetti, the Uruguayan writer, precede his remarks by an allusion to the possibility of love between two men as a legitimate option.

27. Interview April 28, 1986.

28. Habel, *Cuba: The Revolution in Peril,* p. 193.

29. Sonja de Vries, "Homosexuality, Socialism and the Cuban Revolution," *Cuba Update* 15, no. 2 (March–May 1994), p. 13.

30. Taken from a transcript of a video-tape of the UJC session provided by Karen Wald.

31. *Sexo Sentido,* November 14–18, 1994.

32. Interview with one of the founders of the incipient gay organization, the Gay and Lesbian Association of Cuba, who prefers to remain anonymous.

33. To be sure, I was invited to make a ten-minute presentation on "Homosexuality in Cuba, Costa Rica, and Mexico." The chairperson of my session was clearly outraged by my suggestion that there had been homosexual oppression in Cuba and by my insistence that it would have been more appropriate for gay Cubans to have been invited to speak about their own experience. She allowed two Cuban functionaries to criticize me without giving me any opportunity to reply.

34. For example, in March 1995, Cuba's excellent television program on the arts, "La Gran Escena" (The big stage), devoted an entire program to the personal life and work of renowned painter René Portocarrero without once mentioning the role of his lifelong companion, Raúl Milián, whose art was almost as famous as that of Portocarrero.

## Chapter Six

1. According to one survey young women spend between four to six times more time on housework than young males. Rolando Zamora Fernández, *El tiempo libre de los jóvenes cubanos* (The leisure time of Cuban youth) (Havana: Editorial de Ciencias Sociales, 1984), p. 31. In fact, 80 percent of women do nearly all household chores (Deborah Shnookal, ed., *Cuban Women Confront the Future: Vilma Espín* [Melbourne: Ocean Books, 1991], p. 71).

2. See Krause, *Algunos temas fundamentales,* pp. 19, 33–38.

3. See Fidel Castro's speeches to the Third Congress of the Communist Party, *Granma Weekly Review,* February 16, 1986, and to the Fourth Congress of the Cuban Federation of Women, *Granma Weekly Review,* March 24, 1985.

4. See Pérez-Stable, "Cuban Women and the Struggle for 'Conciencia,' " pp. 55–60.

5. See ibid., p. 59. See also Carollee Bengelsdorf, *The Problem of Democracy in Cuba: Between Vision and Reality* (New York: Oxford University Press, 1994), p. 109.

6. Young, *Gays under the Cuban Revolution,* p. 105.

7. Ministerio de Educación, *Manual de educación formal*, p. 19. Contradictory as it may seem, given Cuba's revolutionary pretensions, the Ministry of Education has advised parents and teachers to use "our grandparents" as role models with respect to the manners and forms of correct behavior that should be inculcated in young children. These role models may have helped to preserve personal courtesy and public civility, but they have hardly helped to undermine such oppressive cultural residues as sexism and racism. See also Ravelo García, *Del amor, hablemos francamente*, which emphasizes men's responsibility to be "protective" of women (p. 106).

8. Cited by Fernando Alvarez Tabío, *Comentarios a la constitución socialista* (Havana: Editorial de Ciencias Sociales, *1985*), p. 182.

9. The fact that Fidel Castro always delivers the keynote speech to the FMC congresses speaks volumes with respect to the extent of feminist consciousness in Cuba. So does the sycophantic attitude of FMC leaders such as Vilma Espín, who once told *Claudia*, a Brazilian women's magazine, that Cuban women "love Fidel a lot and he holds women in high esteem, he has confidence in us and encourages us to rise to positions of the highest importance in our country." See Shnookal, *Cuban Women Confront the Future*, p. 30.

10. *Granma Weekly Review*, March 24, 1985.

11. See *Juventud Rebelde*, March 3, 1985. Forty-five percent of Cuban women between the age of twenty-six and thirty-five were found to be dissatisfied with their marriages as compared to only 33 percent of men.

12. *Juventud Rebelde*, August 25, 1991.

13. The absence of an independent public forum for women to express feminist concerns and demands must be one of the explanations (in addition to ideological blinkers) for the extraordinary claim made by Isabel Larguía, an Argentine feminist resident in Cuba, that "in Cuba, there is no violence within the bosom of the family, there are harmonious relations. Now men and children share the burden of everyday tasks, and that lowers the level of hysteria that these conditions produce in other places" (*La Jornada* [Doble Jornada] [Double shift supplement], Mexico City, January 3, 1988). Monika Krause implied that she agreed with Larguía's claim when I raised the issue with her (interview, February 21, 1989). However, in the mid-1990s, new feminist NGOs such as Magín began to raise the issue of domestic violence. A survey of five hundred Cubans revealed that the vast majority recognized its existence, while 42.2 percent believed that there was much violence within

the home. See Mirta Rodríguez Calderón, "Violencia doméstica: En trazos y colores" (Domestic violence: In every shade and form), *Bohemia,* June 10, 1994.

14. Gutiérrez Baró, *Mensaje a los padres,* p. 125. See also Patricia Arés Muzio, *Mi familia es así* (Havana: Editorial de Ciencias Sociales, 1990), p. 16.

15. Cited by Alvarez Tabío, *Comentarios,* pp. 181–82.

16. Alexei Chestopal, introduction to Luis Salomón Beckford, *La formación del hombre nuevo en Cuba* (Havana: Editorial de Ciencias Sociales, 1986), p. 2.

17. Larguía and Dumoulin, "La mujer en el desarrollo," p. 43; *Bohemia,* March 10, 1989.

18. Larguía and Dumoulin, "La mujer en el desarrollo," p. 46.

19. Ibid., p. 49.

20. Comité Estatal de Estadísticas, *Anuario estadístico de Cuba, 1985* (Havana: Ministerio de Cultura, 1986), p. 585.

21. *Bohemia,* November 9, 1990.

22. Fidel Castro, *Granma Weekly Review,* March 24, 1985.

23. The Youth Code, which regulates or sets standards for every aspect of the lives of young Cubans, applies until they are thirty years of age! Once again, however, the concept of a youth code is not unique to Cuba. For example, Costa Rica has a similar code.

24. Mareelén Díaz Tenorio, *Uniones consensuales en Cuba* (Havana: Editorial de Ciencias Sociales, 1994), p. 49.

25. See Marvin Leiner's interview with Abel Prieto Morales, Cuban Vice Minister of Education, in 1971. Leiner, *Sexual Politics in Cuba,* pp. 32–33.

26. See, for example, *Muchachas* (May and October 1985) and *Somos Jóvenes* (October and November 1985).

27. *Bohemia,* February 17, 1989.

28. A notable exception is painting. Even though modern art has not been repressed in Cuba, as it was in the former Soviet Union, homoerotic representations are conspicuous by their absence. The treatment of Servando Cabrera Moreno suggests that some censorship may have taken place. In 1965 he was removed from his post in Cubanacán, Havana's art school, despite his reputation as one of Cuba's great modern painters. Although he was restored to grace in the 1970s, his homoerotic paintings are not to be seen in public spaces. With the exception of the work of the young painter Reynold Campbell, there has been no portrayal of homo-

sexual themes in the public work of the new generation of Cuban painters and sculptors, whose art is oppressively, if unconsciously, heterosexist.

29. See Kelly Anderson and Tami Gold, "Can We Talk? Cuban Mediamakers Size up their Future," *The Independent Film and Video Monthly* (January/February 1992), pp. 18–22.

30. See, for example, Victor Fowler, "El demonio anda por los pucheros," Coloquio José Lezama Lima, Biblioteca Nacional José Martí, December 19, 1991; and Virgilio Piñera, "La vida tal cual," pp. 22–35.

31. The story was originally published in *Unión* and was re-published in pamphlet form by the Ministry of Culture in 1991 in response to popular demand, at least among intellectuals, many of them gays. However, it was not widely available to the public at large.

*Paradiso* was reprinted in 1991. Although the gay stories were removed from the 1987 edition of Piñera's book *Un fogonazo,* there were quite a few references to his homosexuality in the extract of his autobiography that was published in *Unión* (April 1990).

32. See Appendix B.

33. The battle over *Alicia en el pueblo de las maravillas* (Alice in Wondertown), the film directed by Daniel Díaz Torres that was honored in the 1991 Berlin Film Festival, illustrates the point. Its satire of contemporary Cuba outraged Stalinist elements within the Communist Party, who sabotaged the film's distribution within Cuba. Worse still, they almost succeeded in having ICAIC, once the most free-spirited official organization, closed down. However, the resistance of the entire film community proved so effective that it led to the reinstatement as its head of Alfredo Guevara, who had contributed so much to the Institute's early reputation. This was perceived as a good omen, given that Guevara was simultaneously elected to the Central Committee of the Communist Party, the first homosexual whose sexual orientation was widely known to be so honored. Eventually, the film received limited distribution in the main provincial cities.

## Chapter Seven

1. For example, many Cubans in search of lovers and pen pals place personal advertisements in foreign magazines such as *Del Otro Lado* and *Hermes,* Mexican gay magazines.

2. Here, as elsewhere, I use North America (and North Americans) to refer to the dominant white, English-speaking, Christian cultures associated with capitalist commodification.

3. Cuban gays used to complain that any overt show of affection between gay men on beaches could lead to arrest for *escándalo público*. This possibility certainly inhibits their public behavior, but deep-rooted feelings of shame are just as much of a deterrent. There is not all that much difference between the behavior of homosexuals and the police on Cuba's gay beaches and those of Toronto. There may be more sex in the sand dunes of Hanlan's Point in Toronto, but it is certainly not unknown on those of the Cayito. Gays have been detained for kissing or necking on the Cayito, but such police repression is not inconceivable on Toronto's beaches either.

4. Bars with *ambiente* seem to have existed throughout all the vicissitudes of the last three decades. For example, even at the height of the homophobic campaigns of the late sixties, homosexuals were apparently meeting in such visible places as the ground-floor bar of the Capri Hotel. The staff of many bars seem to collude with patrons to ignore official policies. The unofficial attitude of many workers in the service sector is to help ordinary Cubans beat the system. I encountered an example of this in a small bar in the Lenin Park, Los Girasoles, which I discovered by accident in 1986. On that occasion, at least, it was almost entirely patronized by gays and lesbians. The staff were as much party to the *ambiente* as anybody else. The same is true of certain discos, such as El Castillito in Varadero. Even in the late seventies there were discos in Havana—such as L'Atelier, Flamingo, and the Gato Tuerto—that had acquired a gay reputation.

5. Although female prostitution has existed for many years in revolutionary Cuba, it was not until the Sixth Congress of the FMC, in March 1995, that most *jineteras* were officially recognized for what they really are—that is, prostitutes. See *Juventud Rebelde,* March 5, 1995.

6. *Quemado* (burnt) means being identified as a homosexual as a result of associating with people known to be gay.

7. Arenas, *Before Night Falls,* p. 105.

8. See Arenas's scathing references to various prominent Cubans throughout *Before Night Falls.*

9. Some homosexuals have eroticized toilet encounter in Cuba, perhaps as *faute de mieux*. But "tricking" in toilets also represent acts in defiance of straight bourgeois mores, as illustrated by the fact that the famous Colón cemetery has become a popular cruising spot. Many "de-

cent" homosexuals are scandalized and refuse to use certain toilets for these reasons. But there are just as many who delight in recounting their adventures in the more notorious ones. The point is that the sexual practices of Cubans are not all that different from those of Mexicans, Costa Ricans, or North Americans for that matter.

    10. Arenas, *Before Night Falls,* p. 107–8.

## Chapter Eight

    1. The high number of heterosexuals may be inflated because of the reluctance of Cuban males to classify themselves as bisexuals or to admit to having had sex with other males. Cuban females, 28.9 percent of those infected with HIV, may be more susceptible to AIDS because the country's high humidity makes them especially prone to vaginal infection. Furthermore, a majority of them have reported a high frequency of anal intercourse with their heterosexual partners. Raúl Cordovés, "Contra el flagelo mortal," *Bohemia,* February 24, 1989. Heterosexual anal intercourse seems to have a certain popularity in Cuba, especially among Afro-Cubans. It probably became popularized as a means of birth control among slaves in the nineteenth century. See Moreno Fraginals, *El ingenio,* p. 53.

    2. Over four hundred thousand Cubans have been in Africa (not exclusively in Angola) serving as doctors, teachers, technicians, and military personnel. In addition, there are more than twenty thousand Third World students, mainly from Africa, studying in Cuba at any one time. Foreign tourism, mainly from Canada, Europe, and Mexico, constitutes the other potential foreign source of infection. In 1994, over six hundred thousand tourists visited Cuba.

    3. By mid-1993, Cuba had 16 reported cases of AIDS per million inhabitants whereas Costa Rica had 158.8 and Mexico had 150.9 (not to mention the 262 cases in the Dominican Republic and the even more appalling incidence in Haiti and other Caribbean countries). *Surveillance Update: AIDS in Canada,* Federal Centre for AIDS, Department of Health and Welfare (Ottawa, October 25, 1993).

    4. See Leiner, *Sexual Politics in Cuba,* pp. 125–28.

    5. Robert Root-Bernstein, *Rethinking AIDS: The Tragic Cost of Premature Consensus* (New York: Free Press, 1993), pp. 366, 368.

    6. Santana, et al., "Human Immunodeficiency Virus in Cuba," p. 521; Francisco Galván Díaz, et al., "AIDS, Government and Society in

Mexico," in Lumsden, *Homosexuality, Society and the State in Mexico,* p. 105; Ciro Bianchi Ross, "AIDS in Cuba: Patients Speak Out," *Prisma: Cuba and Latin America Report* (10–11-91), p. 6.

7. Cited by Mark Chestnut, "Cuban AIDS Centres Prompt Accusations," *The Advocate,* September 10, 1991.

8. See Eliseo J. Pérez-Stable, "Cuba's Response to the HIV Epidemic," *American Journal of Public Health* 81, no. 5 (May 1991), p. 564.

9. Debra Evenson, *Revolution in the Balance,* p. 32.

10. See Jorge Cortiñas, "Laws That Say So: A Dialogue with a Resident of Cuba's AIDS Sanatorium," *Socialist Review* 23, no. 1 (1993).

11. See Leiner, *Sexual Politics in Cuba,* pp. 133–35.

12. See *Granma* for April 17 and July 9, 1987 and *Juventud Rebelde,* July 9, 1987. See also the Ministry of Public Health brochure, *¿Qué es el SIDA?* (What is AIDS?). To be sure, the reference to "normality" reinforces heterosexist prejudices, but it must be put in a context in which even the majority of Cuban homosexuals refer to heterosexuals as "normal" people.

13. For example, Fidel Castro has several times accused the United States of being responsible for the dissemination of AIDS throughout the world. However misleading and distasteful such accusations may be, his references to the "drug and vice-infected" American culture fall short of explicit homophobia. See *Granma,* September 14, 1988 and October 12, 1988.

14. For example, a recent survey of eighteen to twenty-three-year-old males revealed that only 5 percent admitted to using condoms. Interview, Buró del Sida, Havana, December 24, 1991.

15. *¿Qué es el SIDA?*—the brochure produced by the Ministry of Public Health and sporadically available in certain pharmacies—notes almost in passing that certain sex practices, such as anal intercourse, facilitate the transmission of HIV since they are more traumatic. That is its only reference to a sexual practice that is probably more characteristic of sexual relations between males than between males and females. Its concluding recommendations with regard to sexual practices merely suggest avoiding sexual relations with unknown individuals, with those who are known to change their sex partners frequently, and with foreigners; and they suggest that a condom should be used in any casual sexual encounter.

16. See Jonathan Mann, "Global AIDS: Critical Issues for Prevention in the 1990s," *International Journal of Health Services* 21, no. 3 (1991), p. 558.

17. People who are actually ill are treated in a separate hospital, the Institute of Tropical Medicine, until they are well enough to return to the sanatorium in Santiago de las Vegas or to others in the interior.

18. As is well known, AIDS is not a simple contagious disease. The HIV virus can only be transmitted in limited and specific ways; infection by someone who is HIV positive depends upon direct exposure of the bloodstream to the virus and does not necessarily result even then. Finally, HIV infection leads probably, but not inevitably, to AIDS itself.

19. Cited in *Excelsior,* Mexico City, March 6, 1988. Of course, Pokrovski was proved wrong, at least with respect to Cuba, since the spread of the disease has been checked.

20. *Granma,* April 17, 1987.

21. Once again, Cuba is by no means unique in this respect. Liberal Costa Rica initially required disclosure of sexual contacts. See Jacobo Schifter Sikora, *La formación de una contracultura: Homosexualismo y SIDA en Costa Rica* (San José: Ediciones Guayacán, 1989), p. 269.

22. See Janice M. Swanson, Ayesha E. Gill, Karen Wald, and Karen A. Swanson, "Comprehensive Care and the Sanatoria: Cuba's Response to HIV/AIDS," *JANAC* 6, no. 1 (1995), p. 36. This is one of the most authoritative reviews of Cuba's AIDS program, even though it is occasionally marred by the authors' uncritical willingness to accept official policies at face value—for example, "Government-funded agencies teach positive attitudes toward human sexuality, both heterosexual and homosexual" (p. 35).

23. Interview with Dr. Juan Carlos de la Concepción, April 22, 1994.

24. See Pérez-Stable, "Cuba's Response to the HIV Epidemic," pp. 565–66, and Santana et al., "Human Immunodeficiency Virus in Cuba," pp. 531–33. Two widely distributed AIDS posters are singularly uncreative by Cuban standards. One, "La historia del Chucho" (Chucho's story), focuses on "promiscuity" as the cause of AIDS without addressing the issue of safe sex in any way and typically ignoring the possibility of homosexual sex. Thus it also succeeds in conveying the impression that males are more likely to be infected by their females partners than vice versa, a message that is implicitly sexist as well as heterosexist!

25. See Cortiñas, "Laws That Say So."

26. 69.23 percent of seropositives are between fifteen and twenty-nine years of age. *Bohemia,* October 14, 1994.

27. The Ministry of Public Health claims that HIV antibody tests are not as expensive as they might be elsewhere given that Cuba has devel-

oped its own test (SUMA), which costs a mere thirty-four cents (Dr. Hector Terry, interview, December 30, 1991). However, this figure could not possibly include the labor costs of undertaking and processing the tests, not to mention associated research and administrative expenses.

28. Interviewed at his home in Old Havana during his regular weekend visits. He is about to return home full time so that, as he put it, "I can complete my education and get on with my life." He completely refuted what had been attributed to him by *The Advocate* (January 24, 1995).

29. In addition, every province has its own sanatorium. However, little is known about them. Foreigners are invariably guided toward Los Cocos, even though the sanatorium in San José de las Lajas, which serves the province as opposed to the city of Havana, is not much farther away. It is possible that conditions in Los Cocos are exceptional and perhaps even designed to impress foreigners, as is true of the Hospital Psiquiátrico de Mazorra in Havana, to which all foreigners interested in psychiatric care are shepherded.

30. My assessment of the sanatorium program is based upon interviews with Dr. Hector Terry, Vice Minister of Public Health, Dr. Jorge Pérez, director of the Santiago de las Vegas Sanatorium, and three visits to the sanatorium including a lengthy one on December 39, 1991, at which time I had private discussions with three sets of patients, including four homosexuals. These inquiries have been supplemented by ongoing social contact with other people living with HIV. In particular, I would like to mention Abel Montes de Oca, Regino Teran, Víctor Peralta, and Juan Carlos de la Concepción, who have been long-term patients in Los Cocos. See also Santana et al., "Human Immunodeficiency Virus in Cuba"; Ciro Bianchi Ross, "AIDS in Cuba"; Karen Wald, "AIDS in Cuba: A Dream or a Nightmare?" *Z Magazine,* December 1990, pp. 104–9; and Janice Swanson, et al., "Comprehensive Care and the Sanatoria: Cuba's Response to HIV/AIDS."

31. However much the quarantine program may have been improved in the Santiago de las Vegas sanatorium, popularly known as Los Cocos, it is still a system of incarceration for those who refuse to abide by the conditions imposed upon them. Those who refuse to conform to the liberal conditions of Los Cocos are interned in the much more restrictive conditions of the sanatorium in San José de las Lajas, which serves the province (as opposed to the city) of Havana. And if they escape they still end up in prison in the Combinado del Este.

32. Interview with some of the leading activists in Proyecto Vida, April 1995.

33. See "Componente educativo del programa cubano de control y prevención del VIH/SIDA," National Center for Health Education (Havana, May 6, 1994).

34. For example, although it may well be that Cuban medical experts consciously seek to offer people with HIV or AIDS the best treatment that is currently available, the latter are not given the opportunity, let alone encouraged, to participate in making the appropriate choices. Experience elsewhere suggests that such a policy is not conducive to the promotion of the best interests of those whose lives are at stake.

35. "Soul Searching," *NACLA Report on the Americas* 24, no. 2 (August 1990), p. 31. I myself experienced this phenomenon on my latest visit to the sanatorium on March 31, 1995. When I showed the draft of this chapter to Dr. Jorge Pérez, he was so hostile to the mild criticism within it that there was no point in pursuing the interview. In front of a gay patient, he dismissed me in the following terms. "Since you are homosexual, and I am heterosexual, we will never understand each other."

36. *Granma,* September 9, 1987.


## Chapter Nine

1. For example, apparently Fidel Castro is not aware that one expression of homophobia is to deny that a prominent figure such as Alfredo Guevara could be homosexual, even though he is widely known to be so both within Cuba and abroad. If someone were to ask Castro whether Roberto Robaina (Cuba's attractive young Foreign Minister) was straight, would he deny it in the same manner? It is equally homophobic to insist that there has "never been persecution of homosexuals" in Cuba despite all the evidence to the contrary. See Castro's interview with Ann Louise Bardach, *Vanity Fair,* March 1994.

2. See Bengelsdorf, *The Problem of Democracy in Cuba,* chapter 8 passim.

3. Ibid., p. 169.

4. Medea Benjamin, "Things Fall Apart," *NACLA Report on the Americas* 24, no. 2 (August 1990), pp. 16, 17. See also Andrew Zimbalist, "Teetering on the Brink," pp. 407–18.

5. "Thinking about Cuba," *Social Justice* 19, no. 4 (1992), p. 153. González Casanova's evaluation may sound far-fetched to some in light of the economic collapse that occurred in the 1990s. However, as applied to the mid-1980s it is quite consistent with Dudley Seers's oft-quoted de-

finition of development. "The questions to ask about a country's development are therefore: What has been happening to poverty? What has been happening to unemployment? What has been happening to inequality? If all three of these have declined from high levels, then beyond doubt this has been a period of development for the country concerned." Dudley Seers, "The Meaning of Development," in Charles K. Wilber, ed., *The Political Economy of Development and Underdevelopment* (New York: Random House, 1973), p. 7.

6. Habel, *Cuba: The Revolution in Peril,* p. 35.

7. *Globe and Mail* (Toronto), April 1, 1989. According to the Organization of American States, the number of Latin Americans living in poverty increased from 33 percent of the region's population in 1980 to 62 percent in 1990 (*Excelsior,* Mexico City, February 8, 1994).

8. See Borge, *Fidel Castro,* pp. 222–23.

9. Habel, *Cuba: The Revolution in Peril,* p. 104.

10. Ministerio de Educación, *Manual de educación formal,* for example, makes no reference to expressions of racial prejudice even though these abound in Cuba. The oversight is significant given that the manual has had at least three editions, each of which was studied and debated by hundreds of educators and government officials.

11. For example, although research and teaching related to Afro-Cuban culture can be undertaken in universities, the question of racism in contemporary Cuba is not included in the curriculum. To cover the issue would be tantamount to admitting that racism existed in Cuba, which would put in question one of the purported achievements of the revolution, that it has eliminated all manifestations of racism.

12. See Borge, *Fidel Castro,* p. 222; see also Pedro Serviat, *El problema negro en Cuba y su solución definitiva* (Havana: Editora Política, 1986), which claims that all racial prejudice has been eradicated by the revolution (p. 168).

13. However, Vilma Espín was demoted from membership in the Politburo in 1991. Its current three female members have no particular relation to women's organizations and do not carry much political clout outside their personal relationship to Fidel Castro. See Juan M. Del Aguila, "The Party, the Fourth Congress, and the Process of Counterreform," *Cuban Studies* 23 (1993), p. 82.

14. Marifeli Pérez-Stable, "Cuban Women and the Struggle for 'Conciencia,' " p. 64.

15. To be sure, these and other issues raised by feminists elsewhere

may be discussed within certain circles of the FMC, but they are not allowed to become public political issues.

16. In recent times Fidel Castro has at last begun to acknowledge Cuba's errors in deifying the Soviet Union. What he does not say is that this is entirely the fault of the leadership since Cuban citizens have never been given the facts with which to make up their own minds about the Soviet experience.

17. *Granma,* April 5, 1989.

18. *Granma Weekly Review,* April 16, 1989.

19. Cited by Saul Landau, "After Castro," *Mother Jones,* July/August 1989, p. 46.

20. *La Jornada* (Mexico City), December 28, 1988.

21. To criticize Fidel Castro in public is unthinkable, if only because the sentence for offending the dignity of any public official is three to twelve months in prison, which is raised to one to three years in the case of leading state and Party officials (Article 144 of the Penal Code). To be sure, a similar provision existed in the prerevolutionary Code, but this does not excuse its inclusion in that of a supposedly socialist country. In fact, the 1987 Code actually raised the minimum sentences specified in the 1979 Code (Article 160).

22. *Granma Resúmen Semanal,* June 17, 1984.

23. *Improper Conduct* is a good example of what the Cuban leadership has in mind. Although it made many valid points about homosexual oppression in Cuba, it also "grotesquely" distorted its character by making absurd analogies to Nazi Germany and Pinochet's Chile. On the question of the exploitation of the issue of homosexual oppression for counterrevolutionary ends see Arguelles and Rich, "Homosexuality, Homophobia and Revolution."

24. Policies toward gay social spaces are beginning to change, however, as rapidly as every other aspect of Cuba, as evidenced by a letter received from a Cuban friend in early September 1995. "There's a new disco called El Jockey at Línea and 10th St. which we all go to on Thursdays. The police are there and they don't interfere with anyone. On the contrary, they are there to protect us following some complaints about fighting and thefts. You know how *maricones* behave here, showing off their gold chains and fancy clothes which are the envy of *cheos*. And that is why the police are there. There has been a big change in state policy. The Parque de la Fraternidad is full of gays until dawn and nobody butts in."

25. See Comisión Costarricense de derechos humanos, *Informe de los derechos humanos en Costa Rica,* (San José, 1987); and Jacobo Schifter

Sikora, *La formación de una contracultura*. For example, as late as March 27, 1987, over two hundred gay men were detained by the police in massive raids against the major bars in San José. Such was the fear of asserting their rights that not a single patron offered any form of resistance or challenged the legitimacy of the *redada*.

26. See Lumsden, *Homosexuality, Society, and the State,* and Schifter, *La formación de una contracultura*.

27. See Lumsden, *Homosexuality, Society, and the State,* chapter 3.

28. I am not disregarding the acute economic crisis that presently bedevils Cuba but merely noting that by the mid-1980s the ignorance and dehumanizing poverty that cripple half or more of the population in most Latin American countries had been largely eliminated in Cuba.

29. *No porque lo diga Fidel,* the video made by Graciela Sánchez, a Chicana student in Cuba's International Film and Television School in 1988, could have provided an excellent opportunity to take the issue of homophobia to the public. Although the video was entertaining, balanced, and specifically exonerated Fidel Castro for Cuba's homophobia, it was not distributed within Cuba.

30. See, for example, Amnesty International, *Cuba: Silencing the Voices of Dissent* (December 1992), and Americas Watch, *Cuba: "Perfecting" the System of Control: Human Rights Violations in Castro's 34th Year* 5, no. 1 (February 25, 1993).

31. Information supplied by a recently exiled gay filmmaker.

32. The Cuban public was astounded in 1993 when they realized that two of the principal characters in the imported Brazilian soap opera, "Vale Todo," were a lesbian couple (among other homosexual characters in the serial). When one of them died, half the country went into mourning (and probably more, given Cubans' addiction to *telenovelas*). Unfortunately, an equal number of viewers are also hooked on "Sabadazo," a Cuban program whose often hilarious skits are based on racial and sexual stereotypes. Very few Cuban viewers react to the program in the way that North Americans who have been sensitized to the significance of stereotypes in perpetuating prejudices might do.

33. See Appendix C.

34. Interview with Andrix Gudin Williams, the principal organizer of the Gay and Lesbian Association, March 7, 1995. It is not true that the "government security forces launched a crackdown so brutal that leaders of the group shut it down," as reported in *The Advocate,* January 24, 1995.

35. See Bengelsdorf, *The Problem of Democracy in Cuba,* passim, and Habel, *Cuba: The Revolution in Peril,* passim.

36. Borge, *Fidel Castro,* p. 219.

37. Miná, *Un encuentro con Fidel,* p. 37. At the moment it is utterly inconceivable that the regime would tolerate any public manifestation of dissent as demonstrated by the arrest of a handful of Cubans who attempted to organize a demonstration in favor of glasnost during Gorbachev's visit in April 1989. Cuba's distortion of the aims of the Chinese student movement in the spring of 1989, and its deplorable support for the Tiananmen Square massacre, should dispel any conceivable doubts about how its leaders define civil rights. More recently, Fidel Castro has referred approvingly to the role played by Soviet tanks in "saving" the Hungarian and Czechoslovakian "revolutions." See *Granma,* December 24, 1991.

38. *New York Review of Books,* June 30, 1989.

39. Habel, *Cuba: The Revolution in Peril,* p. 111.

40. See "La democracia participativa en lo político," *Contrapunto* (Miami) 6, no. 3 (March 1995), pp. 8–15; see also Sandra Levinson and William Rose, "Miami Cubans No Monolithic Bloc," *Cuba Update* 14, no. 3–4 (Summer 1993), pp. 3–4. These journals are the two best sources for keeping abreast of political and social developments within Cuba and the exiled Cuban community abroad.

41. *Latin American Weekly Report* (London) no. 42, November 3, 1994.

42. International Gay and Lesbian Human Rights Commission, *Emergency Response Network* (San Francisco), September/October 1994. See also Amnesty International, *Violations of the Human Rights of Homosexuals* (January 1994), pp. 18–19.

43. On homophobia within the Cuban community in Miami, see Jesse Montenegro in John Preston, ed., *Hometowns: Gay Men Write about Where They Belong* (New York: Plume Books, 1992), p. 14.

44. Arenas, *Before Night Falls,* p. 292.

# SELECT BIBLIOGRAPHY

Adam, Barry. *The Rise of a Gay and Lesbian Movement*. Boston: Twayne, 1987.

Almendros, Néstor, and Orlando Jiménez-Leal, eds. *Conducta impropia*. Madrid: Editorial Playor, 1984.

Alvarez Tabío, Fernando. *Comentarios a la constitución socialista*. Havana: Editorial de Ciencias Sociales, 1985.

Americas Watch. *Cuba: "Perfecting" the System of Control: Human Rights Violations in Castro's 34th Year*, vol. 5, no. 1 (February 25, 1993).

——. *Human Rights in Mexico: A Policy of Impunity*. New York: Americas Watch, June 1990.

——. *Tightening the Grip: Human Rights Abuses in Cuba*, vol. 4, no. 1 (February 24, 1992).

Amnesty International. *Cuba: Prisoners of Conscience*. New York, January 1992.

——. *Cuba: Silencing the Voices of Dissent*. New York, December 1992.

——. *Mexico: Torture with Impunity*. New York, September 1991.

Anderson, Kelly, and Tami Gold. "Can We Talk? Cuban Mediamakers Size up Their Future." *Independent Film and Video Monthly*, January/February 1992.

Arenas, Reinaldo. *Before Night Falls*. Trans. Dolores M. Koch. New York: Viking Press, 1993.

Arés Muzio, Patricia. *Mi familia es así*. Havana: Editorial de Ciencias Sociales, 1990.

Arguelles, Lourdes, and B. Ruby Rich. "Homosexuality, Homophobia and Revolution: Notes toward an Understanding of the Cuban Lesbian and Gay Male Experience." Part 1. *Signs* 9, no. 4 (summer 1984): 683–99.

Bardach, Ann Louise. "Conversations with Castro." *Vanity Fair*, March 1994.

Barnet, Miguel. *Biografía de un cimarrón*. Havana: Bolsilibros Unión, 1967.

Bengelsdorf, Carollee. *The Problem of Democracy in Cuba: Between Vision and Reality*. New York: Oxford University Press, 1994.

Benjamin, Medea. "Soul Searching." *NACLA Report on the Americas,* vol. 24, no. 2 (August 1990).

————. "Things Fall Apart." *NACLA Report on the Americas,* vol. 24, no. 2 (August 1990).

Betto, Frei. *Fidel y la religión: Conversaciones con Frei Betto*. Havana: Oficina de Publicaciones del Consejo de Estado, 1985.

Bianchi Ross, Ciro. "AIDS in Cuba: Patients Speak Out." *Prisma: Cuba and Latin America Report* (Havana), October 11, 1991.

Boogaard, Henk van de, and Kathelijne van Kammen. "Cuba: We Cannot Jump over Our Own Shadow." *IGA Pink Book, 1985: A Global View of Lesbian and Gay Oppression and Liberation*. Amsterdam: COC, 1985.

Borge, Tomás. *Fidel Castro, un grano de maíz: Conversación con Tomás Borge*. Havana: Oficina de Publicaciones del Consejo de Estado, 1992.

Brückner, Heinrich. *¿Piensas ya en el amor?* Havana: Editorial Gente Nueva, 1981.

Bull, Chris, and Jorge Morales. "AIDS Crisis in Cuba." *The Advocate,* January 24, 1995.

Bullough, Vern L. *Sexual Variance in Society and History*. Chicago: University of Chicago Press, 1979.

Caballero, José Agustín y Rodríguez de la Barra. "Exposición relativa al matrimonio entre esclavos y otros asuntos relacionados con la población de la isla, así como algunos aspectos de la vida sexual de los esclavos." C. M. Morales no. 9, Biblioteca Nacional José Martí, Havana.

Cabrera Infante, Guillermo. *Mea Cuba*. Mexico City: Vuelta, 1993.

Cardenal, Ernesto. *En Cuba*. Buenos Aires: Ediciones Lohlé, 1972.

Carrasco, Rafael. *Inquisición y represión sexual en Valencia: Historia de los sodomitas (1565–1785)*. Barcelona: Laertes, 1985.

Casal, Lourdes. "Race Relations in Contemporary Cuba." In Philip Brenner, William M. LeoGrande, Donna Rich, and Daniel Siegel, eds., *The Cuba Reader: The Making of a Revolutionary Society*. New York: Grove Press, 1989.

Castellanos, Orlando. "Entrevista con Senel Paz." *Bohemia,* December 7, 1990.

Céspedes, Benjamín de. *La Prostitución en la ciudad de la Habana.* Havana: Establecimiento Tipográfico O'Reilly, 1888.

Chestnut, Mark. "Cuban AIDS Centres Prompt Accusations." *The Advocate,* September 10, 1991.

Chestopal, Alexei. Introduction to Luis Salomón Beckford, *La formación del hombre nuevo en Cuba.* Havana: Editorial de Ciencias Sociales, 1986.

*Código de defensa social de Cuba* (Actualizado). Havana: Ministerio de Justicia, 1969.

*Código de la niñez y la juventud.* Havana: Editora Política, 1985.

*Código penal de Costa Rica.* San José: Editorial Porvenir, 1991.

*Código penal de Cuba (1979). Revista Cubana de Derecho,* vol. 15, no. 27 (April–December 1986).

*Código penal de Cuba (1987). Gaceta Oficial de la República de Cuba,* vol. 85 (December 30, 1987).

Comisión Costarricense de Derechos Humanos. *Informe sobre la situación de los derechos humanos en Costa Rica.* San José, 1987.

Cortiñas, Jorge. "Laws That Say So: A Dialogue with a Resident of Cuba's AIDS Sanatorium." *Socialist Review,* vol. 23, no. 1 (1993).

Daniel, Marc. "Arab Civilization and Male Love." *Gay Sunshine* (San Francisco), no. 32 (spring 1977).

"La democracia participativa en lo político." *Contrapunto* (Miami), vol. 6, no. 3 (March 1995).

Díaz Tenorio, Mareelén. *Uniones consensuales en Cuba.* Havana: Editorial de Ciencias Sociales, 1994.

Domínguez, Jorge. *Cuba: Order and Revolution.* Cambridge: Harvard University Press, 1978.

Evenson, Debra. "Channeling Dissent." *NACLA: Report on the Americas,* vol. 24, no. 2 (August 1990).

———. "'In Cuban Prisons': Another Exchange." *New York Review of Books,* October 13, 1988.

———. *Revolution in the Balance: Law and Society in Contemporary Cuba.* Boulder, Colo.: Westview Press, 1994.

Evenson, Debra, and Aryeh Neier. "'In Cuban Prisons': An Exchange." *New York Review of Books,* September 29, 1988.

*Family Code.* Havana: José Martí Publishing House, 1984.

Federal Centre for AIDS. *Surveillance Update: AIDS in Canada.* Ottawa: Canadian Department of Health and Welfare, October 25, 1993.

Fernández Robaina, Tomás. *El negro en Cuba: Apuntes para la lucha contra la discriminación racial en Cuba, 1900–1958.* Havana: Editorial de Ciencias Sociales, 1990.

————. *Recuerdos secretos de dos mujeres públicas.* Havana: Editorial Letras Cubanas, 1983.

Franqui, Carlos. *Family Portrait with Fidel.* New York: Random House, 1984.

Galván Díaz, Francisco, et al. "AIDS, Government and Society in Mexico." In Ian Lumsden, *Homosexuality, Society and the State in Mexico.* Mexico City/Toronto: Solediciones/Canadian Gay Archives, 1991.

Giralt, Pedro. *El amor y la prostitución.* Havana, 1889.

González Casanova, Pablo. "Thinking about Cuba." *Social Justice,* vol. 19, no. 4 (1992).

Goytisolo, Juan. "Remedios de la concupiscencia según Fray Tierno." *La cultura en México* (supplement to *Siempre*), August 9, 1978.

Green, Duncan. *Faces of Latin America.* London: Latin American Bureau, 1991.

Guerra, Francisco. *The Pre-Columbian Mind: A Study into the Aberrant Nature of Sexual Drives, Drugs Affecting Behaviour, and the Attitude towards Life and Death, with a Survey of Psycotherapy, in Pre-Columbian America.* London: Seminar Press, 1971.

Guerrero, Natividad. *La educación sexual en la joven generación.* Havana: Editora Política, 1985.

Gutiérrez Baró, Elsa. *Mensajes a los padres.* Havana: Editorial Científico-Técnica, 1985.

Habel, Janette. *Cuba: The Revolution in Peril.* London: Verso, 1991.

Hendriks, Aart, Rob Tielman, and Evert van der Veen, eds. *The Third Pink Book: A Global View of Lesbian and Gay Liberation and Oppression.* Buffalo: Prometheus Books, 1993.

Heredia, Carlos, and Mary E. Purcell. *The Polarization of Mexican Society: A Grassroots View of World Bank Economic Adjustment Policies.* Washington, D.C.: Development Gap, 1994.

Hernández, Juan Jacobo. "El HIV/SIDA en Cuba." *Acción en SIDA,* no. 20 (July/September 1993).

Hernández Castellón, Raúl. *La revolución demográfica en Cuba.* Havana: Editorial de Ciencias Sociales, 1988.

International Lesbian and Gay Association, ed. *IGA Pink Book, 1985: A Global View of Lesbian and Gay Oppression and Liberation.* Amsterdam: COC, 1985.

————. *Second ILGA Pink Book: A Global View of Lesbian and Gay Liberation and Oppression.* Utrecht Series on Gay and Lesbian Studies no. 12. Utrecht: Interdisciplinary Gay and Lesbian Studies Department, Utrecht University, 1988.

Jong, Ben de: "An Intolerable Kind of Moral Degeneration: Homosexuality in the Soviet Union." *IGA Pink Book, 1985: A Global View of Lesbian and Gay Oppression and Liberation.* Amsterdam, COC, 1985.

Krause Peters, Monika. *Algunos temas fundamentales sobre la educación sexual.* Havana: Editorial Científico-Técnica, 1985.

Lancaster, Roger. "Subject Honour and Object Shame: The Construction of Male Homosexuality in Nicaragua." *Ethnology,* vol. 27, no. 2 (April 1988).

Landau, Saul. "After Castro." *Mother Jones,* vol. 14, no. 6 (July/August 1989).

Larguía, Isabel, and John Dumoulin. "La mujer en el desarrollo: Estrategia y experiencia de la revolución cubana." *Casa de las Américas,* vol. 25, no. 149 (March/April 1985).

Lauritsen, John, and David Thorstad. *The Early Homosexual Rights Movement (1864–1935).* New York: Times Change Press, 1974.

Leiner, Marvin. *Sexual Politics in Cuba: Machismo, Homosexuality and AIDS.* Boulder, Colo.: Westview Press, 1994.

Le Riverend, Julio. "El esclavismo en Cuba: Perspectivas del tema." In Colectivo de Autores, *Temas acerca de la esclavitud.* Havana: Editorial de Ciencias Sociales, 1988.

Levinson, Sandra, and William Rose. "Miami Cubans No Monolithic Bloc." *Cuba Update,* vol. 14, no. 3–4 (summer 1993).

Liss, Sheldon. *Fidel! Castro's Political and Social Thought.* Boulder, Colo.: Westview Press, 1994.

Lockwood, Lee. *Castro's Cuba, Cuba's Fidel.* New York: Macmillan, 1967.

Loren, Victoriano Domingo. *Los homosexuales frente a la ley: Los juristas opinan*. Barcelona: Plaza y Janes, 1978.

Lumsden, Ian. *Homosexuality, Society and the State in Mexico/Homosexualidad, sociedad y estado en México*. Mexico City/Toronto: Solediciones/Canadian Gay Archives, 1991.

MacGaffey, Wyatt, and Clifford R. Barnett. *Cuba: Its People, Its Society, Its Culture*. New Haven: HRAF Press, 1962.

Mann, Jonathan. "Global AIDS: Critical Issues for Prevention in the 1990s." *International Journal of Health Services*, vol. 21, no. 3 (1991).

Manrique, Rafael. "¿Cómo viven los seropositivos en Cuba?" *Del Otro Lado* (Mexico City), no. 8 (1993).

————. "Cuba gay." *Del Otro Lado* (Mexico City), no. 6 (1993).

Martínez, José Agustín. *El homosexualismo y su tratamiento*. Mexico City: Ediciones Botas, 1947.

Martínez-Alier, Vertena. *Marriage, Class and Colour in Nineteenth Century Cuba: A Study of Racial Attitudes and Sexual Values in a Slave Society*. Cambridge: Cambridge University Press, 1974.

Martínez Casanova, Manuel, and Nery Gómez Abréu. *La sociedad secreta abakuá*. Santa Clara: Universidad Central de las Villas, n.d.

Miná, Gianni. *Un encuentro con Fidel*. Havana: Oficina de Publicaciones del Consejo de Estado, 1987.

Ministerio de Educación. *Manual de educación Formal*. 3d edition. Havana: Ministerio de Educación, 1983.

————. *Memorias del primer congreso nacional de educación y cultura*. Havana: Instituto Cubano del Libro, 1971.

Ministerio del Interior. *Indicaciones para la imposición de multas por contravenciones*. Havana: Ministerio del Interior, 1988.

Ministerio de Salud Pública. *¿Qué es el Sida?* Havana, n.d.

Moreno Fraginals, Manuel. *El ingenio: Complejo económico social cubano del azúcar*. Vol. 2. Havana: Editorial de Ciencias Sociales, 1978.

Mulhare de la Torre, Mirta. "Sexual Ideology in Pre-Castro Cuba: A Cultural Analysis." Ph.D. diss., University of Pittsburgh, 1969.

Neier, Aryeh. "In Cuban Prisons: An Exchange." *New York Review of Books*, September 29, 1988.

Nelson, Lowry. *Rural Cuba*. Minneapolis: University of Minnesota Press, 1950.

Ortiz, Fernando. *Entre cubanos: Psicología tropical*. Havana: Editorial de Ciencias Sociales, 1987.

―――. *Historia de una pelea cubana contra los demonios*. Santa Clara: Universidad Central de Las Villas, 1959.

―――. *Los negros curros*. Havana: Editorial de Ciencias Sociales, 1986.

―――. *Los negros esclavos*. Havana: Editorial de Ciencias Sociales, 1987.

Padura Fuentes, Leonardo. "El cazador." In Leonardo Padura Fuentes, ed., *El submarino amarillo: Cuento Cubano 1966–1991*. Mexico City: Universidad Autónoma de México/Ediciones Coyoacán and Unión Nacional de Escritores y Artistas Cubanos, 1994.

Parsons, John. "East Germany Faces Its Past: A New Start for Socialist Politics." *Outlook*, no. 5 (summer 1989).

Paz, Senel. *El lobo, el bosque y el hombre nuevo*. Mexico City: Ediciones Era, 1991.

Pérez-Stable, Eliseo J. "Cuba's Response to the HIV Epidemic." *American Journal of Public Health*, vol. 81, no. 5 (May 1991).

Pérez-Stable, Marifeli. "Cuban Women and the Struggle for 'Conciencia.'" *Cuban Studies*, no. 17 (1987).

Piñera, Virgilio. "La vida tal cual." *Unión*, vol. 3, no. 10 (April–June 1990).

Quesada Ramírez, et al. *SIDA: Infección-enfermedad por el virus de la inmunodeficiencia humana*. Havana: Editorial Científico-Técnica, 1987.

Ravelo García, Aloyma. *Del amor, hablemos francamente*. Havana: Editorial Gente Nueva, 1989.

Ravenet Ramírez, Mariana, Niurka Pérez Rojas, and Marta Toledo Fraga. *La mujer rural y urbana: Estudios de casos*. Havana: Editorial de Ciencia Sociales, 1989.

Risch, Stephen J., and Randolph E. Wills. "From Cuba and GDR: Positive Views of Gays." *Gay Insurgent*, no. 6 (summer 1980).

Root-Bernstein, Robert. *Rethinking AIDS: The Tragic Cost of Premature Consensus*. New York: Free Press, 1993.

Salas, Luis. *Social Control and Deviance in Cuba*. New York: Praeger, 1979.

Santana, Sarah, Lily Faas, and Karen Wald. "Human Immunodeficiency Virus in Cuba: The Public Health Response of a Third

Schifter Sikora, Jacobo. *La formación de una contracultura: Homosexualismo y SIDA en Costa Rica*. San José: Ediciones Guayacán, 1989.

Schifter Sikora, Jacobo, and Johnny Madrigal Pana. *Hombres que aman hombres*. San José: Ediciones Ilep-Sida, 1992.

Schnabl, Siegfried. *El hombre y la mujer en la intimidad*. Havana: Editorial Científico-Técnica, 1979.

————. *El hombre y la mujer en la intimidad*. 2d ed. Havana: Editorial Científico-Técnica, 1989.

Shnookal, Deborah, ed. *Cuban Women Confront the Future: Vilma Espín*. Melbourne: Ocean Books, 1991.

Simo, Ana María, and Reinaldo García Ramos. "Hablemos claro." *Mariel,* vol. 2, no. 5 (spring 1984).

Sosa, Enrique. *El carabalí*. Havana: Editorial Letras Cubanas, 1984.

Thomas, Hugh. *Cuba: The Pursuit of Freedom*. New York: Harper and Row, 1971.

Thorstad, David. "Tovarich, Chiclets: Impressions of Cuba." *New York Native,* August 3, 1987.

Valladares, Armando. *The Prison Memoirs of Armando Valladares*. New York: Alfred Knopf, 1986.

Vazquez, Israel. "Our Man in Havana." *Lexicon* (Toronto), May 1993.

Vries, Sonja de. "Homosexuality, Socialism, and the Cuban Revolution." *Cuba Update,* vol. 15, no. 2 (March–May 1994).

Wald, Karen. "AIDS in Cuba: A Dream or a Nightmare?" *Z Magazine,* December 1990.

Weeks, Jeffrey. *Coming Out: Homosexual Politics in Britain from the Nineteenth Century to the Present*. London: Quartet Books, 1977.

Yglesias, José. *In the Fist of the Revolution: Life in a Cuban Country Town*. New York: Pantheon Books, 1968.

Young, Allen. *Gays under the Cuban Revolution*. San Francisco: Grey Fox Press, 1981.

Zamora Fernández, Rolando. *El tiempo libre de los jóvenes cubanos*. Havana: Editorial de Ciencias Sociales, 1984.

Zimbalist, Andrew. "Teetering on the Brink: Cuba's Current Economic and Political Crisis." *Journal of Latin American Studies,* vol. 24, no. 2 (May 1992).

# INDEX

*Abakuás,* 48, 205–6, 221n46
Abrantes, José, 90–91, 228n23
*Activo,* 30, 32, 150
Adam, Barry, xxii
*Adorables mentiras* (film), 125
*Advocate, The* (gay magazine), xxii, xxiii, 240n28
Afro-Cubans, 40–42, 147; and Cuban values, 42, 47–51, 205–7; culture of, 29, 41, 42; homosexuality among, 49, 50, 51; improved condition of, 185; no race-conscious movement among, 41–42; racist attitudes toward, 7, 41, 42, 51; religions of, 43–44, 48, 201, 205–7. *See also* Blacks; *Mulatos*
Age of consent: in Cuba, 85; in East Germany, 103
AIDS: awareness education, 175; and blood-donor screening, 168–69; and contact tracing, 171; and control of contaminated blood, 160–61; and Cuba's prevention program, xxii–xxiii, 101, 161–77, 184; education to combat, 166, 238n15; effect of epidemic on recognition of homosexuals, 26; and homophobia, 80, 100, 163–64; and identification of high-risk groups, 168–69; low incidence of, in Cuba, 160–62, 237n3; mass testing programs for, 168–69, 170, 171, 239n26; medical treatment for, 162; program, support for, by Cuban gays, 176; and quarantine program for HIV-positives, 162–64,

167–68, 169, 170, 171–75, 176, 177, 240nn29–31; and safe-sex education, 165–67, 170, 171, 175; statistics, 160, 237n1n3; and tourism, 169, 171, 176, 237n2; and travel abroad as source of infection, 161, 237n2
AIDS Center (Buró del SIDA), 175–76
AIDS Prevention Group (GP-SIDA), 174, 175
*Alicia en el pueblo de las maravillas* (film), 235n33
Almendros, Néstor, xiii, xxii, 162
Amnesty International, 193
Anal intercourse, 166, 237n1, 238n15
"Antisocial conduct," 83, 223n3
Arenas, Reinaldo, 30, 32–33, 72–73, 88, 125, 151–52, 158–59, 202, 218n11
*Are You Beginning to Think about Love?* (Brückner), 105–6
Arguelles, Lourdes, 86
Arrufat, Antón, 59
Artists. *See* Writers and artists

Bach, Kurt, 104–5, 231n15
Barnet, Miguel, 50
Batista, Fulgencio, 54, 57
*Bella de Alhambra, La* (film), 124
Benedetti, Mario, 231n26
Bengelsdorf, Carollee, 180–81, 199
Benjamin, Medea, 176, 183
Birth rates, in Cuba, 21, 22, 120; among teenagers, 217n10
Blacks, in Cuba, xxv, 146–48; discrimination against, 185; homophobia among, 207; lack of

Blacks, in Cuba (*cont.*)
  organization for, 186; prejudice
  against, 20, 41, 42; sexual stereotypes of, 51, 146–47, 147–48. *See
  also* Afro-Cubans; *Mulatos*
Blood: contamination problems,
  control of, 160–61; donors,
  screening of, 168–69
Borge, Tomás, interview with Fidel
  Castro by, 97–99
Brüchner, Heinrich, 105, 106
*Bugarrones,* 30, 31; use of term,
  218n3
Bullough, Vern, 47

Caballero, José Agustín, 50
Cabrera Infante, Guillermo, xxi, 72
Cabrera Moreno, Servando, 71,
  234n28
Carabalí culture, 47–48
Cardenal, Ernesto, 68–69
Castro, Fidel: actions by, toward homosexuals and nonconformists,
  70–71, 73, 74, 75; on Afro-
  Cubans, 42, 49, 220n31; attitude
  of, toward women, 116, 117–18,
  119, 233n9; blames U.S. for
  spreading AIDS, 238n13; claims
  by, about Cuba's progress, 185,
  186–87, 199–200; on Cuba's
  AIDS-prevention program,
  176–77; denial by, of faults in
  regime, 86, 88, 89, 199–200,
  216n3, 244n36; expressed attitudes of, on homosexuality, xxiii,
  93, 97–99, 112, 135, 228n22,
  229n2; machismo and, 46, 53, 61,
  67, 89, 97–98, 129; political ideology of, 12, 63, 64, 100, 187,
  243n16; on sexual relations in
  youth, 90; unconscious homophobia of, 241n1
Castro regime: authoritarian nature
  of, xi, xxvii, 5, 10–11, 18–19, 81,
  87, 93–95, 109–10, 118–19, 128,

  179, 180–81, 182, 185, 188,
  242n11, 244n36; bureaucratic
  nature of, xi, 10, 110, 117, 199;
  development of Cuba under,
  xxvii, 61, 183–84, 191, 241n5,
  243n27; policies of, toward gays
  (*see* Homophobia); and "rectification" process, 12, 188; and religion 45, 221n34n35; survival of,
  questioned, 11–12, 13, 182, 193.
  *See also* Communist Party of
  Cuba; Revolution, in Cuba
Catholic Church, 42–45, 46, 47, 190;
  blocking of sex education by,
  102; in Costa Rica, 44, 102, 190;
  defense of human rights in Cuba
  by, 138; in Mexico, 43, 44, 102,
  190; in Nicaragua, 202
Catholicism, 29, 201
CDRs. *See* Committees to Defend
  the Revolution
Censorship, 5, 72, 104, 105–6, 113,
  232n34
Center for Cuban Studies (New
  York), 112
Children, 84, 85, 230n14. *See also*
  Youth
Cinemas, 34, 138–39
*Civilizados* (gay-positive people),
  123, 139
Class distinctions, in gay community, 148–50; and elites, 149; and
  leveling effect of revolution, 148
CNES. *See* National Center of Sexual Education
"Coming Out," xxvi, 131–32, 133, 134
Committees to Defend the Revolution (CDRs), 13, 61, 67, 71, 94,
  151, 153–54
Communist Party of Cuba, 5, 63–64,
  73, 96, 109, 110, 117, 129, 188; exclusion of homosexuals from
  membership in, 93–94, 98, 99;
  and Fourth Party Congress
  (1991), 180–81; recognition of di-

verse opinions in, 201. *See also*
Castro regime
Condoms, 166, 171, 175, 238n14
Congress on Education and Culture
(1971), 26, 73–74, 75, 81, 122, 151,
225n34
Costa Rica: AIDS in, 161, 165;
Catholic Church in, 44, 102, 190;
civil liberties in, 93, 243n24; class
distinctions in gay community
in, 148, 191; gay liberation in,
xiv, xv, xxiv, 158, 190, 192;
homophobia in, 80, 165; laws
relating to homosexuality in, 81,
82, 83, 189; police behavior in, 87,
135, 190, 196, 243n24; political
and economic system of, xiii; restrictions in, on homosexuals, 77,
189; sex education in, 102–3; social life of gays in, 189–90. *See
also* Latin America; Mexico
Court system, in Cuba, 87–88
Cuban American Foundation in
Miami, 13, 202
Cuban Federation of Women
(FMC), 60, 118–19, 186
Cuban Film Institute (ICAIC), 125,
195
Cuban revolution. *See* Castro
regime; Revolution, in Cuba
Cuban Union of Writers and Artists
(UNEAC), 70, 72
Culture, Cuban, 5–6, 15, 121–29,
191–97; traditional versus mod-
ern, 16. *See also* Mass culture

Dance groups, 124
Díaz, Carlos, 126, 195
Discos, 140, 156, 236n4
Divorce, 23, 118, 120–21; before
1959, 38
Dorner, Gunter, 110
Double dating with lesbians, 156
Double sexual standards (before
1959), 38

Dress, expectations regarding, 6, 25,
31, 75, 122, 218n6
Dumoulin, John, 51, 120

East Germany: acceptance of homosexuality in, 108–9, 230n6; sex
education in, 103, 104, 105,
106–7, 108–9
Economic crisis, in Cuba, life for
homosexuals since, 193–203
Economic embargo by U.S., xi, xviii–
xix, 3, 17, 18, 19, 180, 182, 183
Education: as basic right, xix, 14–15;
effects of improvement in, 121;
and gay university students, 76,
94–95, 135, 212, 229n30; and
living standards, 148; in prerevolutionary Cuba, 38; in rural
Cuba, 19–20; and schools-in-the-
countryside program, 23, 68; sexual (*see* Sex education)
Effeminacy, scorn for, 29–30, 33, 53,
71–72, 95
*Encuentros nocturnos peligrosos*
(play), 127
*Entendidos,* 30, 35–36, 62–63, 71, 131;
before 1959, 57; use of term,
217n1
Espín, Vilma, 60, 110–11, 186,
233n9, 242n13
Evenson, Debra, 86, 228n22
Exiles, 8, 13, 74–75, 76–77, 157, 158,
201, 202

Family, 55–56; constitutional protec-
tion for, 121
Family Code (1975), 24, 115
Family relations, xv, 56, 62, 132, 134,
135–36, 149, 155, 223n1
Fashion, 122, 123
Federation of Cuban Women
(FMC), 10, 110, 111, 112, 186
Feijoo, Samuel, 53–54, 65, 71
Feminist consciousness, in Cuba,
118–19, 233n9n13

Fernández Robaina, Tomás, 205–7
Ferrer, Pedro Luis, 127–28
Fiestas, 8, 48, 134, 142–43, 144, 145,
    150, 156–57, 197
Films, 5–6, 124–25; *Adorables menti-
    ras,* 125; *Alicia en el pueblo de las
    maravillas,* 235n33; annual festi-
    val in Havana, 15, 124, 125; *bella
    de Alhambra, La,* 124; *Fresa y
    chocolate,* 26–27, 112, 125, 192,
    194–95 ; *Improper Conduct,* xiii,
    xxii, 69, 243n23
Franqui, Carlos, 58, 59
*Fresa y chocolate* (film), 26–27, 112,
    125, 192, 194–95

García Lorca Theater, 139
"Gay," use of term in Cuba,
    xxiv–xxv, 131
Gay and Lesbian Association of
    Cuba (GLAC): establishment of,
    197–98; Manifesto (July 1994),
    178, 197–98, 211–14
Gay bars and clubs, 139, 144, 236n4
Gay bashing, 9, 137
Gay consciousness, 130–31, 145, 190;
    age and, 149
Gay liberation: in Cuba, 194–99,
    211–14; and economic develop-
    ment, xiv, xvi; in Latin America,
    100–101; in North America,
    xxiv, 100, 158; and urbanization,
    xv; in U.S., 32
Gay Pride Day of Cuba, 198, 214
*Gays under the Cuban Revolution*
    (Young), 69
Gender roles, 43, 116, 119, 121, 123,
    149–50, 232n1; before 1959, 39,
    55; stereotypes questioned, 114,
    115
Gilly, Adolfo, 188
GNTES. *See* National Center of
    Sexual Education
González Casanova, Pablo, 183,
    241n5

Gorbachev, Mikhail, 12, 187
GPSIDA. *See* AIDS Prevention
    Group
*Granma,* 78–79
Green, Duncan, xxii
Grupo de Acción por la Libertad de
    Expresión de la Elección Sexual
    (GALEES), 198
Guevara, Alfredo, 64, 75, 229n27,
    235n33, 241n1
Guevara, Che, 24, 60, 64, 119
Gunila 95, 196–97
Gutiérrez Alea, Tomás, 125, 195
Gutiérrez Menoyo, Eloy, 201

Habel, Janette, 183, 199
Hart, Armando, 75, 77
Havana: annual carnival in, 4, 34,
    58–59, 144; compared with rural
    Cuba, 19–20; cultural events in
    (*see* Culture); current living con-
    ditions in, 3–5, 9–10, 193–94; pop-
    ular places in, for gays, 137–40,
    145–46; prerevolutionary, 1–2,
    33–36; social events in, 8, 141–44;
    street life in, 3, 7–8, 130, 145; to-
    day, 2–10, 15, 19, 20, 26, 195–99
Havana AIDS sanatorium (Los
    Cocos), 163, 164, 171–73, 174
*Hembrismo,* 43, 119, 217n11, 220n32
Hermanos Saíz organization, 125
Historical perspective, for situation
    of Cuban gays, xxi, xxii, xxvi,
    154, 178–79
Homophobia, 107, 135–36; and
    AIDS epidemic, 80, 100, 163–64;
    among blacks, 207; in Anglo-
    American culture, 36–37; before
    1959, xiv, 28–54; and campaigns
    of 1960s and 1970s, xxi, xxii, 26,
    32, 58–79, 81, 91, 96, 145, 151,
    212; Castro on, 98, 99; and
    Catholicism, 47; and Cuban law,
    85, 86–87, 189; denied by govern-
    ment, 188–89, 192, 244n28;

diminishing of, 114, 151, 178–79, 195, 212, 228n22; effect of, on self-image of Cuban gays, 113; historical and political context of, xxi, xxii, xxvi, 154, 178–180, 181–82; and machista values, 103; meaning of, for Cubans, 32, 218n10; modification of, after mid-1970s, xxii–xxiii, 77–78, 80, 81; and pregnancies, 22; and traditional culture, 6–7

Homosexuals, in Cuba: and Afro-Cuban religions, 205–7; and AIDS epidemic (*see* AIDS); alienation of, from the government, 149, 191–92, 200; before 1959, 28–54, 56–57; Castro's expressed views on, xxiii, 93, 97–99, 112, 135; and decriminalization of homosexuality (1979), 81–82; and gay consciousness, 145, 191, 192, 203, 211–14; increasing tolerance toward, 100–103, 113–14, 145, 146, 189; life since economic crisis, 3–5, 9–10, 193–99; and relaxation of social mores, 22–23; socialization of, with women, 150–51

Human rights: and collective social rights, xvi, xix, 183–84, 191; and Cuban HIV-quarantine program, 174, 176; and individual civil liberties, xvi, xvii, 6, 61, 181, 193, 199–200, 244n36

*Human Sexuality* (Masters and Johnson), 107

Ibos, 47

Identity card policy, for screened blood donors, 168–69

*Improper Conduct* (film), xiii, xxii, 69, 243n23

Inquisition, 42, 45–46

Intellectual life, Cuban, 124–29, 194–95; before 1959, 35. *See also*

Films; Music and musicians; Theater; Writers and artists

International Lesbian and Gay Association (ILGA), xxii, 83

*Intimate Life of Males and Females, The* (Schnabl), 105, 106–7

Islamic culture: and attitudes toward sexual pleasure, 46–47; homosexuality in, 46–47

Jiménez-Leal, Orlando, xiii, xxii

*Jineteros,* 141, 148, 171

John Paul II, 45, 138

Karol, K. S., 74

Krause, Monika, 105, 106, 107, 108, 109, 112–13, 135

Labor Code (1971), 77

Lajonchére, Celestino Alvarez, 103, 104

Larguía, Isabel, 51, 120, 233n13

Latin America: criminal code treatment of homosexuality in, 82; machismo in, 36; oppression of homosexuals in, 179. *See also* Costa Rica; Mexico

Latin American Congress of Sexology and Sexual Education (1994), 111, 112, 167, 232n33

*Latin American Weekly Report,* 202

Laugart, Xiomara, 127

Law of Social Dangerousness, 83–84, 86, 90, 226n1

Leiner, Marvin, 102, 164

Le Riverend, Julio, 50

Lesbians, xxvi, 60–61, 150, 151, 156, 200

*Let Us Speak Frankly about Love* (Garcia), 104

*Lexicon* (gay periodical), xxii

Lezama Lima, José, 35, 126

Linares, Annia, 127

Liss, Sheldon, xxiii

"Lobo, el bosque y el hombre nuevo, El" (Paz), 125, 126, 235n31
*Locas* (queens), 26, 30, 31, 56, 57, 58, 62, 72, 79, 138, 139, 145, 217n1
*Los Cocos* AIDS sanatorium (Havana), 163, 164, 171–73, 174

Maceo, Antonio, 41
Machado, Gerardo, 54
Machismo, 22, 49, 53, 55, 95, 133, 146, 179, 206; in attitudes of homosexuals, 150, 151; before 1959, 29, 30, 36–40; Castro's views on, 97–98; and devaluation of women, 51–52; and homophobia, 218n10; and homosexual oppression, 103; and initial response to AIDS epidemic, 163–64; and softening of machista outlook, 25, 26, 114, 115–29; use of term, 217n11
Magazines: homophobic opinions in, 60, 65, 73, 78–79; youth, 109, 123
Male prostitutes, 141; in prerevolutionary Havana, 34–35. See also *Jineteros*
*Manual de educación formal*, 39–40, 218n6, 242n10
*Marianismo*, 43, 220n32
*Maricones*, 115, 145; current attitudes toward, 58, 60; prerevolutionary attitudes toward, 29–30, 33, 53; use of term, 7, 217n1
Mariel exodus (1980), 26, 78–79
Martí, José, 41
Martínez, Raúl, 71
Mass culture, 5–7, 121–23; and African slave culture, 29; and Catholicism, 29, 42–45, 46, 47; failure of Soviet Union to affect, 17; influence of U.S. culture on, xxiv, 1–2, 16–18, 25; regional cultural differences in, 20; Spanish influence on, 29, 42–43, 44
Mass media, 188; coverage of homosexuality, 104, 109–10, 231n26,

244n31; coverage of Mariel exodus, 78–79
Medina, Mirta, 127
Mexico: Catholic Church in, 43, 44, 102, 190; compared with Cuba, 5, 120, 148, 158, 161, 162, 165, 166, 189; homosexuality in, xii–xiv, xv, xxiv, 81, 87, 100, 189–91, 192; police behavior in, 92, 93, 135, 190, 196. See also Costa Rica; Latin America
Milanés, Pablo, 128, 209–10
Military, Cuban: and conscription, 23; exclusion of homosexuals from, 94
Military Units to Aid Production. See UMAP camps
Ministry of Culture, 75, 77, 196
Ministry of the Interior (police), 75; internal manual (1988), 91. See also Police behavior
Minorities, Cuban attitudes toward, xvii, 7, 180, 181. See also Homophobia; Racial prejudice
Montejo, Esteban, 41, 50, 51
Moslem culture. See Islamic culture
*Mulatos*, 42, 147, 148; use of term, xxv
Mulhare de la Torre, Mirta, 31–32
*Mundo, El*, 65
*Mundo alucinante, El* (Arenas), 72
Music and musicians, 127–28

*Ñáñigos*, 48, 205–6
National Center of Sexual Education (CNES) (*formerly* National Working Group on Sexual Education [GNTES]), 78, 101–2, 103, 104, 105, 108, 109, 110, 111–12, 175–76, 229n31
National Working Group on Sexual Education (GNTES). See National Center of Sexual Education
*Negros* (blacks), use of term, xxv. See also Blacks
Nicaragua, xix, 89, 202

*Ocania: Pasión infinita* (musical), 127
Ochoa scandal, 90, 228n23
Operation Three P's, 58
Oppression of Cuban gays. *See* Homophobia
Ortega, Cardinal Jaime, 138
Ortiz, Fernando, 48, 49, 50, 222n51
Ortiz, Fray Tomás, 46

Padilla, Heberto, 72
Painters and sculptors, 71, 225n28, 234n28. *See also* Writers and artists
*Paleros*, 206
*Paradiso* (Lima), 126, 235n31
Partido de los Independientes de Color, 41–42
Parties (social), 8, 141–44. *See also* Fiestas
*Pasivo*, 30, 150
Paz, Senel, 125, 126, 178
*Pecado Original, El* (The Original Sin), 128, 192, 209–10
Pederasty, 104; penalization of, 85
Penal Code (1979), 83, 91, 104; and decriminalization of homosexual acts, 81–82
Penal Code (1987 revision), 82, 83, 84, 85, 87, 91, 226n6; homophobic bias of, 85, 86; José Abrantes on, 90, 91
Pérez, Amaury, 127
Piñera, Virgilio, 33, 35, 59, 60, 66, 126, 195
Pino Machado, Quintín, 71
Poder Popular (popular assemblies), 94, 96, 105, 188
Police behavior, 57, 62, 86–87, 90, 91–92, 93, 135, 145, 197, 198, 236n3
Popular music, 5–6, 122, 123
Popular Socialist Party (PSP), 63, 223n13
Prejudice: against homosexuals (*see* Homophobia); racial, 51, 146–48, 185–86, 242n10

Prieto Morales, Abel, 73
Prisons, 88–89, 228n20
Project Life (Proyecto Vida), 174–75, 196–97
Prostitution, 141, 171, 236n5; before 1959, 57–58
Public health: and AIDS (*see* AIDS); system, effectiveness of, 169
Public Health, Ministry of, 164, 165–67, 168
Public places: police response to homosexual acts in, 91–92, 93; and homosexual *ambiente* in prerevolutionary Havana, 33–35
"Public Scandal" provision of Cuban law, 84, 91
*Pudor*, 31, 167, 218n5n6
Puerto Rico, AIDS in, 161

Quarantine program for HIV-positives, 162–64, 167–68, 169, 170, 171–75, 176, 177, 240nn29–31
"Queer baiting," virtual absence of, in Cuba, 9, 136–37
Queers for Cuba, 111, 112

Racial prejudice, 51, 146–48, 185–86, 242n10
Racism, 7, 41–42, 51, 222n54
Radio and television. *See* Mass media; Television
Ravenet Ramírez, Mariana, 37–38
*Recogidas* (mass arrests), 57, 71, 86
"Rectification" process, since 1986, 12, 188
*Redadas* (police raids), 57, 58, 86, 135, 142, 198, 227n16
Refugees, from Cuba: in Mariel exodus (1980), xxii, 26, 78–79; in raft exodus (1994), 184
Regional differences, 19–20
Regla de Ifá, 206–7
Regla de Ocha, 206–7
Regla de Palo, 206
Relationships, among Cuban gay couples, 133–34, 157

Resolución Número 3, 71, 77
Revolution, in Cuba: Canadian re-
    sponse to, xviii; future of, 13–14,
    182, 200–202; impact of, on gay
    Cubans, xv–xvi, 179, 191; re-
    sponse of homosexuals to, 61,
    62–63; significance of, in world
    today, xvi, xx–xxi; U.S. reaction
    to, xviii–xix, xxi, 13, 59, 179–80,
    182, 199. *See also* Castro regime;
    Social achievements
Revuelta, Raquel, 70
Rich, Ruby, 86
Risch, Stephen, 105
Robaina, Cristina, 118
Robaina, Roberto, 122, 241n1
Robaina, Sara, 118
Rodríguez, Rolando, 72
Rogers, William, 184
Root-Bernstein, Robert, 161–62
Rural Cuba, 2; disparities of, with
    Havana, 19–20; sexual culture in,
    before 1959, 32–33; social life of
    homosexuals in, 144; women in,
    before 1959, 37–38
Russia. *See* Soviet Union (former)

Safe-sex education, 165–67, 170, 171,
    175, 177, 239n24
Salas, Luis, 87
Sandinista regime in Nicaragua, xix,
    89, 202
Santamaría, Haydée, 75
Santería, 43, 48, 206–7
*Santeros,* 6, 48, 206, 207
Sarduy, Severo, 126
Sartre, Jean-Paul, 69, 74
Schnabl, Siegfried, 105, 106–7, 231n15
"Schools-in-the-countryside" pro-
    gram, 23, 68
*Second Pink Book* (1988), 83, 226n6
Seers, Dudley, 241n5
Sex education: heterosexism of, 104;
    as a revolutionary project, 102;
    and safe-sex, 165–67, 170, 171,

    175, 177, 239n24
Sexual culture, changes in, 20–27
*Sexual Education of the Young Gener-
    ation, The* (Guerrero), 104
Sexually transmitted diseases
    (STDs), 216n7. *See also* AIDS
*Sexual Politics in Cuba: Machismo,
    Homosexuality and AIDS*
    (Leiner), 164
Sexual values, in Cuba, and African
    religious beliefs, 205–7
Simo, Ana María, 74–75
Slater, Philip, 9
Slavery, 40, 47–48, 49–50; and
    homosexuality among slaves, 49,
    50. *See also* Afro-Cubans
Social achievements, of Cuban revo-
    lution, xix, xxvii, 15, 61, 183–84,
    191, 241n5, 243n27
"Social Dangerousness" law, 83–84,
    86, 90, 226n1
Social Defense Code (1938), 82
Sociedad Secreta Abakuá, 205–6, 207
Sótano Theater, 127
Soviet Union (former): collapse of
    communism in, xix, 3, 11–12,
    184, 192; economic support by,
    for Cuba, 63, 183; glasnost in,
    187; homosexuality in, 65; mod-
    est effect of, on Cuban mass cul-
    ture, 17, 103, 230n8; political in-
    fluence of, on Cuba, 180
Spanish colonial regime, 43, 44, 46
Spanish cultural ties, 29, 40
Spanish immigrants, 40, 41
Spanish influence on Cuba, 29,
    42–43, 44, 220n27
Spanish law, discriminatory treat-
    ment of homosexuals in, 82
Stereotypes, of blacks, 51, 146–47,
    147–48
Suárez del Villar, Armando, 224
*Summer of Mrs. Forbes, The* (film),
    124–25
Superstitions, 6, 48, 49

Tabío, Juan Carlos, 125, 195
Television, 18, 20, 123, 124, 127, 244n31
Testing programs, for HIV, 168–69, 170, 171
Theater, 5–6, 126–27, 195, 196–97.
  *See also* Writers and artists
*Third Pink Book* (1993), xxii, 84
Tourism, in Cuba: and AIDS, 169, 171, 176, 237n2; before 1959, 33, 34, 57; effect of, on expectations of Cubans, 16, 18; influence of, on mass culture, 25–26, 140; and *jineterismo*, 140–41
Transvestites, 195–96
Travel abroad by Cubans, and AIDS, 161, 237n2

UMAP camps, 65–71, 81, 89, 212, 224n23; homosexuals in, 66, 69, 70
UNEAC, 72, 152
Union of Young Communists (UJC), 84, 104, 110, 122, 193
United States: AIDS in, 169; cultural influence of, in Cuba, xxiv, 1–2, 16–18, 25; economic embargo of Cuba by, xi, xviii–xix, 3, 17, 18, 19, 180, 182, 183; effect of, on future of Cuba, 182; intervention by, in Cuba before 1959, 29, 54; reaction to Cuban revolution in, xviii–xix, xxi, 13, 59, 179–80, 199
Universities: changes in, 126, 135; purges from (1970s), 71, 76, 212
*Uno Más Uno* (newspaper), 79

Valdés, Ramiro, 75, 90
Valladares, Armando, xxi, 88
Vallejo, René, 70

Washrooms, public, 139, 156, 236n9
Weeks, Jeffrey, xxii

Wills, Randolph, 105
Women, in Cuba: before 1959, 37–39, 51–52, 55; Castro's views on, 97; and Catholicism, 43; changes in sexual behavior of, 22–23; discrimination against, 185; education of, 120; emancipation of, 114, 115, 116–17; feminist consciousness among, 118–19, 233n9n13; in the labor force, 23, 120; and marriage, 118, 120–21, 233n11; official commitment to equality for, 115, 116, 117; paternalism toward, 186; in political life, 60, 116–17, 186, 242n13; role of, within Afro-Cuban religions, 206–7; socialization of homosexuals with, 150–51; violence against, 119, 186, 233n13
World Health Organization, 168
Writers and artists: and abuse of gays in 1960s and 1970s, 59, 60, 70, 71, 72–73, 76–77; and blacklisting of gay writers, 72–73, 125–26, 152; and changes in the literary world, 125–27, 195; homosexuality among, 113, 152; and painters and sculptors, 71, 225n28, 234n28; in prerevolutionary Cuba, 35

Yara cultural center, 126
Yglesias, José, 65–66
Yorubas, 43–44, 48
Young, Allen, xxii, 69
Youth: aspirations of, 16; attitudes of, toward Castro regime, 14, 18–19; changes in sexual values and behavior of, 20–27; cultural values of, 121–23; social and political preoccupations of, 14, 15–16
Youth Code, 121, 234n23